CW01067152

A
THOUSAND
CAMPFIRES

A
THOUSAND
CAMPFIRES

Australian Bush Verse – Past, Present and Future

Edited by
THE ROYAL AGRICULTURAL SOCIETY OF VICTORIA

MACMILLAN
Pan Macmillan Australia

For all those with a deep and abiding love of Australia and an
unshakeable faith in the ability of all its people to happily lead it into a
brave and bright new century.

First published 2000 in Macmillan by Pan Macmillan Australia Pty Limited
St Martins Tower, 31 Market Street, Sydney

Selection, arrangement and all editorial matter
Copyright © The Agricultural Society of Victoria Limited 2000
Copyright © in individual contributions remains with the contributor.

All rights reserved. No part of this book may be reproduced or transmitted in any form or by
any means, electronic or mechanical, including photocopying, recording or by any information
storage and retrieval system, without prior permission in writing from the publisher.

National Library of Australia
Cataloguing-in-Publication data:

A thousand campfires: Australian bush verse - past, present and future.

ISBN 0 7329 1013 7.

1. Australian poetry - 20th century. 2. Ballads, English - Australia.

A821.04408

Designed by Deborah Parry Graphics
Printed in Australia by McPherson's Printing Group

Contents

Acknowledgements

We sincerely thank all those authors and publishers who
generously granted us permission to reprint poems of which
they held the copyright.

The publishers would also like to thank the organisers of the
Bronze Swagman Awards for their cooperation.

Preface

EXCELLENCE IN AGRICULTURE

It is with great pride that the Royal Agricultural Society of Victoria presents this work. We believe it is the most comprehensive collection of bush poetry that has been written and published during the latter part of the twentieth century. We owe a great deal of thanks to Bruce Simpson, Kelly Dixon and Bob Magor, three of Australia's most prolific and talented bush poets, for their works and the time they put into selecting the poetry for this book. Also to Colin Munro, that doyen of Australian rural literature, for his guidance and support, and to the cream of Australia's bush poets who have so generously contributed their work to make the book possible. Finally, our thanks to the Royal Agricultural Society of Victoria's Group General Manager of Agriculture, Jamie Munro Aitken, for producing this anthology of Australian bush verse of the twentieth century and beyond.

Bob Potter
President
The Royal Agricultural Society of Victoria

Editors' Note

There can be no doubt that the bush ballad has made a significant contribution to the cultural heritage of this country. However, after the deaths of the great Australian ballad writers, including Banjo Paterson, Henry Lawson and Will Ogilvie, the popularity of bush verse declined. Publishers lost interest and *The Bulletin*, once the champion of the bush poets, changed its priorities. The majority of Australians were now urban dwellers, although in rural areas there had been little change. During this period of decline, a group of dedicated writers ensured the survival of the bush ballad.

The group included writers of fine verse, among them Jack Sorensen of Western Australia; Colin Newsome and Keith Garvey of New South Wales; and Lex McLennan, Bert Dunn, Richard Magoffin and Dan Sheahan of Queensland. Despite the indifference of the major publishing houses, the group found support in provincial newspapers such as the *North Queensland Register.*

Of late there has been a remarkable renaissance in the popularity of bush verse. There are now many fine bush poets plying their art and the response of the general public has been extraordinary. It is interesting to note that a number of the modern school of bush poets are writing about modern lifestyles and contemporary issues – an approach that augers well for the future of the bush ballad.

In selecting poems for *A Thousand Campfires* we felt it was important to include verses that covered as wide a range of topics as was possible. Although a few of the chosen poems may not be quite as polished as the purists would wish, we consider that the diversity of subject matter more than compensates for the occasional lapse in metrical correctness.

The gathering of material for an anthology is, perforce, an exacting and a time-consuming task. Nevertheless, we found the experience rewarding and our only regret was having to reject a number of interesting poems because of page restrictions.

Bruce Simpson,
Kelly Dixon,
Bob Magor,
January 2000

Introduction

Introducing Volume 2 of *My Country, Australian Poetry and Short Stories, Two Hundred Years (1930s–1980s)*, that amazing lady of letters, Dame Leonie Kramer, writes: 'It is curious, in a way, that while in the first one hundred and fifty years one has a sense of an energetic drive towards the future, a desire to consolidate the gains and to build a vigorous and progressive nation, in the modern period there seems to be an attempt to recover the past and to reflect on its meaning for the Australia of the present. History is the impulse behind much of the writing for the period.'

This book is to take the bush ballad forward into the new century – to offer contemporary writers the opportunity to place their fingerprints on the end of the twentieth century and look into the twenty-first. Perhaps an analogy drawn from the past, in the form of Will Ogilvie's 'The Horseman', can urge us into the future:

Up! Swear by bit and saddlecloth, by crupper, cinch and
    horn.
The spurs our grandsires buckled by our sons' sons shall
    be worn!

In *A Camp-fire Yarn: Henry Lawson, Complete Works 1885–1900*, the then Prime Minister of Australia, William Morris Hughes, while decreeing a state funeral following the death of Henry Lawson on Saturday, 4 September 1922, is quoted as saying: 'He knew intimately the real Australia, and was its greatest minstrel. He sang of its wide spaces, its dense bush, its droughts, its floods, as a lover sings of his mistress … the evening campfire, the boiling billy, the damper and the mutton of stockmen and swagmen, the humour, the pathos, the joys and sorrows, and above all the dauntless spirit

1

of the Australians ... He was a poet of Australia, the minstrel of the people.'

In fact it is recorded in Bill Wannan's *Australian Folklore: A Dictionary of Lore, Legends and Popular Allusions* that it was Henry Lawson, with his frequent and familiar contributions, who earned for *The Bulletin* (launched 31 January 1880) its outback title of 'The Bushman's Bible'.

It was my privilege to sit for a year at A.B. Paterson's desk at school. The Banjo-to-be had carved his name into the head of the desk, alongside the china inkwell. At fifteen, with a bush background, I felt the thrill of history and was hooked from that day forth.

Consequently, I was delighted when asked to judge Winton's Bronze Swagman Award in the Centenary Year of Waltzing Matilda, 1995. In the spirit of this book I draw from that award the last two lines of the final stanza of the poem entered by Beth Nelson of Tewantin, Queensland, 'Can You Hear Me, Banjo?':

> Down countless roads awaltzing, hear this nation – yours
>   and mine
> Salute you Andrew Barton and the next century of time.

Fortified by the love of the bush ballad and convinced of its secure passage into the future, poets and writers Bruce Simpson, Kelly Dixon and Bob Magor, with me as horse-tailer, have taken up the challenge of selecting a number of offerings from bush balladists of more recent years to be on the vanguard of the 'bush story in verse' as it marches proudly across the calendar into 2000 A.D.

R.M. Williams writes in the introduction to his 1992 collection of Australian poetry, *This Beloved Land*: 'By the campfire the one who can recite great verse is the one to hold attention.' But it was not until our little group, overseen by the ever watchful Jamie Aitken, gathered in western Queensland in May 1999 that the title for the collection hit us like a rushing mob. We were reading out loud Colleen McLaughlin's poem 'Redundant', when the opening lines of the third stanza cracked like a whip:

> He has lit a thousand campfires when the evening star was
>   bright
> And has yarned beside their embers, while it slowly slipped
>   from sight.

Here it is … a collection of more recent Australian bush ballads. The mob is ringing – *A Thousand Campfires*!

We do not suggest for one moment that this is the definitive selection. Rather, that it be a spur to newcomers and those who are already making such positive efforts across this nation in the writing and performing of the bush ballad, to double and redouble their efforts.

Vitai lampada traudunt!   Hand on the torch of life!

Colin A.P. Munro
Australian Broadcasting Corporation
Local & Regional Services
January 2000

Geoff Allen

THE QUEENSLAND OVERSEER

When a Queensland man joins a Kimberley camp,
It's said he's from 'inside'.
They wonder if he's galloped stone
And how well he may ride.
But there's men 'inside' can lead the way
And mix it with the best,
And show the old hands in the west
They're equal to the test.

'There's cattle to get,' Sam Croker said,
'We can't wait here all day,
I'll leave old Paddy to bring him out
And lose him on the way.'
'Now, none of that,' the old boss grinned,
'You'll be needing an overseer
To show the way to turn the lead
When the Limestone Stags appear!'

'The Limestone Stags!' Sam Croker yelled
As he rode off in disgust,
'If he's like the rest of them "inside" men,
He'll be lucky to see their dust,
And I'd like to know why it's always me
They blood these new chums on,
That stay a month while you hold their hand
And then they're up and gone.'

'What are you taking him out to ride?
Don't push the bloke too hard.'

'He can take his share of the new broke colts
And a mare left in the yard.
If he can't ride her there's the mule-striped bay
Hobbled on the flat,
And if they don't suit there's Paddy's hack,
Even the kids have sat.'

The truck arrived and out he jumped,
The brand new overseer,
But this was no wondering 'inside' man,
This was a ringer here.
From his steel grey eyes to his Cuban heels,
To the feel of his iron grip,
Cigarette swag and Werner stool,
Here was a man to tip.

'You've missed the camp,' the old boss said,
'They took off yesterday,
But they've left your mount and this old boy
To take you out that way.'
'I'll take myself,' the stranger said,
'I don't require a guide.
I'll cut their tracks and hunt them up.
In less than a good day's ride.'

'The mare in the yard,' the boss began,
But the stranger cut him short.
'I know, old man, she'll buck like hell,
It's called the New Chum Sport.
The fella you got running the camp
Wouldn't be worth his salt
If he didn't try the new man out
With a horse that can somersault!'

He saddled the mare and on he swung,
As she bucked across the stone.
'Here's a man,' the old boss thought,
'Unlikely to be thrown.'
He hooked her hard and rode her out,
Showed his ringing style.
'I think him proper stockman, boss,'
Said Paddy with a smile.

The camp was out in the Limestone Hills
Where the scrub bulls set the pace,
Where stockmen gallop the jagged rocks
In a fearless desperate race
To wheel the lead and make them ring,
No matter what the cost.
If they reach the range where the scrub grows thick,
The branders all are lost.

This day the stockboys missed the lead
And the wild bulls made the hills.
Sam Croker cursed as he struggled on,
Old and fearing spills.
'I should be there to turn them back,
But I'm yellow, old and slow,'
When he heard the rush of a charging horse
And the cry, 'Don't let them go!'

A stranger passed and gave a whoop,
And urged the stockboys on.
Sam watched his rush to the tangled scrub,
Then man and horse were gone.
The stockboys grinned and whipped their mounts,
Now ready for the fray,

And they combed the scrub and wheeled the bulls
As the stranger led the way.

'Nugget will do for a name,' he said
As they moved them in to brand,
'I've took this job as an overseer
But it's your camp, understand.
I'm only here till I get a stake,
I left town pretty quick,
Got in holts with the gendarme mob
And delivered a bit of stick.'

'That's no concern of mine,' Sam growled,
'I like a man that's tough,
Game to fight and claim he's right,
And gallop in the rough.
I hope you stop and lend a hand,
We need your kind out here
To hammer the hocks of these Limestone rogues
And swing them into gear.'

He charged the stags, he raced the stags,
He wheeled the frenzied lead.
The stockboys galloped along behind,
In awe at his breakneck speed.
He tracked them to the stony crags
And forced them from their lair;
He set his horse down stony steeps
Where only a fool would dare.

They ran the bulls, they threw the bulls,
They grabbed them by the tail,
Pulled them down and cut their horns,

Fought them tooth and nail.
They cleared the hills and cleaned the scrub
Of all the old diehards,
And branding irons and knives ran red
Around those bronco yards.

He stayed that year, then off he went
To the country back 'inside',
But old Sam now had a different view
Of how those blokes could ride,
And the boss at times pondered back
To a rogue mare in the yard,
And an overseer in a Werner stool,
Spurring high and hard.

A stranger came to the Kimberley
Who proved he knew the game.
'I'm from "inside",' he smiled at them,
'But we do things much the same.
The hills are steep and the limestone's rough,
And we fight for bulls and stags.
Charge the stone and bash the scrub
To block them on the crags.'

J. M. Allingham

WE'LL GO NO MORE A-DROVING

We'll go no more a-droving when the day has just begun.
No more we'll move the mob off camp to beat the rising sun.
No more our horses' hooves will strike dew diamonds from the grass.
No more the frost will crackle as the leaders quickly pass.

The Burdekin runs deep and cold, steam rising as of yore,
But no-one rides to swing the lead as down the banks they pour.
No horseman shoves the tail along to keep them on the go
While bullocks hang back from the edge and try to take it slow
Till weight of numbers from the top no more the front can stand,
And leaders take a quick cold plunge and splash across the sand.

Coastal mists come swirling in, grey ships unfurling sails.
No lines of ghostly bullocks weave along the droving trails.
No dripping horseman holds the lead and tries to pierce the haze
And keep the mob from going bush through Marlow's scrubby maze.

Through Dead Man's Gully's gentle stream no bullock hooves
    will splash
While trucks and timber jinkers roar as down the range they dash.
No more the packs will lead us down on slipping, sliding feet.
No more we'll see fat bullocks heave when hit by coastal heat.

Now Curlew Flat's been built upon, the Bohle Bend is dry.
We'd like to water in the Ross, but we're not game to try.
No more on watch at Ironbark we'll croon our farewell song
While tired bullocks chew the cud and camp the whole night long.
By then we'll feel the hidden sense that grows and grows and grows,
The bond twixt man and bullock none but the drover knows.

We'd like to take a final count but buildings overlap.
Vet Science holds our 'cool-off' camp before we climb the Gap.
Head stockman Joe now takes the count of bullocks in the sky
While helicopters sweep Ross Plain and big trucks hurtle by.
No more the tiny iron hut the drover's haven makes.
No more we'll toss corn beef aside and dine on meatworks steaks.

Now heli-stirred-up bullocks run up the crush to load.
If they should stop or turn around they'll feel the electric goad.
They race onto the upper deck and slip and push and jam
And once the last one rushes up, the steel doors quickly slam.
And then prime movers pull the crates with bumps and bends
    and jerks.
We hope there'll be no bruising before they reach the works.

Packhorses now are hard to find, packsaddles gather dust,
Horse bells and hobbles hang on nails, the canteens start to rust.
We all now dwell on market trends, Jap Ox and Ausmeat scores
The colour of the bottom line, no-one has time to pause
And think of lowing cattle feeding on to evening camp,
The swinging of the man on watch, the intermittent stamp
Of spare night horses haltered beyond the campfire's light,
The sudden grip of utter fear when bullocks jump with fright,
The tales around the gleaming fire, great rushes, throwing stags,
Horse-tailers slipping hobbles on, packhorses slinging swags,
The melody of horsebells ringing clear across the land,
The low bush sounds and movements that the drovers understand.

Now memories come flooding free of times upon the track,
An era that has slipped away. No-one can bring it back.
Boss drovers are a dying breed, they've had to change their ways,
But we proudly rode the stock routes in those carefree droving days.

THE MAN WHO BRINGS UP THE TAIL

Great tales are told of the stockman bold
    who rides to steady the lead,
And his ringer mate who keeps them straight
    on the wing with his flying steed,
But not one word is ever heard,
    though there's talk till the embers pale,
Of the man whose job is behind the mob,
    the man who brings up the tail.

When the weaners race and the leading face
    erupts in a bursting flood,
Horses prop and chop till they're fit to drop
    and the spurs start dripping with blood.
You can ring them round till the churned up ground
    flies up in a dusty veil,
But they'll swing as wide on the other side
    till someone brings up the tail.

Greenhide Jack drove every track
    from Ord to Lynam's Well.
He'd deliver the lot ere it got too hot
    at the very gates of hell.
When the going's tough and the track gets rough
    on the steepest parts of the trail,
A smart lad you'll need to hold your lead
    but your best man stays with the tail.

The sun sets low and the mob moves slow
    to the wings of the tailing yard,
And horses drag and their riders flag
    from a big day's mustering hard.

Then the whips may lash and the horsemen dash,
    but all to no avail,
At the gates they'll baulk and the lead will fork
    if it gets no weight from the tail.

When skies are clear and the grass is sere
    and the monsoon long passed by,
The outlook bleak and the cattle weak
    and breeders ready to die,
Then shift you can if you find a man
    who will not rant or rail
As he plods away the blazing day
    with those staggering cows at the tail.

You'll find no name in the Hall of Fame,
    nor the lists of pioneers,
Not one tale begun of a job well done
    in the passing of the years,
But there's one whose face has a rightful place
    in the light of the Golden Grail
And his day's work lies
    midst the dust and flies,
He's the man who brings up the tail.

DRAUGHTHORSE MUSTER

Horses dance and prance and fidget, we are on our favourite mounts.
There'll be lots of hard fast riding where a horse's spirit counts.
Saddled early in the half-light, ere the sun sends out its shafts,
Ready for a stirring muster, we are bringing in the draughts.

Heavy horses, bay and brown and black, from the bonny banks of
    Clyde,
Where they pulled the brewery carts and ploughs with heaps of power
    and pride,
Clean legged great grey Percherons from France's fertile lands
Now ranged the warm Australian soil in dashing pounding bands.

In the heated dryish climate they have made the land their own,
Running free and unmolested, their bond with man has flown.
They will take a lot of turning, with riding strong and hard,
Before we get them to the station and safely in the yard.

The horses shun the boree scrub, we leave it on the right.
Once we cross the basalt gully there'll soon be some in sight.
Two men are sent off to the left, the corner is their place,
They'll collect the flying horses as down the boundary fence they race.

We spread across the paddock, keeping each man well in sight.
Soon feeding horses raise their heads and trot about with fright.
They run together in their mobs and leaders, tails held high,
Take them off towards the back and dust begins to fly.

Our pace speeds up, it's vital now we keep the mobs in view.
When they reach the tumbled basalt ridge we don't know what
    they'll do.

Some will gallop straight across but some will swing away
And turn and race straight back again if no-one's in the way.

A big grey gelding leads a pack well forward of the rest.
The man upon the furthest wing can see he's for a test.
He slants his horse towards them, lets the leader keep his speed,
As he comes up to its shoulder with his sturdy flying steed.

There are rocks and grass and red soil holes and gum trees all around,
But the gallant grass-fed stockhorse has his feet well on the ground.
The grey horse, beaten now for pace, starts to veer away;
The rider steadies up a bit, he knows he's won the day.

The rest turn to their leader and follow on his trail
While another rider backing up has now controlled the tail.
They chase them on across the ridge, into the creek they splash,
They reach the further boundary and along the pads they dash.

We check some basalt ridges, behind which horses hide,
We clean them out completely and up the rocks we ride.
No horses graze the poplar swamp, we see right across the plain.
We hope they're in the corner and won't come out again.

The corner now is full of dust, horses dashing round and round,
While the leaders are swung back again when from the mob they pound.
Once we get them settled, running now with mates they know,
We'll hold them all together and down the fence we'll go.

Two horsemen ride into the lead, the fence is on their right.
Two others move along the wing to keep it straight and tight.
The last man will bring up the tail and keep them on the go.
He must hold them all together and make sure they're not too slow.

The mob goes off, a surging mass of horses on the run,
With fetlocks flashing, tails held high, blazed faces in the sun.
Stockhorses reef and plunge and pull as the mob starts off its drive.
This is the utmost riding thrill. It's great to be alive.

The leaders have to judge the pace, too slow and they will spread,
Too fast, they'll get up too much pace and maybe slip ahead.
A racing gelding swings away and quickly dashes out.
He's gone between the wing men ere he knows what he's about.
They block behind and let him be, all on his very own,
He'll soon be feeling lonely once he finds he's all alone.

He gallops off, then steadies down, looks round for some support.
His fear is very evident as on his own he's caught.
A wing man trots out steadily, this is a gentle job.
He circles wide and quietly brings the lone horse to the mob.

They thunder to the basalt ridge and split, the pads to take,
If there are rogues within the mob, this is where they'll break.
The flank men race and prop and swing and keep them flowing fast.
Nothing makes a dash away and soon the rocks are past.

They settle now, a steady trot, we cross the plain all black.
They are following the leaders, nothing now looks back.
There is only one thing left ahead to keep us very tense.
We have to get them through a gate right in the homestead fence.

The right-hand leader steadies up and drops back to the wing.
Straight towards the open gate he makes the leaders swing.
The other leads them through the gate, they follow on the track.
They must be taken carefully or youngsters will break back.

All are through, the mob has spread, we get them in control.
The whole lot's going forwards as towards the yard we roll.
We let the leaders hurry up and push the tail quite hard.
We don't want horses turning back once they have reached the yard.

They gallop in, the dust flies up, horses race and trot around.
The gate is shut and firmly chained, the mob is safe and sound.
Our horses heave and drip with sweat, they have been working hard.
We can now enjoy our smoko for the draughts are in the yard.

Helen Avery

BOOTS

At the ending of each day they're there, outside my kitchen door,
In a struggling line or heap upon the verandah floor …
A line of dusty boots and shoes, a pile of battered hats,
Cast down without a second thought, beside the sleeping cat.

They're dirty and untidy. I should scold for thought and care,
But something strikes a tender chord when I see them lying there.
They're the badges of our labour, the colours of our team,
As we struggle as a family towards our distant dream.

There's a broken pair of T-boots, 'lastic going at the sides,
Crossed and scarred across the toecaps, with the ankles gaping wide.
Nothing's broken in their spirit, they can still stride out with pride,
Kicking at the dust and tussocks, standing tall on acres wide.

There's a cleaner pair, and newer – near the same size as his dad's.
They're my son's, the youthful firstborn, grown a tall and slender lad,
Reaching out for tender manhood, full of dreams and quick to laugh,
Greedy now for life's adventures, taken boldly, not by half.

Then, two pairs of worn-out sneakers, nearer grey with age than white,
From long and dusty days in sheepyards, days on bikes with mobs in
    sight.
Two fair girls with eyes of angels stand beside the men and boys,
Firm and fine they'll face their future, with its sorrow and its joys.

The scruffy pair at the end of the line belong to the small jackeroo,
Bursting his little heart to do whatever his dad can do.
Striding out in giant footsteps, brave enough to sweat and toil,
Hands already chapped and toughened, soul already loves this soil.

Thrown on them, the wide Akubras, darkly stained with sweat and dirt
That cast deep and welcome shadows 'cross each patched and faded shirt.
And the eyes that light beneath them, gaze on distance far and wide,
Hear and feel the touch of Nature, know the land with quiet pride.

THE WAITING

By the iron grey cottage down the dusty street
A struggling tree wilts in the morning heat.
A woman leans in the kitchen door,
Scuffs the broken lino on the floor,
Wipes weary hair from weary eyes …
Man's off in the sheds,
So she waits …

In the shimmering mirage on the plain
The homestead stands stark as a man-made stain.
The harsh, black crow calls raucous and clear,
And the bold sun scorns the new bride's fear.
The woman bends to the sky's fierce glare …
Man's away with the cattle
… She waits.

Where the line runs straight in fine drawn steel,
The horizon melts in distance surreal.
By the iron rain tank in a patch of cool,
A bit of green grows in gentle misrule.
The woman tends to her fragile plants.
She's the wife of a ganger
… She waits.

Wait lonely hours in the long, hot days,
While youth slips away in Time's sweet maze
And the beauty fades, and the dreams grow dim,
But the heart of the woman beats strong within,
She waits for her man to come home.

THE RETURN

My heart's drifting back to the bush again
Where there's room for my need to dream,
Where the soul's not fettered by man-made chains
And the mind sees the grander scheme
In the wide land and a wayward wind and the hot sun burning ...
There are salt tears on this old face, and my heart is yearning.

I want to return to that endless space
Where the edge of the earth meets the sky
In a clean line with the pure grace
Of an eagle soaring by ...
See the grass sway, and mirages play, and the night come winging
With the white stars, then the clear dawn, and a stormbird singing.

Once again I would hear the silence shout
When the midday heat hangs still,
Watch the clouds build when there's rain about
And the dry creek beds fill ...
I need to feel with my own hands the warm dust sifting,
See the stock spread 'cross the Mitchell grass, and the shadows
    shifting.

My heart's drifting back to the bush again,
To a place that I used to know,
When the fire of youth ran quick in my veins
And life seemed a timeless flow ...
Ah, I wish I could ride 'neath the coolibahs when the west wind's
    sighing,
But the day has gone, the night is close, and the old fire is dying.

HE SAID

'The wind's a bastard today,' he said,
Pushed his hat to the back of his head,
Reached for the worn tobacco tin,
Fumbled the pungent weed within.
'From the bowels of hell,' he said.

'Straight from the bowels of hell,' he said,
Spat from his lips a tobacco shred,
Leant on the old verandah rail,
Tough as leather, straight as a nail.
'Cloud's in the north,' he said.

'Clouds are around in the north today.'
He scanned where the distant cloud bank lay,
Rolled the smoke with a languid air,
Bent to the dog and scratched its hair.
'It'll make a mistake one day ...

'It'll make a mistake and rain, it will,'
Put the smoke to his lips, his eyes grew still,
Cupped his hands 'round a gleam of flame,
Drew on the roll till a red glow came,
'... And maybe the dams will fill.

'Yeah, the dams might fill, and the grass might grow,
And the feathers wash white on that miserable crow.
The frogs'll drown, and the ducks'll bog ...'
He reached again to the patient dog,
And he turned on his heel to go!

Frank Bacon

THE ROAD TO COOLATAI

Now that life is slowly fading
Like a rainbow from the sky,
I am sitting dozing, dreaming,
Where the old creek whispers nigh,
Of those days of youth and gladness,
Sure of hand and keen of eye,
When we drove with old Tom Walker,
Down the road to Coolatai.

Long before the days of motors,
When the buggy horse was king,
And their shoes upon the metal
Used to tap and stamp and ring,
Polished bits and shining buckles,
Humming spokes and jingling chains,
And the four big reefing Clevelands
Pulled the buggy by the reins.

Down the long slopes past Bungulla,
Bluff Rock rising grim and high,
Driving down with old Tom Walker,
From Tenterfield to Coolatai.
The world is changing every minute,
I'm out of date and pensioned by.
Could I have one last wish granted,
It would be, before I die,
To grip once more the tight-stretched ribbons,
See the dust and gravel fly,

From flashing hooves of bay and chestnut
On the road to Coolatai.

Anne Bell

MUD-MAP

He'd a wall-eyed dog and a bally mare
And eyes like amber tea.
He sent the dog to hold the lead,
Then drew my road for me.

He smoothed the dust with his brown palm
As the leaders began to ring,
And cast a prick-eared kelpie bitch
Out to the spreading wing.

Where roly-polys, mad old hatters,
Frolic across the sky,
And white as fresh-shorn sheep, the drifts
Of rustling daisies lie;

By lonely tree, by broken gate,
By creek and star and sun,
There on the plain he carefully showed
The way my track should run.

A plover scolded the wall-eyed dog,
The saddles creaked in the heat,
He whistled back the kelpie bitch
To tongue at his dusty feet.

I shook the drover's knuckly hand
And thanked him courteously,
But he'll never know how sharp and clear
He drew my road for me.

Brian Bell

THE GUMNUT DANCE

Old Father Time loves to watch the sights
That changing seasons bring,
Like the rainbow glow of the Arctic nights
And the crocus heralding spring.

The Australian bush gives him one more chance
For a joy-filled annual treat
At the autumn's end, when the gumnut dance
Makes the cycle of life complete.

As the gumnuts waltz in the whispered breeze
To the steps each gorge has fixed,
Cooler night winds howl through the tallest trees
To ensure their seed is mixed.

But Old Father Time still recalls his dream
Of Gondwana's ancient tales,
And the dream came real by a rippling stream
In a gorge in New South Wales.

Old Father Time shed a million tears
For the last dinosaur alive,
But the gradual shift of the long, long years
Helped his favourite pine survive.

As the clash of plates 'neath the mantled crust
Caused the continent's motion north,
Many forms of life had to fade to dust
As replacements ventured forth.

When the cold drove deep Gondwana's heart
Through an epoch's brutal change,
All the pine could do was retreat to part
Of a lonely mountain range.

And a million years was a lightning bolt
That would cause land's mass to move.
Such a fragile tree, feeling each small jolt,
Lay in wait, should things improve.

With its strength confined to a meagre zone
Where the rock and soil seemed right,
Now the gumnut dance threatened each small cone
As the species fought for light.

In a hundred years, only three small seeds
Had a need to come alive.
All the rest could rot in the marshy reeds,
And the pine would still survive.

Now the gum tree lived for the gumnut dance,
And koalas gripped its breast.
Father Time looked on in a wistful trance,
Lest his pine break through the crest.

Then the white man came, ever bold and brash,
To disturb the ancient peace,
With an axe to grind in his quest for cash,
And a wish that wealth increase.

The persistent pine watched its nephews play,
With their gumnuts spread all 'round.
Father Time was pleased, for the game's delay
Meant his favourite's not yet found.

Then a new day dawned when the wistful breeze,
In collusion with the sun,
Helped a caring eye see the ancient trees
And a fight for life was won.

And they named the tree, called it Wollemi pine,
Then in wonder took some seeds,
And the first to shoot, with its crust ashine,
Had a team to meet its needs.

In a few short years, it has grown so tall,
With a thousand more besides.
Now it's up to men to enjoy them all,
Where they grace Earth's mountainsides.

In a stone-lined gorge, where the dim rays reach,
There the pines still fight to live,
Glad their lonely wait was to help to teach
That the best reward's to give.

And Old Father Time knows that man can care,
For he sees his pines growing everywhere.

FROM THE BLUE MOUNTAINS
(DEDICATED TO HENRY KENDALL)

I've spent many years residing in these mountains I adore,
Far from childhood's sardine suburbs where my spirit cried for more.
As I take the living daily in surrounds of sheer delight,
Thoughts of Kendall's creeks and gorges call me out for walks at night.

It's a distant cry from yesteryear, tonight along the ridge.
Progress permeates the city, while the tunnel and the bridge
Link chaotic chain reactions. From the seaside to the heights,
Flashing fireworks flood the skyline in a blaze of city lights.

Pulsing robot-world kaleidoscope! The stories it contains!
It's a phoenix, filtered brilliantly through fossil-fuel remains.
In the patchwork show of light, severe pollution does not show
Till the dawn breaks on the dump bins and the chains of traffic grow.

Like a moth, I feel attracted to the beauty I behold,
But can let my guarded distance watch the restlessness unfold.
More in tune with gentle living, I resist the urgent call
To be just another pinpoint in the phosphorescent sprawl.

As I watch I start recalling how my early years were spent
Caged in multi-storeyed buildings, solving problems as I went
Through an enormous lust for dominance within my chosen field,
Quite convinced that time and tide could easily be annealed.

I recall the frantic meal breaks, buying things I thought I'd need,
Till life's randomness revealed a way my heart could intercede
On behalf of my true spirit. As my feelings were exposed,
Doors were opened wide on attitudes that formerly were closed.

Doors that led me to the shaded mountain village I call home,
Where the night reflects the city's dance of plastic faced with chrome,
Where it's almost safe to walk alone on dim-lit carriageways,
Smelling gently cracking timber in the chimney-winter haze.

But the modern world approaches, with its bustle, grind and push,
Cuts across my meditations on the beauty of the bush,
Letting sadness overcome me, for I don't see any doubt
That we're losing touch with simple things that Henry pointed out.

It's called progress, but a way of life that changes more and more
Makes me wonder at the concepts that society reaches for
As technology's false promise makes the cycle move along,
Bringing loss with each advantage I can see there's something wrong.

While the local shop still operates with diligence and care,
Keeping fragile business going midst political despair,
I see fewer mountain lowries, less king parrots and galahs,
Some are victims of pollution, others scared by noisy cars.

Snakes and possums are a nuisance but they have their rights as well,
Part of Nature's fragile balance in a world of buy and sell.
They're not bound by rates and taxes, and there's much that they
    can give
While our consciences join battle with the way we're forced to live.

Squealing brakes disturb my silence as a goods train snakes downhill,
Vibrant echoes ream the gorges, slicing frosty winter chill,
And it sounds so much like bell-birds that it fills me with remorse
For the children who won't hear them unless progress changes course.

Tony Brooks

POETS AND WRITERS OF SONGS

Poets and writers tell stories of lovers
    and sing of the world and its wrongs,
But the arms of a lover say more than the pens
    of the poets and writers of songs,
But where are the lovers who strolled down the lane
    in the days when the world was so young?
Gone from the stage now, the curtain has fallen,
    there are no more songs to be sung,
The curtain has fallen, the stage is deserted,
    there are no more songs to be sung.

Poets and writers tell stories of children
    and sing of the world and its wrongs,
But the eyes of a child say more than the pens
    of the poets and writers of songs,
But gone are the children who played in the garden,
    and the castles they built in the sand
Have crumbled and fallen, blown by the winds,
    that scattered them over the land,
The four winds have taken the castles of children
    and scattered them over the land.

Poets and writers tell stories of nature
    and sing of the world and its wrongs,
But the song of a bird can say more than the pens
    of the poets and writers of songs,
But the birds that once graced the heavens on high
    have deserted their realm in the air,

No more shall they fly to the trees of the forest,
    the trees of a forest so bare,
The leaves are all withered, the birds have deserted,
    the trees of a forest now bare.

Poets and writers tell stories of friendship
    and sing of the world and its wrongs,
But the hand of a friend can say more than the pens
    of the poets and writers of songs,
But where are the friends who stood shoulder to shoulder
    in the face of the world and its wrongs?
Gone from the earth now, no more shall they listen,
    to poets and writers of songs,
For a cloud that has burst on the Garden of Eden,
    silenced the poets and writers of songs.
Silenced the poets and writers of songs.

THE SCRATCH PULL

Not a very big horse, as working horses go,
A sway-backed bay they called the Trump, he wasn't bred for show.
Ted Faunt the fencer owned him, out Enniskillen way,
And he'd stake the price of a mile of fence no horse would pull the bay.

Les Wilcox had big Baldy, a massive wall-eyed rig,
While Jumbo Harlow's Nancy was as game as she was big.
In burr-cut camp and shearing shed, men argued through the night,
It was Nancy, Baldy or the Trump, each swore that he was right.

A scratch pull was the only way to settle the affair,
So straws were drawn, the match to make, and the rig would pull
    the mare.
The bushman's rules on scratch pulls are pretty loose, of course,
But though it's not laid down in Hoyle, there's one he does enforce.

When the weight is on the collar and the trace chains take the strain,
The teamster must use voice alone, he can't touch the horse again.
So it happened at the shearing shed, Les Wilcox' team was there,
When Jumbo dragged the delver in, his team led by the mare.

Trace chains were hooked together and the teamsters took their stance,
At their horses' nearside shoulder, 'Gee up Baldy!' 'Gee up Nance!'
The mare surged to the collar with quarters bunched up tight,
But the massive rig could not be moved, though she pulled with all
    her might.

With nostrils wide and proud neck arched, the mare first showed
    the strain,
And heart alone was not enough, the break she could not gain.

Then Wilcox sensed his victory, he roared a mighty oath,
That startled all the onlookers and helped retard their growth.

The rig had heard that oath before and with ears laid to the mane,
He towed the mare across the scratch, the victory to gain,
So bets were paid and bets were laid, true bushmen don't renege,
And the date was set a month away for the Trump to pull the rig.

The homestead looked like race day when they settled the affair,
The mob was from the bush Who's Who, led by the Desert Lair;
The Gidyea Prince with four in hand came in to get his mail
And Jimmy Nueman, 'The Trotting Cob', was there to spin a tale.

Old Charlie Gall, the manager, declared a holiday,
So Bull-Fiddle Herb was on the scene to wager all his pay.
'The bush has joys and pleasures that townsfolk never know',
And from battered swags and saddle bags, the rum began to flow.

And horses of 'the good old days' were reminisced about,
Tim Wilcox led big Baldy up, and the Trump came trotting out.
Beside the massive wall-eyed rig, the Trump was but a pup,
But a horse's size is not what counts when the blood is fairly up.

A hush settled on the gathered throng, 'twas serious work at hand,
And the bushmen gathered all intent as the horses took their stand.
With collars filled and trace chain taut, the boss then made the scratch,
He flung his hat down to the ground, the signal for the match.

The teamsters swore as teamsters will, and the crowd, they followed
    suit,
As the game little Trump gave all he knew to hold the surging brute.
Big Baldy heaved and snorted and raised dust for yards around,

His quarters strained and trembled, but the Trump still held his
    ground,

Sweat poured forth from man and beast, the crowd's roar softened to a
    moan,
The mighty Baldy pawed and pulled but the Trump, he held his own.
Then seventeen hands of gallant horse that never had been beat,
Went down upon his fore knees, still proud in his defeat.

So, Ted Faunt backed the Trump up to ease the aching strain,
And Baldy pitched down to his side, never to rise again,
And though Wilcox was a hardy soul, as tough as a gidyea stump,
He wept beside the conquered rig, and cursed the sway-backed Trump.

Now out across the blacksoil plains when the evening sun goes down,
The stockmen gather in their camps and yarn of horses of renown,
They remember the gallant little Trump as the billy goes its round,
And Baldy, who died in harness, fairly pulled into the ground.

Robert Bushby

DESTRUCTO THE COCKROACH

When next in the kitchen you turn on the light
And, racing away to the cracks,
Your friends of the night-time go scuttling past
As, screaming, you leap from their tracks,
Remember the folk who have honoured a champ
And out there in Eulo you'll read
A memorial stone they've erected with pride
To honour the last of the breed.

'Twas in nineteen eighty, excitement was rife,
And a message to everywhere sent
To gather at Eulo where the records are made
To witness a top world event.
The moment arrived, the bets had been made,
And the lizards were ready to race.
They're off! and they're running, and Wooden Head wins!
A creature of beauty and grace.

Then up steps a party with carton in hand
To issue a challenge to stay
And match the great lizard against their young 'roach
They'd trained and prepared for that day.
The crowd was amazed, they couldn't believe
That such an event should be staged,
But it was, and Destructo went flat out and won,
And left the officials enraged.

The cockroach's handlers all shouted with joy;
They jumped up and down in the ring.
The hours of training and faith had paid off –
Destructo the Cockroach was king.
But tragedy shattered the triumph supreme
Before world acclaim had transpired –
In all confusion they stepped on their champ;
The life of Destructo expired.

Now Destructo has gone where all good cockies go,
To the great Cockroach Home in the sky,
And the racing fraternity gather each year
To stand by the graveside and cry.
But it isn't because our Destructo has gone
That brings such dismay to the camp,
It's the shame that forever will darken their hearts;
He beat Wooden Head the world champ!

Ellis Campbell

REMEMBER CHUBBY?

'Simple Chubby!' rang the chorus of the chanting imps who mocked;
Hapless victim stood before us, looking numb and faintly shocked.
Decked out in his worn regalia, passed down by old-fashioned folks;
Simply branded nature's failure – butt of all our stupid jokes.

Spelling was a torture to him, every day at Birchlea school.
Mathematics always threw him, though he followed every rule.
Striving ever with his writing, many teachers thought him slow –
Bore with grace our empty skiting (we were clever, don't you know?)

Last man in when playing cricket, never made the football team –
Without score he lost his wicket, lost his cap and self-esteem.
Sat alone to eat his dinners (tasteless egg in soggy bread);
Ham and salad were for winners, those were things we ate instead.

Finished school with little credit, joined a set where crime was rife;
Drop-out kid – we often said it – without job or social life.
Did a bit of casual labour – sometimes joined the unemployed –
Worked for free to help a neighbour; lacking status we enjoyed.

Clumsy when it came to dancing, always slow to comprehend;
No-one found his ways entrancing, Chubby lacked a lady friend.
Cared not for the trends of fashion, or the voguish smart set's mood;
Viewed the world with calm dispassion, bearing barbs with fortitude.

War clouds welled on the horizon, waves of fear swept all the world.
Frenzied demon's wrath relied on propaganda's lies unfurled.
Allies called their troops to order in the year of '39 –
Grimly faced a mad marauder, crazed with fiendish greed's design.

Came the call to our small township – war's reality was near –
Carting rubbish to the town's tip, Chubby stopped to volunteer.
First of all our district's heroes, without fuss he sailed away;
Long before the chanting cheer rose, certain where his future lay.

'Killed in action,' read the cable. In the scourge of Borneo
Chubby proved that he was able, grimly faced a frenzied foe.
Brave distinction marked his effort on a battlefield of hell;
Died beneath a hailing onslaught; made his mark before he fell.

Earned a medal for his action, posted home posthumously.
Did he find some satisfaction, dying there for you and me?
Every day I sample pleasures, shared with friends and loving wife –
Rich in hosts of worldly treasures; joys unknown in Chubby's life.

Life's a pathway strewn with roses for my family and myself,
But my conscience still exposes many qualms I cannot shelf.
I am swamped by warped conjecture and a nightmare's ridicule;
Haunted ever by the spectre of a chubby kid at school.

Betsy Chape

HORSES ARE SMART

'Horses are smart', the old bushman said.
'I haven't met one without brains in his head;
Some are quite stubborn, others are mean,
And some are no more than a bucking machine.
Some horses are gentle, and many are tough,
On some you ride smooth, but others are rough;
But put aside temperament and get to the heart,
Every nag that I've ridden has always been smart.

'But all of the smart horses, the one for the prize
Was a bloke I called Joe, of considerable size.
With strength in his legs, he flew when he ran,
And on top of all this he could think like a man.
He could figure things out, and make up his mind –
I'm fully convinced he was one of a kind.
He could follow instructions, understand words,
And could always be trusted with fidgety herds.

'Over the years I depended on Joe,
For there wasn't too much that horse didn't know.
I trusted him quite a few times with my life;
He proved a loyal friend in moments of strife.
But I have to admit there was just one time
When Joe let me down without reason or rhyme.
I'd taken a tumble that wasn't his fault,
And quick as a flash he spun to a halt.

'He surveyed the scene; I was out like a light
And I wouldn't be missed at the homestead till night.
So Joe grabbed my collar, pulled me into the shade,
Stood over my body, and that's where he stayed.
He licked at my face, and whinnied at me
Till I came to my senses, only to see
My left leg was broken, my arm was as well,
And everywhere else was hurting like hell.

'One thing's for sure, I needed some help;
I tried to get up, but fell back with a yelp.
"Go for the Doctor," I whispered to Joe,
And sank back in the shade as I heard him go.
Now this is the bit that has got me beat;
Old Joe made a mess of this ordinary feat.
I said, "Go for the Doctor," and I'll never forget
How the silly galoot came back with the vet!'

Louis H. Clark

THE LAW OF GUMBARLEE

They trailed him down through Arnhem Land,
Well on a thousand mile,
But now the police have got their man
He'll have to stand his trial;
For law is law, and sin is sin,
He speared poor old Billie, in
The good old Abo style.

It seemed Gumbarlee's wayward gin,
Some twenty years before,
Ran off with Billie, and that day
Gumbarlee grimly swore,
No matter how long he should wait,
That Billie would meet with a fate
According to the law.

'You must kill Billie,' said the law,
Where laws are strict and few;
The law his fathers scratched on rock,
When ours were scratching too;
But ours found time, and made a clock,
While his just slept beside their rock,
And so he never knew ...

He'll have a good interpreter;
They'll treat him light no doubt,
With fifteen years by white man's law
(He'll never see it out):
He'll pine away and die in three,
Still wondering in his misery
Just what it's all about.

THE BROWN PUP AND THE MAN

I saw them coming down the hill, the brown pup and the man,
The puppy frolicked out in front,
His tail was long, his nose was blunt,
He corkscrewed as he ran.

They stood outside O'Reilly's pub, and through the peeling doors,
The young man walked with steady stride,
The pup flopped in the dust outside,
His head upon his paws.

The day dragged on to early dew; the regular trooped out
But the emperor of his private world
Still laughed and drank; the brown pup curled
His tail around his snout.

Voices! Listen … One was His … The puppy's ears pricked.
'No more credit.' Through the door
The boozer slouched, first thing he saw
To vent his rage, he kicked.

The brown pup yelped his misery, and wormed along the track,
Every fibre fawned his love
For that one God who loomed above,
He rolled upon his back.

His eyes shone up, 'If you meant that, a pup's life's not worth livin'.'
The man looked down, he sobered up,
'Gee boy,' he knelt and hugged the pup;
And the long tail thumped 'Forgiven'.

The man stood up, 'I wish,' he sighed, 'that such remorse could buy
Forgiveness from the lass I hurt.'
He sniffed his nose upon his shirt,
And blinked a stubborn eye.

I saw them going up the hill, the brown pup and the man,
The brown pup frolicked out in front,
His tail was long, his nose was blunt,
He corkscrewed as he ran.

Noel Cutler

GRANDAD'S WHIP

It's hung there on my bedroom wall, since Grandad passed away:
For in this room my mother nursed her father every day.
Though twenty unforgotten years can slip a youngster's grip,
I still recall when Grandad taught me how to crack his whip.

He used it in his droving days when bullocks felt its sting,
And brumbies in the Great Divide have cowered to its ring.
While mickies in the must'ring yard were quick to take the tip
That verbal orders weren't so bad – compared to Grandad's whip.

And at the local country fair he'd put on quite a show,
For ev'rywhere that Grandad went, his whip was sure to go.
A volunteer from out the crowd would brave a bloody lip,
But only cigarettes were cut when Grandad used his whip.

A Sydney flash in either hand, across the body too.
A cutback that I've since found out impossible to do.
He'd crack four-pointers overhead, while on a beer he'd sip,
Yet never spill a flamin' drop. Grandad could crack a whip.

And though I'd yet to start at school, he'd hand that whip to me
And proudly state, 'This tacker is a champion to be'.
With infant might I'd swing that lash and only now can quip,
'That five-year-old was struggling then, to crack his Grandad's whip!'

As recollections fade away, a smile and tear collide.
Though Grandad's gone, his legacy adorns my wall with pride.
Our fancy two-hand cracking now still lacks the showmanship
That kids like me were privy to, when Grandad cracked his whip.

I never learned who plaited it, he bought it second-hand.
The rigid fall, quite brittle now, clings to a single strand.
Its ghostly silence is explained by absence on the tip
Of horse-hair cracker that was used by Grandad on his whip.

With several whips I demonstrate the tricks we do today,
Aspiring to predictions Grandad spoke of yesterday,
And wond'ring if my grandsons will, when I cash in my chips,
Be just as proud as I have been to say, 'They're Grandad's whips!'

CALL ME AUSSIE, MATE!

You might reckon I'm a racist, but I'll guarantee I'm not.
I'm just an Aussie battler who is proud of what he's got.
Australia's multicultural and there's problems come with that,
Like how to look Australian when you want to wear a hat!

Although the old Akubra has its roots out in the bush,
It's failed to make an impact on the inner-city push.
For they prefer the baseball cap – and mate, I must be blunt,
It looks so un-Australian when they wear it back-to-front.

I guess I shouldn't worry over passing Yankie fads
Like crew cuts in the 'sixties when we tried to shock our dads.
A decade later, Beatle boots, with crazy pointy toes,
And hair that grew way down our back – what Mum thought,
      heaven knows!

The fashion scene is what it is – it tends to come and go –
But language is a victim, as the hist'ry books will show.
And though I am a patient man, there's one thing I despise –
It's Aussies greeting Aussies with a 'How you going, guys?'

I reckon television's got a lot to answer for,
The way that it manipulates and tries to mould our lore.
You'd think that our producers would be keen to sow the seed,
But most would rather follow than go out and take the lead.

Although it's in its infancy, Australia's growing up.
It's time we stopped accepting foreign matter in our cup.
We lead the world in medicine, technology and sport.
So why this masochistic trend to sell our culture short?

And while Australian customs *are* as rare as dingo eggs,
A growing nation's heritage begins on shaky legs.
If you're a proud Australian (as are most Aussie folk)
Then don that old Akubra, and remember – I'm a bloke!

Frank Daniel

CANDLE IN THE DARK

When I was just a youngster I'd lie in bed so quiet,
Listening to crickets and night owls, dogs barking in the night,
The leaves against the window, wind hissing through the pines,
The choofing of the Cooma Mail, south bound on frosted lines.

And when the clouds came over that brought torrential storms,
My room would dance a pantomime of darkened ghostly forms.
Then I'd call out loud for Mother as I lay there, stiff and stark,
And she'd hurry in to comfort me, a candle in the dark.

In my teens, as wisdom came and truth was prone to hurt,
When learning was experience and toil and sweat and dirt,
Some moments of my childhood still lived in silent form,
The terror of the lightning and the thunder in the storm.

As I grew older through the years, sometimes in my dreams
My mind would fill with memories, near bursting at the seams.
Or sometimes just a passing phase, perhaps a chance remark,
Would rekindle thoughts of Mother, with her candle in the dark.

We all know life's swift passing has its comfort and its pain,
So my years were filled with sunshine and at times a little rain.
The grandeur of fulfilment, the pride of doing well,
The loss of cherished loved ones and the tears that often fell.

Now that my time is done I know my prayers are not in vain.
At the end of that long tunnel, the light is clear and plain,

For way off in the distance, midst a soft and hallowed arc,
Stands the form of my dear Mother with her candle in the dark!

Richard R. Davidson

LAST CAMP

When the last big mobs deliver down beside the Jasper sea,
And the sheep and goats are yarded, as we have been told they'll be,
When the horses are unhobbled to run free for evermore,
Then all the old-time drovers will camp there, by the shore.

And they'll build a mighty campfire that will boil a thousand quarts –
If they speak in different lingoes they'll have many common thoughts,
For their trade transcends the boundaries of colour, race and creed,
And horses buck and cattle rush, whatever be their breed.

There'll be stockmen from the Cooper where it hardly ever rains,
Drovers from the Snowy Mountains and the Riverina plains,
From the pampas, from the deserts, from the jungles and the snows,
They'll muster at the Big Gates when the final trumpet blows.

And they'll praise the shining waters that are never known to dry,
And they'll laud the star-tipped grasses, green and sweet and belly high,
They'll extol the blessed country where the season never fails …
And when they tire of giving thanks, why, won't they tell some tales.

They'll tell of treks across the veldt, of longhorns on the trail,
How they held the plant together in a Gobi Desert gale,
How they blocked the lead at Meetuck Hole, when the
    Tobermoreys rung,
Or sweated grass in a Jordan pass, when Abraham was young.

And the master of the drovers who is known to all the crew,
Boss of Jacob, Lobengula, the Duracks, Mohammed too,

Will walk beside the campfires in the evening's cooking smoke
And smile a quiet and kindly smile, and listen to them joke.

And I hope there'll be a place for me
And all my old bush mates,
When they hold that final muster
There beside the golden gates.

THE WINDMILL MEN

We've heard the tales of the stockman true,
    who saddles the roughest colt,
And we've laughed at the English jackeroo –
    presented as a joke
(Though he tamed the land in the days gone by,
    and battled with drought and flood;
And left is the white man's heritage,
    which he bought with his new-chum blood).
The swagman, bagman and rouseabout,
    the man that steadies the lead,
The overseer and the station cook,
    and the rest of the outback breed
Have had their stories, their hopes and dreams
    sung by the old bush bards,
And many have told of the teamster bold,
    and the men who built the yards.

But this is the song of the greasy coots
In the old felt hats and the blucher boots –
The men who have never been told of yet,
Who earn their tucker in grease and sweat:
THE STATION WINDMILL MEN.

And mostly camped at the back of the run
    (we're sought by many and loved by none),
Where the boss and the stockman pass us by
    while we shiver or sweat 'neath a worn-out fly.
Where the flour tastes of kerosene,
    and the rum is tainted with diesoline,

Far from the town and our misspent youth
    (further from heaven and love and truth):
THE STATION WINDMILL MEN

When you spur the outlaw out of the yard,
    there's plenty to cheer you on.
There's a bouquet too for the jillaroo
    who marries the squatter's son.
The drover's wife has a place in life
    (as we learned at the old bush school).
There's even a niche in the outback lore
    for a Paddy riding a mule.

But without us coots in the greasy boots
Who toil with spanner and block,
The water points would be scarce indeed,
And so would the station stock.
REMEMBER THE WINDMILL MEN.

There's a thrill in riding a flashy colt
    (while the rest of the camp look on);
There's glory riding the station crack
    in a hard-fought finish home.
But the ride on thirty foot of tail
    from the ground to the cap in a summer gale
While the ginpole creaks and the guy ropes whip
    is an unsung, unsought and thankless trip
RESERVED FOR THE WINDMILL MEN.

The ringer's fires will burn tonight
    with their mythical mystic glare,
The horse bells chime in the creek tonight,
    and the poets will be there.

But we'll be camped by some lonesome rock,
   on downs selection or desert block,
Working with pinchbar, hammer and chock,
   keeping the water up to the stock:
THE STATION WINDMILL MEN.

TRYIN' TO GET A QUID

The old man sat on the tractor seat,
There was dust in his hair and grease on his feet,
And he said, 'This job has got me beat,
Tryin' to get a quid.

'The pressure's low and the engine's hot,
The tracks are loose and the gears are shot,
But this old bitch is all I've got,
To try and get a quid.'

He turned down the bank with an awful roar,
And he made for the other side full bore,
And he opened the taps as he hit the floor,
Tryin' to get a quid.

But the scoop got snagged on a big white rock,
And he swore and cursed as he did his block,
Put the governor over the safety stop,
Tryin' to get a quid.

She blew right up when the con rod broke,
And the old man died in a cloud of smoke.
As he passed he said, 'It ain't no joke
This tryin' to make a quid!'

But ... he was insured for twenty grand,
Which the company paid on his wife's demand,
And she said as she took the cheque in hand ...
'At last he's got a quid!'

THE GRAVY TRAIN

I lived for years in the bush – far out – and I starved for lack of rain
Till I slipped the yoke that had kept me broke and caught the gravy
    train;
Now the bridle may rot on the stockyard rail, the shovel in the drain,
And the crowbar rust in the yellow dust, or ever I work again.

The ringers shall strive with the starving stock, but I will not be there –
I'd rather the pub than the gidyea scrub; and I'll weep in my icy beer
When I think of the years I left behind, of the futile fruitless fight
To wrest a home from the stubborn loam, before I saw the light.

We are 'the backbone of the land', the politicians say.
There's plenty of sweat and a ton of debt, but bloody little pay;
There's flood and fire and dust and drought, tears and an overdraft,
A wornout wife and a wasted life, rewarded all the graft.

So I've got a job with the council mob and I live in a house rent free,
And I drive from the bar in a council car, when I go home to tea.
The cattle may die by the dried-up dam or perish on the plain,
The bank may sweat about the debt – I'm on the gravy train.

Kelly Dixon

THE LAST OF HER LINE

Hold her here in the shade, where I'll take off her shoes,
Let me fondle her brow one last time,
Then just lead her away, to the big willow bend
And be kind to this good mare of mine.

Oh, the best little mare ever jangled a bit,
She has mustered the scrubs her last time.
Now her shoes, like old Minstrel's, a keepsake will be
Of old Memories – the last of her line.

The last by old Minstrel, the best blood around,
With her stride ever sure, ever free.
Old Memories was magic, through bonewood and box,
And her hoofbeats were music to me.

In the heat of the muster you'll all miss the mare,
When a dozen are winded and lame.
Search though you might, for the rest of your life,
You will never find one quite so game.

Never spur stung her girth, for she needed no goad
With her courage, and temper so fine.
Mark a mark that will last, o'er the grave where she sleeps:
Vale – Memories, the last of her line.

A grander mare never my bridle will claim,
My saddle a sweeter one know.
When she sleeps her last sleep, by the bend in the creek,
Where the clover and wild sorghum grow!

In the station horsebook, write in gold if you can,
Write that she was the last of her line –
The last filly by Minstrel, so mark the grave well
For old Memories – the last of her line!

FOOLSCAP TOMBSTONES

With fading ink brandings, and covered in dust,
Forgotten up here on this shelf out of view –
These old station journals and cheque lists and such,
Naming those pound-a-week people I knew.

The names of old ringers and fencers and breakers,
Camp cooks and drovers, a housemaid or two,
Firing old memories, these old station journals,
Are shrouding the names of bush people I knew.

Names long forgotten by company shareholders,
Written in ledgers up here on this shelf.
Cheque-butts bear witness to pound-a-week battlers
Who did precious little to better their self.

Names of hard toilers, bad boozers and brawlers,
There are one or two names of good horsemen I knew,
Indelibly etched in these old station journals –
Abandoned, and held by a ribbon of blue!

Copies of records required by head office –
Monthly reports from a man held 'in trust'.
Fragile old entries on musty old foolscap,
Now home for red hornets, and red Cooper dust.

Credits and debits, in copperplate pencilling,
Statements of earnings and entries in red,
Adjustments, corrections, reversals and afterthoughts,
Mentions of musters and days that are dead.

Close to my hand lies a volume of history
Listing some names, seldom spoken, deceased.
Dead though they may be, today they come back to me,
Reading these pages, so dusty and creased.

And who in head office now values this history –
History with which these old journals are filled?
How many shareholders still drink to the memory
Of the pound-a-week ringer, a station horse killed?

The bush-bred young housemaid, now where has she wandered?
The scribe who composed these four-weekly reports?
And where is the dogger, the drover, the blacksmith,
The others who form a parade through my thoughts?

Ah! Old station records all tattered and dusty,
Though banished from sight here, neglected, alone –
You are fragile, yet stronger than flowery epitaphs,
Man ever chiselled on marbled headstone!

Well I'll dust you and mend you and care for you now.
I'll place you out there at the front, in full view –
And every so often I'll come by and squander
Some time with these pound-a-week people, and you.

READING THIS LETTER

There's mist in the valley, I hear the creek singing,
And I hear the cry of the mournful curlew.
I can see clouds on the tops of the ranges,
Tonight ... as I'm reading this letter from you!

Oh! I can hear clearly the thunder of hoof beats,
I'd give all I own for a quart pot of tea.
Visions of home you have painted in pencil,
Here in this letter you've written to me.

Smoke from a campfire of cypress comes drifting,
I can see rose bushes dripping with dew.
I hear the butcher bird trilling the dawning,
Tonight ... as I'm reading this letter from you.

A wedgetail on vagabond wings I see soaring,
Mustering the clouds in his realm of blue.
Blossoms from beefwood and bloodwood are falling,
Tonight ... as I'm reading this letter from you.

Foals in the pasture are wheeling and playing,
Proudly, the brood-mares go galloping free.
I can hear horse-bells and I can hear hobbles,
Forever the sweetest of music to me.

It soon will be branding time, out on the station,
You wrote how the Mitchell is waving and gold.
You say there are cleanskins in hundreds to muster,
And the fats from Kianga are already sold.

You've broken the filly we bred from old Mystic,
I read how she works like her dam used to do.
I see the heelers, and I hear the stockwhips,
Tonight ... as I'm reading this letter from you.

Oh! I can see Murphy, his moleskins in tatters,
Heading some pikers away from the scrub,
Or riding a rough one just broken to saddle,
Or shouting the bar in the old Federal pub!

Ah! It's goodbye the days of the camp and the muster –
Goodbye the days when I rode like a king –
Racing a good one through boulder and bracken,
Or bending a rogue when he burst from a wing.

I crave one last yarn, one last drink with old mates,
One last ride down those old tracks we all knew –
Just to leave far behind the despairs of this town,
Where, tonight ... I am writing this letter to you!

A wedgetail on vagabond wings I see soaring,
Mustering the clouds in his realm of blue.
Blossoms from beefwood and bloodwood are falling,
Tonight ... as I'm writing this letter to you.

ONLY WILD HORSES

So you've wheeled them out, and you've killed the foals,
You've crippled them too, in the rocks and holes,
As you've yarded at last the mob.
You have chivvied and raced and cursed at them
From the scrubs to the creek, to the scrubs again –
Oh! proudly you boast of your job.

Unseeing you are of the mares' torment
As they search the winds where their weaners went,
And nicker in deep despair.
The stallions, no longer proud, stand mute,
Beaten and cowered, does a poor dumb brute
Stir in your breast a care?

Born to the freedom of limitless plain,
Bred by the shelter of valley and range
And spawned by one careless deed –
Branded a pest, to be cruelly slain,
Their bones may bleach, yet their blood will stain
Your conscience and mark your greed!

When the night winds howl, and the bonewoods toss,
And the cold air sharpens the Southern Cross
While your prized herd grazes your grass,
Will you sometime fancy you hear the tread
And savour the dust, as a thousand head
Of brumbies – in your dreams, pass?

A DRIFTER'S GRAVE

No bagpipes to skirl and no bugle to chorus,
No solemn-faced preacher with Bible to pray,
No cortege to follow his bier to the graveside.
Few ever will sight this lone place where he lay,

Where musterers found him, five miles from a water,
Guided by carrion birds to this place.
A lost soul who wandered away with a bottle,
To perish out here, where the dust devils race.

A quickly dug grave and a pile of red gibbers,
No headstone of marble to tell passers-by –
Some rough-hewn bush rail, by a blaze on a mulga,
To show where this unknown forever shall lie.

The dingo at evening will howl to a soulmate,
The night birds will twitter a ghostly refrain,
Where sometimes the stockmen, in search of stray cattle,
May pass now and then by this lonely red plain.

The suns of the summers will bleach the bush railings,
The winds of the winters the grasses shall dry.
The spring rains will nourish wildflowers a moment,
By this grave where an unknown, a nameless will lie.

Beyond the wild bush and across the wide oceans
Perhaps far away on some strange foreign shore,
A wife or a mother, a sister or brother,
May weep for a lost one they'll see never more.

YESTERDAY'S GHOSTS AND ME

Sometimes at night I go down to the place
    where the Georgina waters are quiet,
When the birds are all camped on the coolibah limbs,
    and the moon casts a ghostly light
When the night breeze whispers through the silken grass,
    and stars paint a silvered roof,
While a lone swan trumpets his sad refrain –
    to the beat of a distant hoof.

It is then, only then, I hear the bells
    and the chime of the hobble-chains.
When I close my eyes, I can see the sweep
    of those rolling Barkly plains.
The pungent scent of the horses' sweat! –
    and the redhide reins I still feel –
And I hear the jingle of Wave Hill spurs,
    on some long-dead drover's heel!

There comes to me, too, the lilting sound
    of a watching drover's song
As I swear I can see a travelling mob,
    fifteen hundred strong –
Where the Buchanan wanders –
    Flinders and Mitchell, waving stifle high,
Like they used to be for my ghosts and me,
    when we'd beaten the Murranji!

The lancewood cracks like lightning bolts,
    and a bellowing cook I hear
Thundering hooves, a red dust cloud,
    and the smell of nighthorses' fear –

The roaring rush of a maddened mob,
    from a camp where the bullwaddie grew,
And the sound of the bells on the plant at night,
    those awe-filled nights we once knew.

I picture the spread of a Kimberley mob,
    with the wings a mile apart –
On the sundrenched plains of the Tableland,
    and it gladdens a drover's heart.
Ah! a camping mob on a moonlit night,
    with the Southern Cross on high,
And the sights and sounds of the rosy dawns,
    of those wonderful days gone by!

Yesterday's ghosts are always there,
    they wait, 'cause they know I will be
Where the lone swan trumpets his wild refrain,
    and old campsites I can see –
It is there the music of hobble-chains,
    and the Condamines sweet and free,
Comes, borne on a breeze from the droving days –
    to yesterday's ghosts and me!

TRAPPED

Drought, and December, the third year of famine,
Claiming the last of the weaklings, the poor.
Stark now the bones, lying bleaching and marking
Pathways of torture which lead to the bore.

The timberline shimmers, a smudge on the skyline,
The raw savage sun heats the red gibber plain.
No vestige of pasture or cleanskin or brumby –
The dust devils herald the morning again!

Away where the lancewood entwines with the mulga,
Where seldom the long-searching stockmen now ride,
The wilga and currajong, boxwood and heather,
Give shade in the noonday – where bush cattle hide!

Away to the westward, mirages are dancing –
Illusions of water the lost soul to craze –
And fifty miles north on the brassy horizon,
The range on the boundary is muted in haze.

Missed every muster since he was a yearling,
A monarch – he dwarfs the top rail of their yards –
His scalpel-like horns are a challenge to any
Who covets a wife from the harem he guards.

Disturbed by the scents and the sights at the water,
Drinkless, he holds his mob three days and more.
Mistrustful of gateways and hateful of mankind,
He puzzles what dangers encircle that bore.

Ah! but drought and December test even the bravest,
Of hearts, in this place where the dust devils breed.
By evening the old bull is coaxing his charges
To muster their spirits and follow his lead.

Softly, so softly, he calls to his matrons.
Quietly they nuzzle the calves to their feet,
Dejected, they break one last time from the timber
To follow their Lord from that leafy retreat.

They leave their last refuge of boxwood and wattle,
For the long painful trek to the borehead again.
No longer majestic, their leader now shambles,
This last time he leads them 'cross gibber and plain.

At moonrise they huddle behind the old leader,
Who nervously sniffs at the scents he so hates,
But thirst is the victor, he loses, and falters –
Like Judas he leads the mob through the steel gates!

Nimbly, a stockman leaps down from a beefwood,
He swings the big gates and they lock with a snap.
The warrior ushers his mob to the trough
Where they drink and surrender to man and his trap.

At sunrise, the manager straddles the top rail.
He gloatingly studies the pitiful mob.
Then turns to his stockmen – now thoughtfully standing –
None hearing him mouthing his praise for their job.

SULLIVAN

I was somewhere back in the bygone days,
  when I met with a saddlemate –
A tall, tough bloke with a Tim Carr stool
  and a rolling horseman's gait.
He was lean and brazed by the western sun,
  and his swag was cigarette thin.
His bridle touch was his trademark too,
  along with his larrikin's grin.
We met in the bar of a backblocks pub,
  where the Warrego waters flow,
Or it might have been on the Paroo side –
  it's been forty years or so
Since that distant day in that distant town
  when Sullivan first came in.
He ordered a drink and winked at me,
  and gave me that larrikin grin.

We eyed each other as strangers will,
  then Sullivan offered his hand.
He'd come, he said, from the Dawson scrubs,
  and mentioned a famous brand.
Some trouble it seemed with a woman back there,
  some vixen's hot caress
Had signalled the need for him to move –
  and cancelled his old address.
Sullivan said he had run stock camps
  'way down on the Dawson side',
And I knew from his build and the Tim Carr stool,
  Sullivan knew how to ride.
Even the clothes that he wore so well,
  and the boots so shiny and neat,

Told me enough of the kind of bloke he was,
    and his tiny feet –

Were certain signs of a horseman true,
    and the hat which crowned his head
Bespoke his place in a rider's world,
    where never the fearful tread.
And I could tell from the belt that he wore,
    'twas a dinner-camp hobble too –
That Sullivan came from a place where
    only the best of the men will do.
We camped that night on the edge of town,
    and we yarned till the stars grew pale.
Between us a bond was formed that night,
    which years have never seen fail.
We rode and romped our way through life,
    our coin we gambled and spent,
And seldom did ever we walk away
    with a cheque from wherever we went.

Side by side we would tackle a task,
    or back to back in a brawl,
Stirrup to stirrup I rode the west,
    with Sullivan – grandest of all –
Of the mates I made in my younger days,
    when our lives were wild and free,
When a good stockhorse meant more than gold
    to Sullivan and to me!
We both had known a lover or two,
    in some two-bit outback town,
But women don't fit with a rambler's life,
    boozing and knocking around.
Sullivan never had time to stay
    too long in some fair one's arms

And I was the same in those far-off days,
   no women had ever the charms

To coax us both from the cattlecamps,
   from the shanty and the lonely shed
To the hearth and its cheery fireplace –
   we favoured our swag instead.
Many's the heart that Sullivan broke,
   with his reckless vagrant life,
But Sullivan sooner would love his horse,
   than settle with home and wife.
Not once in the years that we knocked about,
   did I ever see Sullivan thrown
From a bad bush horse or a playful colt,
   he belonged to a class of his own.
He always offered to 'take a twist'
   from something I could not best –
Between us we rode anything that came,
   in those camps of the golden West.

No charging mick in a branding yard,
   and no bull in some frowning scrub
Struck fear in the heart of Jim Sullivan then,
   nor a brawl in some seedy pub.
Sullivan sooner would fight than eat,
   'twas told in the camps and the town
But he'd always offer a helping hand
   to a foe he had just knocked down!
Then in '54, the Korean War
   seemed to beckon to me and to Jim.
He felt he should 'fight for our freedom and flag'
   and I wanted to follow him.

When those bugles called Jim Sullivan
    strode to the Inchon front and its mud,
Where he lost his life in a filthy trench,
    all stained with Australian blood.

The screaming shell and the sniper's round
    are things I never have known.
The booby traps on the battlefield,
    where the grim grenades are thrown,
Were part of the hell that he would live,
    and part of the price he'd pay,
Yet he smiled his larrikin's grin at me
    when he went off to war that day.
My health too frail to follow my mate,
    I stayed behind to curse –
Where I fretted that Sullivan went to war,
    but today I know what is worse.
Each Anzac Day when the brass bands play,
    I know what they're playing for,
And I still see that grin on a larrikin's face –
    when Sullivan went to war.

I met with a veteran from Sullivan's mob,
    who had known the horrors as well –
The firefights and the shrapnel burst,
    and the mines in that snow-filled hell.
The Yalu River he said was cruel,
    but Sullivan soldiered on
Against fearful odds, with a worn-out gun,
    and most of his comrades gone.
Now the long parades, and the marching bands,
    the banners and bugles sweet,

The medals on veterans' ageing chests,
 the streamers which litter the street,
All take me back to another time –
 when Sullivan first walked in
To that run-down bar in that western town
 and gave me his larrikin's grin.

FOR A PATCH OF GRASS

When years were dry and the routes were bare,
With no grass to be seen from here to there,
'And the teams must eat' was the teamsters' claim
From here to there it was all the same.

When wool from the sheds was branded and baled,
The teams went out, and they seldom failed,
When grain was headed and bagged and sewn
It was hauled by teams, and never once known.

Was a wagon-load lost by some careless lout.
It was work well-done, when the teams went out
To a distant shed on some hungry run,
Or some battler's block, with the harvest done.

'The teams must eat,' was the time-worn claim
And to steal some grass was a kind of a game
For the teamster's boy, with the bell-tongues tied,
And his trusty pliers he would always hide

Should a squatter ride to the camp to seek
Were the horses out on the grassless creek …
Or grazing, rich, on his well-fenced land,
With a fence laid low by the horseboy's hand?

When dark came down, and the squatter's horse
Left his hoofbeats there by the watercourse,
Then the wires tight would be all tied back
To a strainer post, and the boy would smack

The rumps of the horses and let them pass
Through the waiting gap to the welcome grass,
And the squatter, asleep in his mattressed bed,
Would dream a curse on that teamster's head

Whilst the boy camped out, on the cockie's land,
With the horses he loved dear close to hand,
And he'd loosen the hobbles at first daylight,
Then drive the mob to the campfire bright

Where the teamster would smile and hook the chains.
Then he'd face once more those beckoning plains,
His horses ready for Heartbreak Pass,
Their bellies all full of the squatter's grass.

And down the track a squatter would wait
On his thoroughbred hack, by his boundary gate,
To say hello, and smile at the kid –
But wide awake to what teamsters did!

'Well, the team must eat,' was the teamster's claim,
And to beat each other was rather a game,
'Twixt the teamster's boy and the squatter class,
A game played out for a patch of grass!

MULLIGAN

Mulligan's team was a sorrowful sight, his horses and harness too;
His wagon tyres were always loose, and his wagon, a faded blue,
Was held together by greenhide lace and pieces of rusted chain,
And Mulligan's house was an old-time hut, out on a blacksoil plain.

Though Mulligan often had taken the sweat from another teamster
    horse,
He always claimed to a questing soul that 'the owner approved', of
    course.
Many a trooper had tried to pinch old Mulligan for such a crime,
But technical points of law, it seemed, beat the troopers every time!

Mulligan wandered the wagon tracks in the timeless land out there,
Seemingly hauling the loads of freight for cockies who did not care.
Mulligan managed to meet the times, due mostly, they said, to Luck –
Times laid down for the load to meet with a steamer or railway truck.

The Devil, some claimed, was saddlemate to Mulligan and 'tis true –
No other teamster dared do the things that Mulligan used to do.
Despite the best of the gear they owned, the hearts of their horses bold,
None could better his feats or fists, or equal the tales some told

Of Mulligan's rides in the dead of the night with troopers at his heel,
Or how he had shaped from coolibah limbs new spokes for a wagon
    wheel
With only a rasp and a piece of glass and a broken-handled axe,
Or how he was always ready to help other teamsters along the tracks.

Shanty-keepers along the way spoke Mulligan's name with pride.
Never their doors they closed to him on the tracks of the Paroo side.
Overproof rum was Mulligan's choice, oft brewed in a shady still,
The strength of which was enough, some said, a drover's dog to kill!

It chanced one day that a drover wild with a mob from a Queensland
 run
Reined his horse by Mulligan's team and thought he would have some
 fun.
He cleared his throat and firmly spoke, 'I won't call the law this time,
But I see you've got in your team today a bloody good horse of mine.

'If you drop the chains and just turn him out, no trooper ever will
 know,
'Cos bushmen most have a sin to hide, and we give each other a go.'
Mulligan grinned and assured the bloke he was sorry, 'but would he
 mind
Dismounting his steed and dropping the chains, to leave the horse
 behind?'

The drover worriedly did just that, and a gelding nuzzled his hand,
Then shook himself, as a horse will do, and rolled in the welcome sand.
Mulligan called to his team to start, and away to the south they strode.
The drover wolfishly grinned awhile, then back to his mob he rode!

Mulligan's boy was just sixteen years and, puzzled, he failed to see
Why his dad was rude to the droving man and the horse he did not free.
He voiced his thoughts to his father then, who said with a grin, 'because
With this team of ours, I wasn't too sure, just which bloody one it was!'

This is one of a thousand tales of Mulligan in my youth,
And I venture to state few would know where fiction marries with truth.
But I know for sure many legends lived – the folk of the bush know
 too –
Though we bury 'em deep, they will still rise up – those Mulligans
 always do!

THE PRIDE OF THE PLAINS

Taylor's team was the pride of the plains,
    in a time when the horse was king –
A time when as kids, in my bush hometown,
    we waited for teams to bring
The four-square loads from the shearing sheds
    to the waiting, whistling trains.
We'd wait for days just to catch a glimpse
    of Taylor's Pride of the Plains!

Taylor's wagon was always smart,
    and painted in two-tone green.
Jim Taylor's horses were kept well-shod,
    and no truthful teamster had seen
Twenty-four punches better than they,
    which tensioned the singing chains,
When the wheels were held by the clinging mud
    on the blacksoil Barcoo plains!

The seven-inch tyres on Taylor's rig
    were polished by gravel and shone
With a sheen like mansion's silverwear,
    when chanderliered lights are on!
The spokes and felloes of every wheel
    were lined and scrolled, and the chains
Were painted green like the coaming rails,
    fixed to The Pride of the Plains.

Twenty-four chestnuts, evenly matched,
    all pulling as hearts would burst.
Twenty-four punches never were whipped,
    and never were railed or cursed –

Loved by the master they trusted and loved,
    that trust unsullied by stains.
We kids would sooner miss dinner and tea
    than the sight of The Pride of the Plains!

Many's the time when my sister and I
    just wagged it from school to spend
An afternoon where the teamsters camped,
    down in the river's bend,
Where we'd thrill to the music of Condamine bells
    as horses grazed the grass,
And we always seemed to know just when
    The Pride of the Plains would pass!

Though the teamsters knew we should be at school,
    they too had been kids, they said,
And all loved the teams and the wagons too,
    with twenty and twenty-four head.
Like us they lived for the chorus of bells
    and the chime of the hobblechains,
Like us, they secretly loved the sight
    of Jim Taylor's Pride of the Plains.

But time moved on, and the trucks were born,
    and a melancholic haze
Now blurs my view of the splendid scenes
    of the horse and wagon days –
When dawning's echoed the tramping hooves,
    and the ring of the straining chains,
And a couple of bush kids risked the cane
    just to wave to The Pride of the Plains!

Gone are the days of my childhood now –
    the teams and the wagons too –
But that diesel smoke cannot mark the way
    like the horse-dung used to do.
Though their trucks are labelled Midnight Miss,
    and another is Love's Tearstains,
They never will capture this horseman's heart
    like Taylor's Pride of the Plains!

Bert Dunn

BLUEY AND I

Once Bluey and I from the 'Whispering Bore'
Went hunting the 'roos for the jackets they wore.
We had but one rifle, an old .38,
But true as a hair if you pointed it straight.
My mate, so he said, with the rifle or gun,
On trap door or target was second to none.
We soon found some hoppers as busy as bees.
All feeding like steam with their heads to the breeze.

'Be careful,' I whispered, 'and don't miss a shot.
There's seventeen there and you might get the lot.'
So resting the gun in the fork of the tree,
The aim that he took was a caution to see.
Then he fired not once but the full magazine,
But not a 'roo dropped of the whole seventeen.
Stock still they all stood, save a pair of young does,
Who were prancing around on the tips on their toes.

Then 'Dammit' I cried as the kangaroos fled.
'It seems that you're wasting our powder and lead.
You say you're a shooter – you're blind as a bat.
Why, Warrigal's gin could do better than that.
I wonder what's wrong with your shooting,' I cried,
'For it's plain to see that your bullets go wide.
But where are they going, you never hit one.'
'I know,' he replied, 'but they're leaving the gun.'

Annoyed with his shooting, to say I was wild
At this stupid rejoinder was drawing it mild.
'Oh! give me the rifle,' I said to my mate,
'And I'll knock a few over before it's too late.'
So snatching the rifle I strode on ahead,
To show him my skill with powder and lead.
We hadn't gone far when we found them again,
All quiet as mice on the edge of a plain.

With magazine loaded and one in the breech,
We crept within range of a regular peach –
A monster old buck fully six feet in height,
And slinging his weight around looking for fight.
I snapped off the trigger the moment he stopped,
And kept my eyes open to see if he dropped.
But he stood like a statue, not caring a hoot,
Although I shot five or six times at the brute.

Oh I fired away till my shoulder was black,
Till the seventeen fled with their ears laid back.
Then Blue remarked as he stifled a grin,
'Next time we go out we'll fetch Warrigal's gin.'
When back at the camp, empty-handed and sad,
We looked at the boxes of bullets we had
And plain on the cover – believe it or not–
Was '38 calibre loaded with shot'.

THE BALLAD OF BRONCO BILL

Now Bronco Bill on a horse's back
Was a king in the cattle domain –
He could run a trail where a myall black
Would lose it in half a chain.
No weakling he, nor a bush-bred fool,
No midget of seven stone –
In a 'knuckle up' in a two-up school
He could easily hold his own.

Let winners smile and the losers weep,
You could gamble the game was fair;
You could stake your money and go to sleep
If Bronco Bill was there.
But he thought one day he would take a change
From the bridle, the stockwhip and brand,
So he turned his back to the Selwyn Range
And the charm of the cattle land.

Then he waved farewell to the Western downs
And the dazzling skies of blue,
And he drifted down to the coastal towns,
Like most of the stockmen do.
There he met a maiden of beauty rare,
As fair as the bloom of Spring;
A bold brunette with eyes and hair
As dark as the raven's wing.

Though lacking the charm of the 'Gippsland Girl'
She was pretty enough, you bet,
For she set poor Bronco's head awhirl
The moment their glances met.

Then for five long years (she was false indeed,
Though tempting and fair of face),
Though tears may fall and your heart may bleed,
She led him a maiden's chase.

Till at last he said, 'We must now decide
The day of our wedding to be.'
'But you're not number one,' the girl replied,
'And you're not even two or three.'
Then Bronco Bill gave a painful start.
And reached for his bridle reins,
And he rode away with a sinking heart,
And made for the Bunda Plains.

On women he frowned wherever he went,
And deeper he plunged in the swift descent,
Till drink was his only bride.
T'was little he cared if he bought a fight,
For his love was a painful dream;
And he scolded the publicans left and right,
And ordered 'em round like steam.

There were pitying friends in scores of course,
But his ruin went on unchecked,
Till even the girl felt deep remorse
And wept for the life she wrecked.
He died, of course? No, he never died –
That wasn't the way with him –
And you'll find him now in the regions wide
Where the western stars grow dim.

Well, a broken man? No, he isn't broke,
For he fights like a fiend from hell,

And he'll crack a joke or lend a smoke,
And fight for a mate as well.
Then he lived it down? Of course he did
(And wouldn't you do the same?),
For Bronco counts himself well rid
Of the girl who was lost to shame.

Should you ever meet him you'll find a friend
Who'll shout you a drink or a feed,
And he'll stick to a mate to the journey's end
Wherever the track may lead.
But touch with care on his love bereft,
Or a dark girl's charming smile,
For remember he carries a dirty left,
And it mightn't be worth your while.

Gary Fogarty

THE HUT

There's a hut near Mondeorilby, out amongst the bull-oak stand,
That for years has stood neglected, now it rots there in the sand.
With its solitude unbroken, 'cept for those who come by chance,
And the timid bushland creatures who just add to its romance.

The dawn's light paints the shadows like a master artist's stroke,
As the mist on winter mornings drifts away like campfire smoke.
While the magpie's early calling drowns the echoes of the past
Around the remnants of this bushman's hut, history's shroud is cast.

The roof is sagged and rotting and the chimney's all askew,
The doorway stands unguarded and the wind just whistles through.
The rough hand-hewn timber speaks aloud to those who know
The foundations of our nation are standing here on show.

And while learned scholars rave aloud about the great 'bush myth',
They denigrate the memory of our world-renowned wordsmiths.
In their marbled halls of learning, in an academic bliss,
Dispensing words of wisdom while the truth they squarely miss.

They're entitled to their theories, and they're entitled to their say,
But they should not have the mandate to lead our youth astray.
As they mourn our lack of culture, 'cause it does not suit their style,
And ignore the bush that bore us and ignore the bushman's guile.

For despite their lofty intellect, despite their learned ways,
They miss true understanding of the bush and all her ways.
And despite their push for progress and for true ideals that last,
They gaze in blinding ignorance at the lessons of the past.

But life's a better teacher than the best of public schools,
And those who learn her lessons will not be labelled fools.
They protest this desecration with a brush or with a pen,
So that truth shall not be altered, not least by learned men.

For the bush gave us a spirit and forged a nation's soul.
It gave to us a vision, and set for us a goal:
That everyone should have fair chance, that all should give their best,
No matter dressed in dungarees, or tailored suit and vest.

For in that hut near Mondeorilby, out amongst that bull-oak stand,
There's a monument for all of us, now rotting in the sand.
And I'll keep its presence guarded, 'cept from those who come by
    chance,
In case they mock the memory, or tarnish the romance.

YOU'LL FIND IT IN THE BUSH

Have you seen the blue dog darting, through the brigalow scrub and
    dust,
With iron will and jaws of steel, for when the scrubbers bust?
That's courage, and you'll find it in the bush.

Have you ever faced a bar-room brawl, and saw the odds too late,
Heard the soft step at your shoulder, and the words, 'I'm with you
    mate'?
That's friendship, and you'll find it in the bush.

Have you mustered up the wild-eyed colt and drawn the girth straps
    tight,
Then thrown your leg across him, and prayed with all your might?
That's excitement, and you'll find it in the bush.

Put the bay mare at the timber, that is growing thick and stout,
With only touch of hand or heel to swing the lead about?
That's skill, and you'll find it in the bush.

Have you ever searched your wallet and been wondering what to do,
When someone slips a tenner, 'cause they've been busted too?
That's compassion, and you'll find it in the bush.

Have you ever stood a line of fence, beneath a blistering sun,
And the aching of your muscles has proclaimed a good day done?
That's commitment, and you'll find it in the bush.

Have you seen the dawn's light glistening on the cobwebs dripped in
    dew,
As a soft breeze stirs the tree leaves and the whole world wakes anew?
That's beauty, and you'll find it in the bush.

Have you seen the old cow nuzzling at her new born baby calf,
Seen him struggle awkward to his feet, and can't suppress a laugh?
That's life, and you'll find it in the bush.

So you think this world's in trouble, think our country's had its day,
Then you haven't been inducted in the good old country ways.
For there's an answer, and you'll find it in the bush.

Keith Garvey

WETHERS

I've shore poor ewes and daggy lambs,
Angora goats and merino rams,
Gluey cross-breds as tight as clams,
   And wethers.
All me aches come alive again,
In me back there's a horrible pain
When I think of the endless strife and strain
   Shearin' wethers.

In nightmare dreams when the vampire feasts
And bats and owls honour pagan priests,
Me slumber is haunted by terrible beasts,
   Big rough wethers.
Out there the Gwydir its passage wends
Past ridges red where the blacksoil ends,
In memory again me torso bends
   Over big wethers.

High as the rails around the yard,
Wrinkly and weighty and wide and hard,
Waitin' to kick when yer lower yer guard,
   Wilful wethers.
Strugglin' and strainin' at every blow,
Crazy from feedin' on indigo,
Spawn of the devils down below,
   Bloody wethers.

Tryin' the temper of every gun,
Battin' for twenty-five a run,

Biggest bastards under the sun,
     Stinkin' wethers.
Now I'm retired and shear no more,
Still at times me muscles get stiff and sore
When I think of the torturin' times I shore
     Thumpin' great wethers.

Wicked red eyes and horns like knives,
Bred to shorten the shearers' lives,
And yer feel like swingin' a bunch of fives
     At the wethers.
Stampin' their feet and blowin' their noses,
And I'll warn yer, before me story closes,
If yer think that shearin's a bed of roses,
     Try rough wethers.
     '— the wethers!'

THE MIGHTY FLASK OF RUM

When yer battlin' wethers on the endless plains out west
And the wool is filled with seedy foxtail grass,
And they strain and kick like donkeys till yer swear yer'll give 'em best
And yer reckon shearin' sheep's a bloody farce.
Or in cold Monaro mountains when the mist is like a cloak,
Where the clammy mornin' dew gleams white and wet,
Where yer work on woody weaners till yer heart and back are broke
And yer dungarees and flannel reek with sweat,
While the wilful wind comes whistlin' like a banshee up the chutes
And yer're prayin' fer the final bell ter come,
So yer joyfully can stagger, fairly tremblin' in yer boots,
Ter the hut where waits the Mighty Flask of Rum.

Black and brutal brew from Bundaberg where grows the sugarcane,
Guaranteed per bottle 40 overproof,
Easin' every tortured muscle of its weariness and strain
With a kick that's strong enough ter lift the roof.
Take a shower and change yer clobber, then yer have another snort
Before lurchin' ter the dinin' room to eat,
Feelin' rowdy and resourceful now yer aches and pains are naught
And the steamin' roast of mutton is a treat.
Then yer sink in ter the blankets as the night falls dark and still,
Quite forgetful of the tiresome days ter come,
And yer slumber sound and peaceful while the mornin' hours grow
    chill
With beneath yer bunk the Mighty Flask of Rum.

But yer crawl out blind and bleary when yer hear the breakfast bell,
Sadly sober with no stomach fer the job,
And the tucker makes yer bilious and yer head's as hot as hell
And the tools are blunt and every sheep a snob.

So yer curse the grinnin' rouseabouts with banal words and bad
While silently yer swear ter drink no more,
And yer reckon that the hangover's the worst yer ever had
Since the very first occasion that yer shore.
Men who foller up the shearin' are a brainless mob of fools
Yer decide as, with expression sad and glum,
Yer take up the battle bravely till it's time ter drop the tools
And find comfort in the Mighty Flask of Rum.

THE SHEARIN'S ON AGAIN

Put a crimp in bluey, boys, the shearin's on again,
The musterers are saddlin' up on every hill and plain.
See the kelpies workin' wide where the big mobs spread,
Pushin' up the laggard tail or castin' far ahead.
The cook is in the kitchen, stokin' up the coals.
Mincin' stringy stag-meat for curries and rissoles.
Time to leave the Cross behind, gaudy girls and beer,
Roll yer swag and scarper, the shearin' time is here.

Put a crimp in bluey, boys, the shearin's on again,
Holidays are over now, it's time to catch the train,
Get the combs and cutters out, clean away the rust.
Western sheds are kickin' off, it's back o' Bourke or bust.
That's the place where every day the big guns cut the deuce,
Land where men are mostly men and laws are fast and loose.
Let's go where the rouseabouts pray all night for rain.
Westward where the brolga's dance, the shearin's on again.

Put a crimp in bluey, boys, there's money to be had,
Cash for willin' workers and battlers goin' bad.
Mulga wethers big and rough, hard merino ewes,
Providin' pain and backache for fellers on the booze.
Dainty little hoggets, good for fifty every run,
Encouragin' the learner who desires to be a gun.
Tighten up your dungarees, show a willin' heart,
Hop in, boys, and get a quid, the shearin's due to start.

Put a crimp in bluey, boys, the shearin's on again,
Dry and sunny weather makes the rouseabouts complain.
Ninety bucks a hundred now, hear the squatters squawk.
Fraser's in the discard, here's success to Mr Hawke.

See the ringer knuckle down, he's a hungry cow,
Streams of sweat and brilliantine pourin' down his brow.
Stokin' up on aspirin and rum to ease the strain.
Duck yer heads and graft, boys, the shearin's on again.

THE SHORTHORNS

White or dappled or red as flame,
From the hills of Durham the shorthorns came
Over the salt seas wide
To the timeless country a world away
Where the brigalows glitter silvery grey
And the world's best stockmen ride.

Selective breeding the strain improved,
Slowly inland the big mobs moved
Under the dust-wrack brown.
With quality constant in every line
On runs from the Gulf to Condamine
The shorthorn won renown.

Down where the Snowy runs deep and dark
By Monaro mountains cold and stark
Where wombats make their home,
Or where western rivers wend their way
Under the gums on a summer day,
The placid shorthorns roam.

Shiny and sleek from springtide graze
On Queensland pastures by lonely ways
Where Warrigul lurks unseen,
Watch them fatten where foothills rise,
Switching their tails at the countless flies
That swarm from the verdure green.

Strong resistance to blight and pest,
Veterinary officers all attest
Temperament calm and bland,

Showing the way where weight prevails
When butchered carcasses hit the scales
For export to foreign land.

Over the plain at fall of night,
Ghostly hulks in the fading light,
They move from the scrub to feed.
Many a nation starved for beef
Has cause to thank with profound relief
The famous shorthorn breed.

THE GHOST RIDERS

Darkness falls on a rodeo, ending
A day of excitement and thrills,
And contestants' mistakes are defending
Quite regardless of bruises and spills,
No Brahma or saddle-bronc fearing,
Never heeding the moment of truth,
Riding wild, unafraid and uncaring
With the reckless demeanour of youth.

And I wonder, as memories come wending
Through the dust of a past that has gone,
Were the ghosts of old riders attending
From a faraway yard looking on
Where the trees on the Jordan are shady
Under the heavenly mountain and ridge:
Were you watching us, Boomerang Brady?
Were you cheering our efforts, Ben Bridge?

Old man Skuthorpe would have to be present
To relive all his days that were great,
And in style both flamboyant and pleasant
Comes the Queenslander, dark Billy Waite,
To the bar where the champions palavar –
All excitement when fortune has smiled.
Are you knocking a beer down, Bill Carver?
Are you bucking the spurs, Charley Wilde?

For a spell Billy Timmins may tarry
And his presence is sure to be felt,
Plus the Englishman known as Wild Harry
Who lies buried on Africa's veld.

Many more of renown I could mention,
Though for long years departed they are,
How comparing their skills caused dissension
In discussions at showground and bar.

In their day they were fearless and famous,
Still their legendary feats linger on.
Soon the short years that claimed them will claim us
And the pride of our youth will be gone.
So good luck, every rodeo rival,
And a toast to the hard life we know
At the end of our earthly survival.
May we go where the ghost riders go.
May we go where the ghost riders go!

Bill Glasson

A CHILD SHALL LEAD THEM

Now this is a tale that has been relayed
From the days of 'away back when …'
Of Mary, a pleasant, attractive maid
Who could work with the best of men.
She would hold her own in a mustering camp
And shine in the stockyards too,
But she fell for Edward, a no good scamp,
As good girls so often do.

The church bells rang, he knew all the ropes,
For he was already wed.
He filled her head with unlikely hopes,
'We'll go to the west,' he said,
'And take up a block by the Condamine,
It's a land that is fit for kings.'
With hook and sinker she took his line,
For love does the strangest things.

Quite sadly, her life was unkind and rough,
She was killed when her stockhorse fell.
Though her 'married' life had been long enough,
For his secret was not kept well.
They buried her out by the Overflow,
Where the Moonie and Lancewood meet,
On a ridge where the gum and the cypress grow
And the scent on the air is sweet.

Now Ted, as you've guessed, isn't worth much space,
He worked with a droving team.

Chased different women from place to place
And went, more than a bit, off beam.
He drank like a fish, and in time he paid –
He was killed in a drunken fight –
Or was it the curse of a dying maid
That finished him off that night.

A story started, I'm not sure when,
That each month when the moon was bright,
The Moonie Ghost knelt beside the men
Who camped near her grave at night.
They were not believed, too much rum or wine
Was their problem, the sceptics mused.
But the drovers switched to the Condamine
And the Moonie was seldom used.

Drinking Moonie water, they also thought –
It's a tale that they still believe –
Made lying almost a favourite sport
And made beautiful girls deceive.
Now some Moonie-ites lie like a pig in dirt
And distort on the grandest scale,
But for most … well a little white lie won't hurt
And can often improve a tale.

A lifetime went, prickly pear arrived,
Some gardener's foolish joke.
The squatters came but could not survive,
For even the banks went broke.
Then cactoblastis, with better flocks
And farming, brought wealth again.
The brigalow belt was cut into blocks
For our eager ex-servicemen.

I drew a block of the virgin land
Where only the 'pikers' ran,
And I found her grave in the cypress stand
Where this sad little tale began.
It was there I felt something brush my arm —
A branch? Or her ghostly glove?
Then an anguished moan quickly shook my calm.
Was it just the belahs above?

A few old locals had heard her tale,
Some claimed to have seen her face.
They told me her ghost haunted every male
Who came by her resting place.
'Her soul can't rest,' one old drover said,
Enjoying his spectral flight.
'She was so deranged by that mongrel Ted,
She's as mad as a min-min light.'

Well, we had a couple of haunting years
With that poor little long lost shade;
We heard knocks and whistles and moans and tears
From the ghost of that misused maid.
But one morning I woke and my youngest girl
Stood quietly by my bed,
Brushing away at a golden curl,
And these are the words she said:

'Dad, I had a dream that won't go away,
A lady stood close to me.
And she asked if a little girl might pray
So her soul would at last be free.
I said all of the Protestant prayers I know
And some Catholic ones that I stole.

Then the lady just faded away so slow.
Oh! I do hope I saved her soul.'

Down the Moonie road, near the Eighteen Mile,
On a ridge by the Overflow,
You might find her grave if you pause a while,
Where the wattle and wildflowers grow.
And if you should camp for a night or more,
You'll awake to the birds' refrain,
But you'll not see the ghost that the drovers saw,
For only her bones remain.

This tale is as true as a tale can be –
Of that you need have no fear –
Though the Moonie river, I must agree,
Was my water supply for years.
But my darling girl with the golden hair
Will swear what I've said is true.
She's a church-going lass, but to be quite fair,
She has drunk Moonie water too.

PAROO

I was only a lad when I met Paroo,
With a mob on the stock route he so well knew,
Which happened to run through my father's land,
And, as drovers to me had the 'Clancy' brand,
I stayed and I showed him through.

A friendly fellow with hair of grey,
We rode together and yarned all day;
And the tales he told, whether wrong or right,
Were tales that filled me with sheer delight
As the bullocks marched on their way.

A few years later, my school days done,
I got the word from a neighbour's son
That Paroo was trying to find a hand,
To take a mob with the Quilty brand
Down south to the Boatman run.

With the war begun, men were hard to find,
So he signed me on to the droving grind.
We crossed the Flinders below old Kings,
And headed north to Euroka Springs,
With the horses, and me, behind.

The cattle were ready, we hit the road,
Though rainy weather our progress slowed.
We settled the mob and our time we took,
Three drovers, me and the babbling brook,
In the days when the drovers rode.

As the wet fizzled out and the roads got drier,
We made good time through Kynuna Shire
And the days and weeks, why they fairly flew,
As I soaked up the stories of old Paroo
At night, round a gidgea fire.

Three months on the road – to Paroos' delight –
We made Clara Creek, with the pub in sight.
He bought some rum, but it made him sad,
And for once his story was mean and bad
And went on until late that night.

He had dealt in horses way back before
The start of the '14–18 war.
The Indian Army had bought them all
And he made good money, he did recall,
But he wanted to make much more.

He bought up over a thousand head
And went up to his eyes in debt, he said.
He hired a ship called the *Hindu Queen*
That was run by a villain, both bad and mean,
Who was known as Truthful Ted.

The horses were loaded, his plans all made,
He hoped to corner the Bombay trade.
Well fed and fit, they would make good mounts
And their sale would swell out his bank accounts,
But fate is a fickle jade.

With only a few days left to go,
A radiogram with a tale of woe
Read, 'The price of horses has slipped to hell,'

And the agent added, 'Go home and sell,
Or hold for a year or so.'

His credit was gone and his cash was low,
Which the world and a boy would quickly know,
But then a thought to his belfrey sped:
The insurance cover, a score per head,
Might give him a second go.

He had staked his career on a decent sale
And lost, he was now facing years of gaol,
So he paced the deck in an awful stew
All night, till the Devil beat old Paroo
And he slid down the crooked trail.

The daylight came and his scheme was planned;
A storm to starboard, to port some land.
To the captain's cabin he quickly hied,
He quietly knocked and was let inside,
And the villains were hand in hand.

Five hundred pounds was the murderer's price
For this lowest point in a life of vice.
The charges were laid and an S.O.S.
Contributed to the plan's success,
Then muffled explosions twice.

They lowered the boats and then made for shore
As the *Hindu Queen* found the ocean floor,
While the shrieks of terror the horses gave
Would follow Paroo to his distant grave
And haunt him for evermore.

Soon the tropical storm with enormous drive
Had the lifeboats struggling to survive,
And Truthful Ted with his load of pelf
Went down with his boat on the Maldive shelf,
But Paroo made the shore alive.

And that was his tale, I am sad to say;
He fell off to sleep almost right away.
I rode his watch with a troubled mind,
Upset, for it's hard for a lad to find
That his idol has feet of clay.

With a hair from the dog in the early morn,
He rode after the horses, sick and drawn.
In an hour or so, as he'd not returned,
I followed his tracks, feeling quite concerned,
In the chill of a winter's dawn.

I found him lying beneath a tree
With a fractured skull and a broken knee,
But he whispered softly, 'The old grey horse
Got square for them all at last.' Remorse?
Well, not that a lad could see.

He died in his boots where the gum trees grew,
The greatest fellow I ever knew.
He was tempted and fell, but you don't forsake
A chap for making just one mistake.
Especially when I'm not sure how true
Was the tale of my drunken friend, Paroo.

THE FIREPLOUGH TEAM

Back in the years between the wars,
Away on the western plains,
Where the water poured from the flowing bores
And trickled along the drains,
Where the big red roo, with a nervous glance,
Filled up on the Flinders grass,
While the brolgas showed us their fairy dance,
And outshine any dancing class.

We had over a thousand miles to go
And were sure of a few delays;
Today you would say we were rather slow,
For it took us a hundred days.
We were pulling a plough with a ten-foot beam
Over downs where the bushfires roar,
With twenty-eight draughts in the fireplough team
And the tailer had sixty more.

We would muster the horses at break of day
And start ere the hot sun showed,
With the plough screwed down in the heavy clay
To make sure of a grass-free road.
For a job well done would mean this, my son,
We'd be back next year for sure.
Though we bowed or took off our hat to none,
We took pride in the name we bore.

Ten shillings a mile was the ruling rate
And we thought we were paid in full.
Today they plough with a Cat D8
And charge like a wounded bull.

But when bushfires raged, as they did back then,
On *our* tracks, they could all depend;
When western fellows were really men,
And the horse was still man's best friend.

THE PILTON VALLEY

The quiet's sometimes broken by the rustling of the leaves,
You will almost hear a spider as her web she deftly weaves;
In the distant valley, cattle quietly low, and now and then
You can hear a bellbird calling, soft and sweetly, to his hen.
There's a narrow, tinkling mountain stream, meanders slowly by,
Lots of ferns and wildflowers bloom and grow among the trees so high.
In a world of hare and madness, torn by war, disease and strife,
I have found peace and contentment and some quality of life.

There are motor cars and tractors, but they seldom raise the dust;
There's a dance hall at the corner and we go there when we must.
No hotels, and massage parlours are unknown out our way,
And – thank God – the nearest racetrack's over thirty miles away.
Cranky neighbours? An odd one, but there'll be narks in heaven, mind.
Let me add that on the whole, a better bunch you'd never find.
Set among the mountain ranges, where the cooler breezes blow,
It's delightful, quite the closest thing to Heaven that I know.

I have never been an angel and I hope they never wake,
For I'd hate to be like Lucifer, expelled, for goodness' sake.
I just want to stay and listen to the magpie's tuneful notes
And throw bread out to the parrots, with their green and crimson coats.
The rat-race sometimes beckons, when my cash is running low,
And bank managers suggest at times that maybe I should go,
But I feel sure with the rain we've had, enough to bog a flea,
That if I can stick to Pilton, Pilton's sure to stick to me.

PAMELA'S LETTERS

'My dearest Patricia, a hurried line,
    would you like a week here in May?
The season is good and the weather fine,
    and Henry will be away.'
Well Patricia arrived and we rode around
    and she met all the local push
She was still good fun and we laughed and clowned,
    but I don't think she liked the bush.

I well understand that it can be hard
    to adjust to our flies and heat,
Or the dust from the sheep and cattle yards,
    while a fly-blown ewe's not sweet.
Though I love it when city friends visit here
    and welcome their company,
Our sense of adventure today, I fear,
    is not what it used to be.

When I was a girl and the world was wide,
    our dad drew a brigalow run,
So I went out with him and camped beside
    a creek the block we'd won.
The howls of the dingoes I'll not forget,
    nor the sound of the night owl's call,
But in spite of the death adders being a threat,
    I fell for it warts and all.

The eagles were soaring up overhead
    and the roos hopped away in shock,
When, with Dad and my brothers Bill and Ted,
    we rode over our virgin block.

And I wonder how Pat would have liked the life,
    our toilet was rather crude,
And spiders, mosquitoes and ants were rife
    and a camp oven cooked our food.

We built, in a week or a little more,
    a fifty-by-fifty shed,
And that shed, with it's wall-to-wall earthen floor
    became home on our brigalow spread.
We ran some wires from here to there
    and hessian soon made a wall.
We bought a stove in quite good repair
    and a loo, with a seat and all.

Next the scrub was pulled and the yards were built
    and we steadily stocked the run;
Then Mother arrived, with a touch of guilt,
    for much of the work was done.
Her job had been selling our coastal farm
    and she really had done us proud,
So we furnished the shed with finesse and charm …
    well as much as the dirt allowed.

There was no TV for we had no power,
    but a copper from ages past
Supplied hot water so we could shower
    and smell like a flower at last.
Our shed was as fresh as the new-mown hay –
    daily watering kept it cool –
And my sister Roz, on her holiday,
    declared it beat boarding school.

We worked long hours from dawn till dark,
  keeping up with the jobs we'd planned.
We had our first drop of lambs to mark
  and a nice lot of calves to brand.
The weekends helped keep our young hearts bright
  for we went to the local hop,
And we swam and fished, when the fish would bite,
  or we went into town to shop.

When the creek was flooded we'd swim across
  to pick up our mail and stores.
A raft and line, with some minor loss,
  brought them back to the homestead shores.
Then a year-long drought and despair was near
  as the stock all began to die.
All the fun went out of our life that year,
  we thought God had passed us by.

But the clouds rolled in and the rain poured down
  till the paddocks were lush and green.
A smile took the place of Dad's worried frown
  and the creek was a lovely scene,
Full of yellow belly and cod galore,
  and gone were the wounds of drought.
Then to make things better, the boy next door
  asked Dad could he take me out.

Time drifted by and our house was built
  by the boys, under Dad's control,
Where the gums grew tall in the rivers silt,
  by a beautiful waterhole.
But twenty-odd years have wandered on
  and I married the boy next door,

While Mum and Dad have sold out and gone
    and the dingoes we hear no more.

'My dearest Pamela, thank you, dear,
    for a week that was really swell.
I have lost four pounds and my eyes are clear,
    it is years since I've felt so well.
There were so many things that I thought were great –
    that beautiful bower bird's nest
Full of flowers and diamonds to please his mate,
    I really was quite impressed.
Our swim after working the whole day long;
    Oh I fell for your bush, my dear ...'

Well, isn't it great to be proved dead wrong.
    She can come for a month next year.

THE NEW FARM

We'd been looking round for ages,
Reading 'Farms for Sale' in pages
Of the *Country Life*, and papers from Toowoomba out to Bourke.
When an agent rang and said he
Had a place if we were ready,
'It's your style,' he said, 'a beauty, it just needs a bit of work.'

In a valley quite secluded,
Ringed with hills that weren't denuded,
We were driven to inspect it, dozing as the agent jawed.
An old family, it appears,
Had lived there for sixty years,
But since they died off there'd only been an absentee landlord.

There were calves tied up and bawling
And the rain was softly falling
As we drove up to the homestead that had been locked up for years.
All the gutters, loose and battered,
Leaked, for they were torn and tattered;
It looked like a poor old lady left forsaken, shedding tears.

Very old and sad and musty,
All its roof was loose and rusty,
And a cow was camping underneath an awning out the back.
There were broken windows banging
Like a drunk, the front door hanging
And the long grass tried in vain to hide a fallen chimney stack.

Roses grew in wild abandon,
Ten feet high, in bloom, but hand in
Hand with Bathurst burr and thistles that had not been cut for years.

Out the back we found an orchard
Looking sad and rather tortured,
But the old place seemed to somehow smile a welcome through
    its tears.

In the paddocks there was clover,
All the tanks were running over
And the cattle looked as if they were all going to the show.
Del and I walked miles around it
And she said, 'Old man, we've found it.'
Then the sun shone on the homestead and we saw its tears go.

There were contracts, banks and hassles,
We cleaned up and dreamt of castles,
Cut the grass and nailed the roof down, pulled the lino from the floor.
That was when the ghosts all met us
In old papers and love letters
Of the boys who sailed off bravely to the '14–18 war.

And we got an understanding
Of the old place we were landing,
For the folk who built the house had left their story everywhere.
We relived their doubts and fears
As we read of Armentières,
And a letter from the boy who'll stay forever over there.

Now it's clean and full of gear
And we're sure it's pleased we're here,
With a cheery fire burning and its windows clean and bright.
In the orchard, trees are bearing,
You can tell that someone's caring,
And once more it's warm and friendly and we're sure our choice
    was right.

And the ghosts now are all sleeping,
We no longer hear them weeping;
If they call they'll come as friends to have a wander round and see
The old house with love a'glowing,
Roses pruned and cattle lowing,
And perhaps one day we'll have it as they wanted it to be.

Marco Gliori

MATES

I've never known the mateship that is forged in times of war –
I'm a middle-class consumer with the tax man at my door.
But still I'm sentimental, and the thing I hate the most
Is to come across Australians who have given up the ghost.
Those fly-by-night pretenders who desert their losing teams,
Who jump on board the bandwagon – not knowing what it means
To stand beside a wounded friend regardless of their fate …
If they had they'd understand the meaning of a MATE!
I've got mates from Loserville with not a cent to spare,
Yet they offer something priceless you can't buy anywhere.
They'll never patronise you with false compliments you hate,
But rib you like a ratbag just to prove that they're a MATE!
They're dags for all occasions and the dribble never stops,
With suggestions and solutions – everyone they have is 'tops'!
They're tipsters with a 'sure bet' that comes a day too late …
And I'd have prob'ly choked 'em if each one was not a MATE!
I've met those lurking vultures who come swooping when you fall –
Who hound you like a dingo when your back's against the wall.
They're last to come and see you when your struggle's going wrong –
They're busy starting rumours where they'll sell you for a song.
But in your bleakest moment, when the Reaper starts to dance,
When fighting in the frontline with the seat out of your pants –
Search beside you in the trenches and darkness will abate,
Swallowed by the brightness of that spark you call a MATE!
They'll raise you in an instant with that old familiar grin
That guides you back to sanity when life is closing in.
I've launched a prayer to heaven and I've screamed a curse to hell,
But neither one will argue – so I give me mates a yell!
I treat 'em as I find 'em and they take me as I am,

While trashing all and sundry like we didn't give a damn.
But in the end we do declare the earth would be just great …
If everyone upon it went and found 'emselves a MATE!

THE STAND

I have ridden the waves of good fortune,
But now I have crashed in the sand,
While the foam of this mismanaged country
Rolls over the man on the land.

I am not reaching out for your pity,
I would not relinquish my pride,
But my faith in this land that I love
Today must be placed to one side.

We're primary producers, they tell us,
Having export potential abroad,
Yet they cannot develop a system
Where potential is offered reward.

Instead they rescinded my contract,
The bank has forgotten my name.
It's not that my produce was wanting,
But guess who'll be copping the blame?

Yet I read where we sell off our country
While imports have risen again.
As I try to work out that equation,
The answer I get is insane.

So, today I must make declaration
With those who have taken my stand.
We've been left for the dingos to feed on;
They've abandoned the man on the land.

And I dare say the future looks gloomy
As we sit and ponder our loss.
We've made the biggest mistake of our lives ...
We sought to place trust in the boss.

The boss, who reclines in his office,
With the might of his government pen,
Forging the policy papers
That have seen the demise of good men.

Good men who've surrendered the comforts
That modern-day living has shown,
And women who've broken their backs
To give it a crack on their own.

Now the taste in my mouth is disgusting
As I chew on lies that I read,
That manipulate tides of opinion
And hinder the help that we need.

I have never forsaken a neighbour,
I've played the game fair and square,
But I'll throttle the mongrel who says
The roots of my labour aren't there.

And be damned if I'll be retreating,
I'll rise and speak out while I can,
Praying God will see fit to stand by me
And look out for the man on the land.

A COUNTRY MOTHER

He would give the blind the gift of sight,
The deaf the chance to hear.
He would change the winds and turn the tide away.
Yet God will not concede me
One simple selfish wish
And take me home to Mother for a day.

For as I lay here dreaming
On a beach so far from home,
Where the cattle trails and dust are seldom found,
My heart is heading off again
On board a battered truck
Rattling over worn and well-used ground.

I see the lush and fertile fields
Where the speckled milkers feed
And familiar smells of countryside prevail,
Then up ahead, the homestead
Where all is going well
For the family dog is slapping down his tail.

I cross the soft uncultured lawn
To pause below the porch,
Smiling at a sight I've seldom seen –
Those arms outstretched to meet me
In the front yard of our house
Where the daffodils adorn the gardens green.

I know she yearns to see me,
To hold me once again
And share the times since we have been apart,

To laugh at silly memories
That mothers oft recall
Of the days when children's laughter filled their hearts.

And though I've sought to travel,
Collecting unheard tales
From strange and distant places where I roam,
I would trade them all tomorrow
For a country mother's love
And the promise of a day with her at home.

Janine Haig

DIRECTIONS

He was in some far-off paddock doing something to a fence
When he called up on the 2-way in a voice all tight and tense:
'I've got a punctured tyre and the spare is flat as well.
It's hot, I'm out of water and my day has gone to hell.
I need another tyre – there's a couple in the shed,
So look at them real careful; bring the one with the thickest tread.
Could you throw it in an old ute and bring it out to me?
I know it's quite a bother – there's no other choice, you see.

'If you go along the road across the creek heading east
And follow it until you reach the carcass of a beast,
Then chuck a left along the track – it's rough but pretty straight –
So take it easy as you go until you reach the gate.
The gate's an old wire mongrel so undo it with great care
(When I get the time it's on my list to be repaired).
Head West along the fence-line till the big dam comes in sight,
Then when you reach the pig trap, spin the wheel and chuck a right.

'Take care across the gully – it's better if you creep,
Put the ute in low range cos it's slippery and it's steep.
When you reach the bore drain you will see it's pretty clogged,
Find second gear and give it some – or else you might get bogged.
There's a stony ridge ahead then, where the road is hard to pick,
But if you keep on heading northish where the mulga's pretty thick
You'll come out on a grassy plain – where all the grass is dead,
Then you'll see some tangled wire and old fence posts up ahead.

'And over to your left you'll see a big old gidyea tree,
And underneath it, red with rage,
A bloke in shorts – that's me!'

Geoff Hendrick

A MINOR POINT OF LAW

I had an altercation, just a minor point of law,
With a chap in Kununurra, though his verbal skills were poor.
I'm an educated fella and enjoy a good debate,
But this chap was not aspiring to let logic shape his fate.

It soon became apparent from his lack of self-control
That rhetoric would be wasted, and my wit was far too droll.
He was clearly agitated, for his nostrils flared and shook,
And I thought perhaps some pages might be missing from his book.

His face betrayed frustration with each premise I'd propose,
And his body language told me I was starting to impose.
His temper was outstanding, then it finally slipped its brake,
And I wondered for a second if I'd made a slight mistake.

A lightning blow descended and convinced me that I had,
For, though rather busy bleeding, I could tell this chap was mad.
Then a storm of action followed, first his fists and then his feet,
He 'discussed' things with passion that did not admit defeat.

I was forced into conceding that, when this chap had a beef,
He excelled at innovation, using elbows, knees and teeth.
His style was controversial, of a disenchanting kind,
And I knew that my best interests were the last things on his mind.

On the brink of Krakatoa, or the burning sands of hell,
I would have found more solace than with this chap, I could tell.
I retaliated bravely, when he seemed about to tire,
With creative bursts of reason aimed to wrest me from his ire.

Though his theories quite confused me in the way they were expressed,
He appeared in better humour as our 'argument' progressed.
Later, they informed me, he grew bored with our debate,
But was able to find comfort in my limp, unconscious state.

On subsequent reflection from my Health Department bed,
I thought this chap more suited to an outback shearing shed.
Certainly, in court you don't expect such fierce debate,
For I'm a flamin' lawyer, and this chap … the magistrate!

W.G. Howcroft

THE BALLAD OF DROVER JACK

Old Jack was a drover, a noted hard case,
With marks of his calling etched deep on his face.
His visage was battered, much-weathered and lined,
His manners were crude and his speech unrefined.

Now Jack was a boozer, a lover of beer,
Whose fame as a tippler had spread far and near.
Whenever in funds he'd embark on a bout
That lasted as long as his money held out.

One night the old toper, as full as an egg,
Fell down a deep cutting and busted a leg.
Next day he was rescued and, looking half dead,
Was taken and placed in a hospital bed.

A day or so later, his leg in a cast,
His mind turned to binges and sprees of the past
And, missing his cronies and tied to his cot,
A craving for grog soon assailed the old sot.

The matron came in and, in accents urbane,
Inquired was he comfy and free of all pain,
'Would you like a bottle?' she then kindly said,
Arranging the pillows and smoothing the bed.

'My oath!' cried the oldster, his mind fixed on beer,
'I'll bring one fer you when I gets outa here.
But while yer about it, good friend that yez are,
Best make it a dozen ... *just one won't go far!*'

THE RAILWAY HOTEL

When Joe was a young 'un, his cheeks flecked with down,
He drew his first pay cheque to head into town.
Then up spoke his father: 'Son, heed my words well –
Keep clear of the girls at the Railway Hotel.

'Those harpies will fleece you of all that you own,
They're wicked and wanton with hearts hard as stone.
Believe me, young fella, the road straight to hell
Begins at the door of the Railway Hotel.

'They'll ply you with whisky, with beer, rum and gin,
Then when you're half sozzled they'll lead you to sin.
They're skilled at seduction, at this they excel –
Those trollops who tempt at the Railway Hotel.'

'Gee whiz!' cried our hero, with awe on his face,
'So *that's* what goes on in that old wooden place!
Our parson has warned me of women who dwell
In dens of ill-fame like the Railway Hotel.

'It seems I can still hear that old preacher's words
On drinking and gambling, bad language and birds.
But where did he gain such vast knowledge, pray tell,
Of girls like the ones at the Railway Hotel?'

Joe caught a fast pony and girthed it up tight,
Then, bidding his father a hasty goodnight,
He sprang in the saddle and galloped pell-mell
For his destination – *the Railway Hotel!*

MY CHOICE

You can talk of tropic sunrise,
Waving palms and all of that,
Or the miracle of morning
Mists above the River Platte.

Not for me those far-off places
For I'd far, far rather see
That old mallee moon a-shining
Through a eucalyptus tree.

Some folks rave of Taiwan temples
And the sands of Suva Bay,
Or a Moslem mosque by moonlight
In some country far away.

Give me tree-lined tracks at sunset
And the sound of rustling wheat,
Plus the peaceful, plodding patter
Of my homebound horse's feet.

Venezuela, Valparaiso,
Vera Cruz and Everest,
Patagonia, Puerto Rico,
All are lauded as the best.

But I'll settle for the magic
Of a magpie's song at dawn
While I watch the furrows turning
In the soil where I was born.

There are those who sing the praises
Of the sands at Waikiki.
Others claim the beach at Bali
Is the only place to be.

Well, I've done me share of tripping
And I'd swap the bloomin' lot
For a wallow in our house dam
When the weather's good and hot!

Madagascar, Magdalada,
Mandalay and Mozambique –
Where unsettled souls go striving
For the happiness they seek.

Yet at hand's a kindly country
Where the mopokes call at night
And devoted sheep dogs greet you
At the morning's early light.

Saunter slowly through the scrublands
With no special aim in view
While you watch the wildlife wonders
In their rural rendezvous.

Here the bush birds build their bowers
And, on aimless afternoons,
You can linger there and listen
As they trill their tranquil tunes.

Samarkand and San Marino
Have attractions I'll agree,
But I'm blowed if they can better
Billabongs and billy tea!

Set your sights on Surakarta,
Take a trip to Trinidad –
Old frequented lanes I'll follow
Where I lingered as a lad ...

TILL THE CURLEWS CALL AT NIGHT

Sutherland studied the cloudless sky
And solemnly shook his head.
'I sees quite plain there will be no rain
With the way things are,' he said.

'I've watched the weather an' weighed its ways
An' knows what I knows is right,
So I says out bold this drought will hold
Till the curlews call at night.'

The weeks went by and the drought dragged on
And dark was the farmers' plight,
The dams ran dry 'neath the brazen sky
And no curlews called at night.

Sutherland asked the bank for a loan,
His manner was most polite:
'I'm broke ter hell, but 'twill all be well
When the curlews call at night.'

The banker shied like a startled steer
And slammed the dividing slide:
'You'll get no cash with your balderdash
About curlew calls,' he cried.

Sutherland trudged to his old tin shack
Where he hanged himself in fright,
And such is fate, local legends state
That the curlews called that night ...

DONOVAN AND ME

The mallee trees were merry as
They nodded in the breeze,
And happy hares and rabbits were
A-nibblin' at their ease.
The deadly nightshade was in bloom,
And brassy blue the sky.
'I thinks we'll have ourselves a drink,'
Said Donovan to I.

But soon the breeze became a gale,
The dust began to roll
And quickly thru' the patch of scrub
Its gritty fingers stole.
The hares and rabbits vanished and
The trees we couldn't see.
'I thinks we'll have another drink,'
Said Donovan to me.

A darkness settled on us as
The wind still wilder blew,
While somewhere in the seething sand
Our flapping tent fly flew,
And eerie were our feelings as
The land went drifting by.
'I thinks we'll have another drink,'
To Donovan said I.

THE FAILURE

The old man strode down the dusty road,
His lined face set and grim.
Long years of strife in a fierce-fought life
Were mirrored deep in him.

Tho' bouts of drought when the feed ran out
And wheat crops paled and died
Had left their mark on this patriarch,
He held his head with pride.

He'd faced each test in his toilsome quest
To tame that torrid land,
And battled on when all hope seemed gone,
'Mid debts and seething sand.

His face was grey on that fateful day
When credit he had none,
And the creditors sold his last foothold
On hard-fought soil he'd won.

In a city bank, where computers clank,
An entry then was made.
Cast in letters red, it simply said:
'He failed to make the grade!'

J. M. Hulbert

THE RUNNING OF THE DOG

Old Harry had been growling and the big dog with his howling
Made the moonlight nights a nightmare when you couldn't get to sleep,
And the corpses from the slaughter on the flats and at the water
Any morning on the muster were enough to make you weep.

He wasn't one for dreaming so he did a little scheming.
He would mount the men on good'uns every time they took a ride.
Then perchance one early morning, and they wouldn't get much
    warning,
They would sight the yellow terror and they'd likely get his hide!

He had them train their horses on the strangest of all courses,
Chasing emus on the claypans and the roos across the holes.
For to start on such a mission on a nag without condition
Was to invite disaster on the toughest of all goals.

The dingo full of cunning, though he didn't mind the running,
Knew full well that any failure would be paid for with his life.
But they couldn't breed them tougher, more enduring, or much rougher,
With his ancestors surviving through some thousand years of strife.

So it chanced one morning early, with their horses fit and burly,
Jack and Tyson made a sighting, they were riding up the creek.
Ewes and lambs were bleating madly and the dog had torn some badly,
And the author of the trouble was not very far to seek.

'Quick, get off and shorten leather, tighten girths and don't ask
    whether
We will take him on at tandem or will tackle him on face.

137

For there's only one thing certain, that before the final curtain,
He will lose us or we'll kill him, it will be a mighty race.'

Fast the dog went for the timber with old Tyson, tall and limber
Right behind him, on his hammer, and the old grey mare was flat
As he ducked and dodged the branches, sure you wouldn't like his
    chances.
He was on and off the saddle like a circus acrobat.

Then across a broken gully and his rep he didn't sully,
For old Tyson was a demon when he started on a chase.
So young Jack stayed right behind him, in the place you'd hope to
    find him.
If you tried to head that ringer you would end up in a case.

The red dog was all bustled, for he never had been hustled
By a rider on a chaser who was never off his tail.
And he left the timber's shelter and he went off helter-skelter
To the refuge of the gilgais where a horse was like to fail.

Then old Tyson rode to bend him to a course that aimed to send him
Out into the open spaces where a horse is sure to win.
But he hit a pothole fairly, midst the grasses long and curly,
And the grey mare catapulted in a somersaulting spin.

They hit heavy when they landed, on the ground they both were
    stranded –
Out forever from the contest, on that score there was no doubt.
As the boy rode past him madly, Tyson called out to him sadly,
'I'm alright, Jack, go and get him, then come back and dig me out.'

And the dingo now was failing but the bay mare who'd been trailing
Early in the contest now was getting pretty hot.

She was bred to stay forever, and this time 'twas now or never.
There was no thought of failure, in this fierce and testing spot.

The bay mare quickly caught him, with her flailing hooves she
    fought him,
Struck and pounded at his body till he lay upon the ground.
Never was there joy in killing, and although the chase was thrilling,
Horse and rider both were lucky that they came through safe and
    sound.

Back to Tyson, still in trouble, mare and rider on the stubble.
When Jack saw then from the distance both were lying deathly still.
Over him she was a-straddle, he was pinned beneath the saddle.
Both were glad to do some resting after such an awful spill.

Jack dug ground beneath each gaiter with a 'western castrator'—
This instrument would now be called a stock three-bladed knife.
The some huff and puff and straining gently still to ease the paining,
First one leg and then the other, horse and man were out of strife.

And old Harry … rest his ashes … didn't issue any sashes
For the running of a dingo was what stockmen had to try.
As a contest it's the roughest and the odds they are the toughest,
Never far from this condition: three to start and one to die.

For whenever stockmen gather, get their horses in a lather
When they wheel them in the timber and they hold them on the face,
Though you spin the tallest story just to coat yourself in glory …
If you haven't run a dingo, then you're just not in the race.

Neil Hulm

KIANDRA GOLD

I searched for the gold in the mountains,
I starved and I dug like a slave;
Through the freeze of Kiandra's long winter
I worked my way close to the grave.

I searched for the gold and I found it;
I came out with a fortune last year,
But I left just a trifle uneasy
And it isn't the gold that I fear.

It's the land that will make you tread careful;
It's the weirdest big land that I know,
From the bare face of old Kosciusko
To the deep roaring rivers below.

Some say to live with it, don't fight it
When the snow clouds form up in the sky;
But if caught and your tucker bag's empty,
You'll fight and you'll fight or you'll die.

You came to get rich, then get richer,
You feel like an outcast at first;
You hate it like hell for a fortnight
And then you are worse than the worst.

You find a good friend on the diggings –
A good mate in the hills is a must –
But the first sign of gold you're a loner,
You're suspicious, there's no-one you trust.

I've watched from the plains of Kiandra
The Eucumbene full to the brim;
I've watched the pale sun at her setting
As her lovely mixed colours grew dim.

The moon set the great white tops gleaming;
The stars danced and jumped through the night,
You feel you could reach out and touch them,
With the Milky Way ever so bright.

The brightness of winter will blind you
And the snow-covered land is locked tight;
There's a fear that you can't seem to fathom
And it grows with the silence of the night.

Now my money has slipped through my fingers,
I had somehow found friends by the score.
I'll be glad when the last of it's finished;
I'll go back to Kiandra once more.

The gold is well hidden and waiting;
How I'm struck with the fever of old,
Yet it's not just the gold that I'm wanting,
It's the thrill of just finding the gold.

To a land way above the great tree-line,
To a land full of beauty to share;
I'm quite sure when the Good Maker made it,
He took time and meticulous care.

Jim Kelly

THE RINGER'S FAREWELL

Farewell to the trails of the great outback,
The long, dry stages on the Rankin Track,
To the all-night watch 'neath a stormy sky,
When the cattle were bad and the stakes were high.
In the broken ground where you held your breath,
For a falling horse meant a flirt with death
'Neath the galloping hooves as you onward sped
To the rolling thunder of a thousand head.

To the sprawling stations and the small bush towns,
From the coastal ranges to the open downs,
To the cattle yards where bellowing blends
With the bawling calves in the branding pens;
To the breaking in that follows the rain,
And the favourite colt you wished to train,
To the comrades made in the saddle days
Who proved their worth in a host of ways.

To the band that plays on the receding shore,
As the transports leave for the scene of the war –
For the tune was sung in the days of old,
When the fires burned bright and the nights were cold.
As the troopship swings in the rising tide
A voice drifts over the grey ship's side,
And the Ringer's Farewell comes loud and free
As the convoy sweeps to the open sea.

Denis Kevans

THE TICKTACKER'S BENEDICTION

Now, if you went to Randwick, in the good old days of yore,
You'd see ticktackers working on the Flat.
They'd signal changing prices, by waving arms or hands,
Or flag 'em with a sugar bag or hat,
And if there was a plunge horse, they'd quickly semaphore
The latest betting on the bookies' stands –
Who was shortening in the market, who was 'blowing like a gale',
The ticktackers wave their arms and hands.

If there was no backing for a favourite on the day,
They'd say he's blowing, 'blowing like a gale'.
'Like a hurricane' he's blowing, they would ticktack to their mates,
'No money for him, dead as a doornail;
He's dead as Tutty Karmo, or the pharaoh, he is dead,
Not a cracker for him, not one single sprat,
He's blown out in the betting, he's D-E-A-D, dead!'
The ticktackers would signal from the Flat.

Now, a mate of the ticktackers was laid out in the church,
And his two good mates sat mourning for his fate,
When a very nervous reverend rushed out to bless his corpse
And wave his arms above their china plate.
'I can't believe he's dead, mate, he was so fit and well,
I can't believe that Mickey's dead, old son.'
'Dead? There's not a penny for him! Did you see the brewer's yeast?
He's just blown from twos to 33 to 1!'

143

Mark Kleinschmidt

REVENGE

Slumped in the blood-soaked grass I sat
With her head upon my knee.
That velvet muzzle had breathed its last,
Those gentle eyes had turned to glass,
And I fondled the ears that would never cast
Again, for beast or me.

The track in the scrub clear marked the path
Of the bull that had gored her flanks.
He'd ripped her guts in a lonely creek,
She'd stood her ground with a mortal shriek,
Then carried me clear on her dying feet,
My tears her only thanks.

How I cried for that mare with the gamest eye
And a heart that had passed the test.
No finer horse was ever astride
The ragged heights of the Great Divide;
No finer friend had ever died
'Neath the brow of the mountain's crest.

Oh the blade of anguish twisted deep
At the stroke of that last caress.
Then a serpent stirred within my soul
As anger rose to take control
And vengeance was my only goal;
My sights on cruel redress.

And the rogue that tore my beauty's flesh
Was mine for black revenge.
I tracked him through the fading light,
Beyond the lonely, moonlit night,
Then cornered for that final fight
To death, to death avenge.

A mindless killing – lust took hold
And I screamed with every breath.
He must have known he couldn't win
For his mortal bawling raised a din,
And he fell to me as she fell to him,
But his was a slower death.

And when at last that madness ceased
To shake me like a leaf,
Beyond a brooding, distant hill,
My little mare was lifeless still
And I stared with numbness at the kill
That hadn't eased my grief.

And I mourned that mare with the gamest eye
And a heart that had passed the test.
For no finer horse was ever astride
The ragged heights of the Great Divide;
And no finer friend had ever died
'Neath the brow of the mountain's crest.

THE DAMP-EYED BLOKE

They laughed at him and his teary eye
As he read of tragic days gone by.
Clean-nailed hands laid down the book
And he met their eyes with a misty look:
'There's many a man with a core of steel
That goes to water when tough's the deal,
And many a cove with a soft, soft heart,
Who comes to the fore when the rough stuff starts.'
They laughed again at the words he spoke
And shook their heads at the damp-eyed bloke.

Those rough tough men of the mustering camp
Had no time at all for an eye that's damp.
And that first-day fella with the fresh-shaved look,
The neat-rolled swag and the bag of books,
Was opportune for a spot of jest
And they wagered high he'd fail the test.
Only the cook, with a contrary nod,
Said, 'I'll put a fiver on the hapless sod.'
They chuckled, almost fit to choke.
They'd crucify that damp-eyed bloke.

The dawning saw the ringers grin
As they caught the horse to suck him in.
Old Charcoal's gentle when first he's rode,
But when clear of the camp he's wont to explode;
He'll rattle your teeth as he bucks around
And jar your spine when he hits the ground.
But they didn't let on to the new chum there
As they threw him aboard with never a care.
Then Charcoal was lashed with the end of a rope
And they laughed at the back of the damp-eyed bloke.

The horse shot off straight into the trees,
Hooves churning dust through a flurry of leaves.
The ringers rolled round, their sides set to bust,
But their mirth was cut short when out of the dust
Came Charcoal and rider, unable to steer,
Smack bang through the middle of all the camp gear.
Blankets and wraps flung this way and that,
Clothes were trampled all over the flat.
The only two spots those hooves never smote
Were the swags of the cook and the damp-eyed bloke.

Cookie just smiled and raked in the dough
As the new chum dismounted that rough so-n'-so.
The ringers stared round, dismay in their eyes,
Mouths dropping open to welcome the flies.
They knew that it must be beginner's good luck,
How else could it be? Old Charcoal could buck.
They planned and they schemed, and agreed on a way
To fix the new man, they'd lose him today
Out there in the bush, and have time to gloat
While waiting in camp for the damp-eyed bloke.

They swept through the scrub and round through the rough,
Checked out the creek-flats and down by the bluff.
Not once was he sighted, that object of scorn,
They chuckled with feeling and thought him forlorn.
By the end of the day he still hadn't shown,
So they started the mob of cattle for home
And entered the camp with eyes all agog;
The 'lost' man had beaten them home with a mob
About twice the size, but he didn't gloat,
They just copped a wink from the damp-eyed bloke.

Now the ringers were smart; at least they weren't dumb.
By now they had twigged he was no new chum
But they still hadn't learnt, you just cannot guess
A book by its cover, a man till the test.
And what did they see as they took a fresh look –
A man who could muster, yet cry at a book.
And where would he be when the bull tried to gore?
He'd probably 'snatch it' straight out the back door.
Would be wiser by far to look like a goat
Than depend on the likes of the damp-eyed bloke.

The first watch was taken, so close was the air
That the men all looked up to the clouds brewing there.
By the way they had gathered, some rain looked a chance,
Then lightning began to flicker and dance.
Across from the distance the thunder rolled low,
And wind off a storm had started to blow.
'Get everyone mounted, don't spare the time.
If the mob rushes now there'll be life on the line.'
They all knew the tone when experience spoke,
And it came from none less than the damp-eyed bloke.

The horsemen rode off as the mob stirred in fright
At the lightning so close that it lit up the night.
They circled and crooned to soothe the unease,
But fear, once felt, is hard to appease.
Then a thunderbolt struck with a crack and a boom
And terrified cattle rushed fast through the gloom.
If ever a cool head, then now was the need
As the ringers spurred hard to get to the lead.
And right to the fore as they took on a slope
Was bloody old Charcoal and the damp-eyed bloke.

The lead of the mob was nearing the bluff,
And for most of the ringers, well that was enough.
They reined in their horses and quietly withdrew,
And looked on in fear at the last silly two
Who battled to turn them, to make the mob veer,
Then Curly went down in front of a steer.
The ringers withdrawn were still as a post,
Their faces downcast and white as a ghost.
And the cry from poor Curly came out like a croak
When he screamed for the help of the damp-eyed bloke.

Old Charcoal responded to the stab of the steel,
Shouldered the steer, sent him head over heel.
The rider plucked Curly from the path of the rush
And set him down safely, no fanfare or fuss.
Then he spurred on ahead and uncurled his lash
And worked 'mongst the leaders with a crack and a slash.
From this way and that he worried the lead,
Bodies bounced off his galloping steed.
He worked like a thresher, drew blood with each stroke,
Till they turned from the fury of the damp-eyed bloke.

He circled them tight till they came to a halt,
Old Charcoal still prancing like a fresh-broken colt.
The ringers were sheepish as they took up the herd,
From the man on the black, there wasn't a word.
And none from them either, they knew they mistook
For weakness the fact that he cried at a book.
And Curly was grateful to just be alive,
He knew he'd seen death in the very next stride.
And those ringers, as they settled the cattle, had hope
To, one day, be just like the damp-eyed bloke.

INFIDELITY

With passion I flirted unfettered,
Abandon seized hold of my heart,
Lured by the lust and excitement
Of conquest, yet all else apart,
The sight held me, breathless and captive,
My intention was not to betray ...
But I fought with the strength of a zephyr,
And wisdom was left by the way.

Her curves were bold and inviting,
She lay like a siren sublime,
With secrets and places of pleasure
And promises older than time.
She was young and alluring and tempted
Me sorely to forfeit my own
For fruits and favours fallacious,
Of wild, youthful beauties unknown.

There's a wonder in mountains and canyons
That incites a soul to romance,
The chuckle of fresh water chatting
To rocks as it swirls in a dance
Through white-frosted meadows at sunrise,
'Neath the black velvet blanket of night.
To see and to drink in the beauty –
Of such is the heart's pure delight.

And I nibbled that fruit of temptation,
But spat it before I was cursed.
One sip from the rim of that goblet
Was more than enough for my thirst.

For the draught that is real and sustains me,
The yield of that glorious vine,
Is the soul, the breath and the heartbeat
Of life, this outback of mine.

THE TRANSIENT

I've seen the fiery western skies
Trail the sun away,
I've seen the east go softly pink
To usher in the day,
I've seen a sky of thunderous black
Grudgingly give forth,
Or months and months of powder blue
And the bone-dry watercourse.

I've seen the flooding in the creeks
From scuds along the range,
I've seen the clouds so little give
'Cept rainbows on the plains,
I've seen the grass grow thick and green
Then dry to golden hay,
I've seen the soil, its soul laid bare
And, lifeless, blown away.

I've seen a lot in this life of mine,
These four-score years and one,
Nights beside a friendly fire
And long days in the sun.
I've lived my days so full and free,
I've put my time in well,
And now beside this old ghost gum
I bid my spirit dwell.

I'll rest content beneath the tree,
My kingdom will not change,
The evening sky will still flush red,
And sometimes it will rain,

And sometimes there'll be bone-dry creeks,
And sometimes plains so green,
This land of stunning contrasts,
Awaiting souls unseen.

Ken Knuth

YOU CANNOT LOVE AUSTRALIA TILL YOU'VE SEEN THE LAND OUT BACK

Well I've read about the city
And the conservation move,
Where they march and carry banners
'Save our trees and Kangaroos'.
They believe they love their country
But I think they're off the track,
For they cannot be fair dinkum
Till they've seen the land out back.

They should see a country sunrise
As the east grows red and bright
When the bush stirs from its slumber
As the treetops catch the light,
Then the wallaroos and whiptails
Bound towards the mountain tall
And the dingo bitch howls to her mate
Across the lava wall.

They don't know what they're missing
Till they've seen the morning dew
As it settles in the hollows
Where the air you breathe is new.
And they've never known the fragrance
Of the sandalwood in bloom,
Nor the sweet scent of the wattle
When it blossoms after June.

They ought to see the flowers
Growing wild here in the spring,

Hear the butcher birds in chorus
And the bush canary sing,
See the distant misty ranges
Rising like a rolling sea,
And the golden rays of twilight
Painting shades on rock and tree.

If they could only listen
To the mopoke's call at night,
Hear the curlews' eerie wailing
And the plovers' crying plight,
Hear the whistle of the wild duck
As he looks for some lagoon,
And the colours of the sunset
Beats a Disneyland cartoon.

They've yet to know the feeling
At a far out muster camp,
With your mates all telling stories
As the stars turn on their lamps
And the smell of burning gumwood
Mingles with the billy tea
And the moonrise o'er the river
Is a sight they'd love to see.

So come on, my city cousins,
While you have some youth to spare;
You can't see what's in the offer
Feeding pigeons at the square.
The country folk will show you
When they see you've got the knack,
For you cannot love Australia
Till you've seen the land out back.

THE SYDNEY JILLAROO

She was born in Parramatta, on Sydney's western side,
And she'd never heard of a curlews' call or seen a bullocks' hide,
But she caught a steaming mail train that was labelled northern
    bound,
And shyly she stepped off the train in Queenslands' western downs.

She couldn't start the lighting plant or cook a curried stew
Nor handle any station chores like other jillaroos.
The father of the family then, his patience almost through,
He thought that he might send her back, this Sydney jillaroo.

Three sons were on the family team, the youngest boy was Tim;
She caught the twinkle from his eye and passed it back to him.
Against his father's stern advice he drove her to a dance,
And soon the fire had quickly spread, their very first romance.

The father rose and shook his fist, his face was crimson red,
'You'll wed a cocky's daughter, son,' the angry dad then said.
But Timmy's trust was in his heart: her love for me is true.
The church was full of empty seats, the wedding guests were few.

Through droughts and seasons bountiful, four children did she raise,
She slowly learnt to milk the cows, and fork the stable hay,
She learnt to ride the station colts, and cook a curried stew.
Far in the west, she stood the test, this Sydney jillaroo.

One day the family gathered round, the old man's race was run,
A gentle smile stole from his eyes, to see that she had come.
He called her meekly to his side, he knew she'd understand,
And never since his wife had died, held he a woman's hand.

'It's time to cross the great divide, my earthly days are few,
For years I've kept it in my heart, to say these words to you:
You are the answer to my prayers, the girl I never had,
My dearest wish before I go, to hear you call me Dad.'

And now her face is often seen at social town events,
For she's the local member in the Queensland parliament.
Old-timers smile a cunning smile, the story they review,
The day that girl stepped off the train, the Sydney jillaroo.

Darcy LaMont

OLD JACK

Battered and old and tarnished with sin,
A floppy old hat, a whiskered old chin,
Legs slightly bowed from years on a horse,
Who is this fellow? The duffer, of course.
Winks at the barmaid as he sips at his beer;
She knows all the stories and thinks him a dear,
For once he was famous for the way he could ride,
And few of the locals could stay at his side.

Way in the ranges, the back of the Towers,
The birthplace of rivers, where birds build their bowers,
In a lonely old station, the back of beyond,
Watered in good years by a bit of a pond,
Old Jack did his duffing, he was king of 'em all.
He stole from the big bloke, never touching the small,
And many a digger at the end of his beat
Gave thanks to the duffer for a bag full of meat.

His old eyes are reddened by days in the sun,
His shoulders are sagging through working the run,
The old cattle dog sound asleep at his feet
Dreams of the good days and plenty of meat,
For Jack's on the pension, he camps in the town,
Too old now for duffing and knocking around.

Keith Lethbridge

MUM'S DRIVING LESSON

In the prime of his life, when a man takes a wife,
And the family fortunes are thriving,
When he reckons he's set, it's a pretty safe bet
She'll bring up the subject of driving.
'It's a bother,' she'll say, 'that when you go away,
I'm stuck with the cooking and mopping.
When there's bargains in town, I feel badly let down,
'Cause I can't take the car to go shopping.'

So of course he'll agree. 'She'll be apples,' says he,
'I'll show you the ropes in the morning.'
He's still very green and he hasn't foreseen
That little red beacon of warning.
So, early next day they're up and away
Before the old rooster stops crowing.
A full frontal attack, with the kids in the back,
And they haven't a clue where they're going.

Dad's patient and calm – 'This'll do us no harm' –
But the kids are a little bit smarter,
Bewildered and glum, as they witness their mum
Hit the headlights instead of the starter.
The wipers are next, though it's not in the text,
Then the horn and the left indicator,
But at last they're away, lurching into the fray
Like a moon buggy leaping a crater.

Now Dad's turning pale, as the brakes seem to fail,
And the steering's gone wild and erratic.

He's losing his touch, so he yells, 'Hit the clutch!'
But she thought it was all automatic.
It's a little too late as they clip the front gate
And they didn't need Dad to remind them,
With the rear bumper down, throwing sparks off the ground,
And the letter box trailing behind them.

Dad's doing his block and the kids are in shock,
As deep in the vinyl they cower,
But strange to relate, Mum's feeling just great,
With a sense of invincible power.
Her foot hits the floor, doing ninety or more
(Miles per hour, not your wimp kilometre),
But they're heading for town so, 'For God's sake slow down,
And stop fiddling around with that heater!'

Now the Reverend Oates is rehearsing his notes
As he crosses the road for his sermon.
He's pedantic and tame, but he's lifting his game:
'Slow down, you detestable vermin!
When Pharaoh ignored the wrath of the Lord,
He was cursed to the fourth generation
With serpents and frogs, and incurable wogs,
On the road to eternal damnation!'

But Mum's in a trance, as she dreams of romance,
And at last she's a woman of action.
She squeals with delight as she runs a red light
And the cops are an added attraction.
Dad offers a prayer as he tugs at his hair
And his features are frozen in terror.
Now he dives in the back as Mum threads through the pack
With a fractional margin for error.

It's a terrible sight as she swerves to the right,
But she hasn't completed her folly.
She's itching for more, as she racks up a score
Of two dogs and a vegetable trolley.
Now she's letting it rip down the median strip
As her sanity starts to unravel.
An unorthodox route, with the cops in pursuit,
And their motorbikes churning up gravel.

With the dust and the smoke, it's a fair dinkum joke,
But the law doesn't find it amusing.
After coffee and cake at their ten o'clock break,
It was time for some serious snoozing.
But it's not for the pace that they give up the chase,
And it's not for the lack of endeavour.
If someone gets killed, there'll be forms to be filled
(And you reckoned old plod wasn't clever).

Far away from the town, Mum doesn't slow down,
Boadicea prepares for the battle,
With a blood-chilling yell, like a demon from hell,
As she charges the on-coming cattle.
And in the back seat Dad's accepted defeat,
But that isn't the end of our story.
Now the children as well, coming out of their shell,
Are goading their mother to glory.

They've left the main track and there's no turning back,
With the wife and the children gone feral.
Now they're out of control, in a crocodile roll …
It's a pageant of panic and peril.
Do you know how it feels to skid round on two wheels,
Just an inch from destruction and ruin?

Then the first words you hear, as the dust starts to clear,
Are: 'Well darlin', how am I doin'?'

* * *

So, young married folk, though you think it's a joke,
Don't try this at home, I beseech ya.
Provided, of course, you're not seeking divorce …
Bring in a professional teacher!

WHEN DIGGER CAUGHT THE WOG

A drought was in the outback
And the days were hot as hell,
But Digger found employment
At the Murchison Hotel.
Well, they couldn't really pay him
But he always got a feed.
The grog was automatic,
And his bunk up in the attic
Seemed to satisfy his need.

So he kept on washing dishes
And sweeping out the bar,
And he often said to Cobber
He was better off by far,
With his prime accommodation
And his access to the grog.
Yes, things were rolling Digger's way
Until that sad and sorry day
When Digger caught the wog.

His gut was in a turmoil,
Bloated tighter than a drum,
And he had a premonition
There was even worse to come.
He was aching like a boxer,
He was shaking like a dog,
But his greatest single fear
Wasn't death or diarrhoea
But to lose the taste for grog!

So he went to see a doctor
Who was visiting the town,
And he got some medication
Just to keep his tucker down,
And the doctor, sympathetic
When he heard of Digger's plight,
Gave instructions to the letter,
That he never would get better
Climbing up those stairs each night.

Now Digger was a rebel –
He was reckless, he was bold –
But a bloke in his condition
Does exactly what he's told.
So he took his medication,
Regulated his affairs,
Drank his grog in moderation,
And with total dedication
He avoided climbing stairs.

It was later in the season,
With the weather still depressing,
When the doctor did his rounds
To see how Digger was progressing.
He found him broken-winded,
Pathological and pale.
When he should have been in clover,
With the wog completely over,
He was frazzled, fraught and frail.

'Thank God you came,' said Digger,
'I was just about to croak!
Those instructions that you gave me

Were beyond a flamin' joke!
I took me medication,
And I said me daily prayers,
But it fairly wore me out,
Climbin' up the water spout
Just to keep away from stairs!'

*   *   *

Now the drought's still in the outback,
And the days are hot as hell,
But you won't find Digger camping
At the Murchison Hotel.
He prefers the open country
And the solitude, he swears;
And it mightn't look so grand,
With the spinifex and sand,
But … it's got no flamin' stairs!

COBBER'S TALKING DOG

There are many good yarns on a dusty track
And all of them can't be true,
But I've spent years in the great outback
And can verify quite a few.
I once sat down on a crocodile
In mistake for a fallen log;
I spent two years with a camel team;
I've mustered bullocks and skinned 'em clean,
But the most remarkable thing I've seen
Was a genuine, talking dog ...

* * *

'Hey, can't you read?' the barman said.
'No dogs allowed in here!'
But Cobber just grinned and shook his head
As he ordered a jug of beer.
'This ain't no ordinary, pot-lickin' mutt
What's developed a taste for grog.
That's canine royalty there, y' know,
The star of many a country show
From Badgingarra to Bendigo:
The original talking dog!'

The barman was an agreeable bloke
With a liberal point of view.
'I'll play along with yer ratbag joke,
But how can y' prove it's true?
I know there's a horse that can count to three
And I've witnessed a dancing frog.
I've heard of a boxing kangaroo,

A billy-goat playing the didgeridoo,
And a snake what swallows a billiard cue,
But never a talking dog!

'I'll tell yer what, we'll give him a try.
You can stay, on the one condition.
If your smart alec dog can identify
This classical rendition.'
He lifted a record from the shelf,
And a needle from the jar,
And while Cobber scratched his receding hair
And settled back on his rickety chair,
Sweet, classical music filled the air,
And wafted through the bar.

The magical, lifting melody
Of Chopin's Polonaise.
The old dog listened diligently
And his eyes began to glaze,
And Cobber sipped from his pewter cup,
Just as happy as any lark,
While every customer turned around,
With eyes transfixed on holy ground,
To face that wise, inscrutable hound,
And Cobber's dog said ... 'Bark!'

'Get out of here!' the barman roared,
'And remove that mongrel, too.
It's plain to see he's a total fraud,
And the same applies to you.'
So Cobber adjourned outside the pub,
In misery and disgrace,
Then, like a lovable, lop-eared pup,

Clutching his master's pewter cup,
The faithful animal lumbered up
And licked his whiskery face.

He paused to scratch a determined flea,
Then rolled back a mournful eye.
'I'm sorry, Cobber old mate,' said he,
'But I gave it a dinkum try.
I'm not that much of a classical dog,
So I possibly missed the mark.
I could name each one of Tchaikovsky's songs,
With Handel or Mozart I'm rarely wrong,
But I could have sworn that was Bach!'

* * *

So life rolls on in the great outback,
According to yarn and rhyme,
And those of us still on the dusty track
Are pretty well past our prime.
A lot of good mates have gone to rest
Where the creeks run high with grog,
And those few hardy remaining men
Regret that we'll never see again
That fine example of man's best friend:
That incredible talking dog.

THE LEGEND OF MOTHER McQ

You can reel off the names of the champions of old,
The peerless drop-kickers, the brave and the bold,
Clune, Harvey, Les Mumme, to name but a few,
But they can't hold a candle to Mother McQ.

*   *   *

We were well into shearing at Minderoo station
And Aussie Rules football was sweeping the nation.
On Sundays we aimed for our own recognition
By fielding a team in the bush competition.

Young Henry, the tar boy, was down in attack,
While Cobber was stationed at centre-half-back.
McCarthy, the presser, was known as a stayer,
While Mildew, the cook, was a back-pocket player.

We had no reserves but we gave it a fling,
And even old Digger was named on a wing.
Such a motley collection, we thought it a shame,
And felt we were certain to lose every game.

But as bad as we were, and conditions adverse,
The other three teams were a flamin' sight worse!
So picture the pleasure, out Minderoo way,
When we found ourselves playing on grand final day!

Old Digger was struttin' and starting to brag,
And Cobber was planning to auction the flag,
But joy turned to gloom and we cancelled the keg
When Mildew fell over and fractured his leg.

To start a grand final with seventeen men,
Was like trying to float the *Titanic* again.
A new cook was coming on grand final day,
And Digger said, 'Crikey, I hope he can play!'

We prayed and we sweated till one thirty-five,
When Mildew's replacement was due to arrive,
And then the old wagon came full into view,
And into the sunshine stepped … Mother McQ!

McCarthy was shattered, and young Henry swore,
And Digger said, 'Struth, it's me mother-in-law!'
But Cobber said, 'Boys, this is Mother McQ.
A flamin' good cook, and a strong woman, too.

'Her stews are delicious, her damper first class,
And from seventy yards she can pinpoint a pass!'
Then Mildew limped up, with his leg in a cast:
'Just think of it, woman, we need you at last!'

Old Mother McQ stood there gasping and blinkin',
She twigged straightaway that the boys were fair dinkum.
She wasn't a quitter, I'd like you to know.
'Look lively!' she shouted. 'Let's give it a go!'

We took to the field at a quarter past two,
And leading us on was old Mother McQ.
Right down the back pocket, she stood her position,
All panting and sweating and out of condition.

She got in the road of a nuggety rover,
Who lifted an elbow and bundled her over.

She lunged for a tackle but missed by a yard.
She tripped on a boot lace and hit the deck hard.

She flew for a mark but the ball wasn't there.
She cursed like a trooper and fought like a bear.
Then in the last term, with a minute to play,
We were five points behind … and the ball came her way.

A lumbering ruck man came thundering through.
He sneered: 'You remind me of Mother McQ!
You can't take the blame for your miserable looks,
But you play just as bad as the old buzzard cooks!'

He should have stayed silent … if only he knew,
For he woke up the demon in Mother McQ.
She charged in a fury, too angry to speak,
And knocked the big ruckman right into next week.

She picked up the ball and she plunged through the pack,
Not veering, not swerving, and not looking back.
The ump was distracted because of the ruction
While Mother McQ laid a trail of destruction.

And then, with a drop-kick that nearly brought rain,
She split the big uprights and won us the game!
The crowd was ecstatic … they both gave a cheer,
And Digger said, 'Mother McQ, have a beer!'

*   *   *

And so, when they write of the legends today,
The games won and lost, both at home and away,

The champion wing-men, the half-forward-flanks,
The heroes, the wizards, the crackpots, the cranks,

The classic grand finals, the narrow defeats,
The red-blooded spectators glued to their seats …
There's one final chapter that's long overdue:
The flag that was won by old Mother McQ!

James B. McKenzie

'KALIMNA' OR
THE FATE OF ROBERTA FITZGERALD

Out across the wide plain where the mulga scrub grows
And the sound mostly heard is the call of the crows,
On a mound was a name in white pebbles spelt out
And the name was 'Roberta Fitzgerald'.

An old man shuffled by in the dust of the road
And I asked of the name in the letters that showed.
'It happened,' said he, 'in the year of the drought,'
And he told of Roberta Fitzgerald.

'And that was the time with the wind in the north
And the smoke hazed the sun and the stockmen rode forth;
At the homestead the children were left in the care
Of the young girl, Roberta Fitzgerald.

'A touch of the tarbrush had shaded her skin;
In a far-away tribe were the rest of her kin,
But her father was white, from a station out there,
And he named her Roberta Fitzgerald.

'And they fought the red raider with beater and rake,
But the swirling wind carried the fire 'cross the break,
And the children ran down where the water had lain
In the tank, with Roberta Fitzgerald.

'But the tank was near dry and she clawed at the mud.
In the hollow she laid them with hands that were blood;

With her body she shielded them safe from the flame,
That brave girl, Roberta Fitzgerald.

'And the children came out when the men galloped back
And the homestead was smouldering, smoking and black,
But she never would laugh with those children again,
That girl named Roberta Fitzgerald.

'Then a signal rose up and her tribe gathered there
And the lubras all wailed and they tore at their hair,
And her people would never more speak of the name
Of "Kalimna", Roberta Fitzgerald.'

'Kalimna' is Aboriginal for beautiful.

Colleen McLaughlin

SILVER AND GOLD

The grass is long on the training track
And the hay has gone from the well-filled stack,
There are empty stalls in the stables red
And the pastures fair where the stallions fed.
When the dark comes down and the curlews cry
And the Cross is bright in the southern sky,
And the world is hushed – if you have the ears –
You can bridge the gap of the bygone years.
You can hear the ring of the plated hooves
When the moonbeams run on the rusted roofs,
You can see the gleam of the bridle bars
In the silver light of the watching stars.
And a horse goes by with a coat of gold,
And his rider wrapped from the morning cold,
As the dawn light breaks and the rails are white
And the darkness fades and the world is light.

The stables stand with their roofs of red
As they did way back where the colt was bred.
The track is ringed with the Queensland plains,
But his forebears walked in the English lanes
Where the banks are starred with the primrose gay
And the skies are soft on a summer's day.
The colt was the pride of the old man's heart
And this was the trial for his first big start.
He shook his head, and he mouthed the bit,
And he played, to show he was feeling fit.
And he saw the track like a band of green,
And he gathered speed like a gold machine.

And the clock clicked off and we knew that day
That a colt of the best had come our way.
He carried the silks of the old brown boss
For many a win and seldom a loss.
And he and the place were the district's pride,
But his heart went out when the old man died.

The colt was sold and the money spent,
But no-one followed the old man's bent,
The grass grew long and the paint peeled back
And the rails fell down on the training track.
But sometimes now, if you have the ears,
You can hear the calls, and claps and cheers
That began way back on a frosty morn
When a gold colt ran in the silver dawn.

RODEO

Waterholes are full again, sweetly sing the frogs,
Hidden are the bleaching bones in the sucking bogs.
Talk along the mulga wires tells of rodeo,
The grass is green, the sky is blue. Yippee, let us go.

Let us polish bit and spur – saddle, bridle too –
Let us clean our roo-hide boots until they shine like new,
Let us take our fancy hacks from where the rivers flow
Towards the little western town – towards the rodeo.

Fancy hacks and hunters, too – drafters, fat and sleek –
Tossing heads and flowing manes, fiery eyes and meek,
Jingle, jangle, stirrup irons clashing side by side,
Pound of hoofs and swirl of dust. Into town we ride.

Flash of movement in the ring – horse and beast and man
Striving for supremacy, as the bush-bred can.
Bucking, squealing, twisting broncs, riders spurring high,
Yells of gay encouragement reaching to the sky.

Bawling bullocks, charging steers, riders in the dust,
Brushing prickles as they rise, grinning as they must.
Gallant horses, gallant men, thrilling to the show,
Colour, movement, life and fun – this is rodeo.

Jogging home when all is o'er, down the dusty track,
North and south, and east and west, men are going back,
Back to work and drought, maybe, as the slow months go,
Until the rains will bring again another rodeo.

REDUNDANT

He's old and wrinkled and his hair is white as snow,
And his mates are calling quietly from wherever good mates go.
But loath he is at leaving, for it seems to him a sin
That his saddle should be idle while his heart's still young within.

For his heart's still young within him, though it's many years ago
Since he started jackerooing where the western rivers flow.
He has seen those rivers flooded, he has seen them parched and dry,
While the starving cattle perished underneath a burning sky.

He has lit a thousand campfires when the evening star was bright,
And has yarned beside their embers while it slowly slipped from sight.
He has heard the horse bells ringing, 'bove the silver song of frogs,
Heard the lonely curlew crying and the howl of yellow dogs.

He has known the days of summer, when the grass was green and high,
And the thunder clouds were thrusting snowy heads up in the sky.
He has known winter mornings when the floating scarves of mist
Were lifting from the valleys to the peaks the sun had kissed.

He has mustered sleepy bullocks from the flats where clover grows,
And the river chatters gaily with its weight of melted snows.
He has galloped through the bone wood on the track of long-horned
     cows,
Felt the thrill of pounding hoofbeats and the sting of slashing boughs.

But those days are left behind him, though the sound of bawling steers
That comes to him on breezes tells the tales of vanished years.
They say he's old and useless, save for doing simple jobs,
But he knows he could be riding in the lead of racing mobs.

The colts they catch are not for him, until they're worked and tried,
But the lads who take the youngsters cannot ride as he could ride.
And he feels a helpless anger that it's him they leave behind,
With a mob of lonely weaners and the womenfolk to mind.

So perhaps he'll leave his saddle and his bridle on the rack,
Call his dog and roll his bluey, and he'll wander down the track
To the land beyond the sunset, glowing bright across the plain,
With the hope that when he gets there he'll be useful once again.

THE GOLDEN RAILS

The rails beside the pearly gates are slim and gold and bright.
The bars are polished, smooth and worn, and shining in the light.
Behind are paddocks, wide and green, where little rivers flow,
The golden sliprails guard the land where all good horses go.

And here will come the ones we rode – old Satin, Gleam and Gay –
The horses from the cattle camp – the likes of Swing and Sway.
And here will come the truest friends that ever mares have foaled,
The faithful steady plodders that are worth their weight in gold.

There's room for all the drovers' teams that know the dusty tracks,
The barren stock routes leading down from the cattle runs out back.
They'll canter up the winding track and whinny at the rails,
And greet their mates with little squeals and flirt of heads and tails.

The old faint scar of girth gall and the snowy spots of hair –
The saddle marks of service all the best of horses bear –
Shall be noted and recorded, and the rails will clatter down
For chestnut horse and dappled, for the black and bay and brown.

No saddles here shall scar their backs, no bits their mouths shall feel,
No streaks of blood shall stain their flanks from the stabbing, spurring
    heel.
The winds will be their bridles, and for shoes they'll have the stars,
And grass is green through all the days behind the golden bars.

So let them come, those faithful friends, from the mountains and the
    plains,
Each horse who felt a rider's hand and answered to the reins.
And when the day is dying and the sunset slowly pales,
Hear the ghostly horses galloping behind the golden rails.

A BOY'S WAY

We rode one day, when the rains had come,
    from dawn till the sunset's glow,
By rolling plains where the bluegrass waves
    and up where the lancewoods grow.
For spring had come and the yearling colts,
    as free as the winds were free,
Were mustered up to be roped and tied
    and seared with the Diamond D.
They were wild as hawks and the racing mob
    was led by a chestnut mare,
A lovely thing with a ton of pace
    that came from her sire, Declare.
An outlaw mare – she had thrown a man
    and maddened herself with fright
(He caught his foot as she plunged away,
    and hung from the iron all night).

We yarded the colts as the darkness fell.
    Next day as we put them through,
A stranger's voice from behind us said
    ' 'S there anything I can do?'
We looked around and a sunburnt kid,
    with freckles and sandy hair
And bright blue eyes 'neath a battered hat,
    was jauntily standing there.
Said Mace (our boss) to the freckled kid,
    'Now what do you want with me?'
'I'm out of work,' was the lad's reply.
    'Can I come to the Diamond D?'
And Mace, he laughed. 'I've a dozen men –
    that's more than I need today.

You get a feed from the cook, young man,
    then you'd better be on your way.'

He turned to go, then he wheeled around
    and came to the boss's side.
'Would you have a horse that's been pensioned off,
    that a bloke like me could ride?'
And Freddy Mace, with a silly grin, said,
    'Give him The Dancer, Dad.'
'That chestnut mare,' were the boss's words,
    'is yours if you ride her, lad.'
We bridled The Dancer and led her up
    and saddled her in the crush.
The kid got on and we let her out –
    she came with a flying rush
And bucked and squealed when she felt his weight,
    and reared till she toppled back.
The kid crawled out by a stroke of luck –
    we thought that his spine would crack.
He tried again – it was just the same –
    said Mace, in a kindly way:
'Just leave her now – have another go,
    tonight, if you want to stay'.

The kid was game and he did his best,
    but never a chance had he
Of sticking The Dancer long enough
    to ride from the Diamond D.
Twice more he tried. On the second morn
    The Dancer was sick and sore.
We don't know yet what the trouble was –
    it hadn't been seen before.

'Now here's your chance,' said the horse boy, Jim,
    'a baby could ride her now.
Just come along to the horse yard, boys,
    and Mickey will show us how.'
The kid went white, and his changing voice
    came shrill on the morning air.
'You cut that out. Do you think I'd try
    to saddle a real crook mare?

'I couldn't ride when she was well –
    I won't when she's down and out.
I'm going now.' And he turned away,
    but stopped at the boss's shout.
'You stay, young man. You can have a job,
    for someone is moving on.
No horses here will be knocked about –
    so Jim, you had best be gone.'
And Mace walked on and the freckled kid,
    he followed as if on air.
The boss looked around. 'If you want that horse
    you can have her, for all I care.'

*   *   *

So Mickey came to the Diamond D.
    He tended the chestnut mare
Till the sickness passed. And then one day,
    when all of us chaps were there,
He saddled The Dancer and rode to work.
    We gawped as we saw them go.
For how he had managed to win her trust
    is more than we'll ever know.

THE STRANGER

Now Gina dwelt where the western peaks are fired by the setting sun.
She lived and ruled like a cattle queen on the plains of Nindah run.
And she was fair as the sweetest flower, and loved for a hundred miles,
But vainly men from the whole wide land had tried for her winning
　　smiles.

It chanced one day, in the summer time, she rode on a brumby colt –
A silver grey with an iron mouth and a tendency to bolt.
A stranger watched, from the ageless hills, as over the plains she rode;
He was not keen on the girl herself, but the grey horse she bestrode.

A stranger came to the Nindah yards as the sun went down to rest,
He sat a while like a traveller at the end of a weary quest.
And Gina Leigh, on the silver colt, with a careless gesture said,
'If you want to stop, you will get a feed, and ask for an empty bed.'

The stranger stayed and, as men were scarce, he joined with the
　　stockmen band.
'Twas mustering time and the new recruit was willing to lend a hand.
The more he saw of the silver colt, the more he admired his ways
And waited for a chance to try him out, one of these busy days.

He got his chance. On a winter's morn the colt was saddled and tied,
Restless, and stamping impatiently, ready for Gina to ride.
The stranger looked – there was no-one near – he quickly undid the
　　rein
And swung aboard, and he ran his hand up the silver horse's mane.

The colt stood still. Then he grabbed the bit and left like a silver streak,
With drumming hooves and an iron mouth, for the timber along the
　　creek.

And fear stole into the stranger's heart as the branches lashed and tore,
The grey colt swerved with a mighty leap – and the stranger rode no
  more.

Now he lies at rest by the riverside, where the she-oaks croon and sigh,
And whisper low at the dead of night, when the ghost wind passes by.
And Gina Leigh, with an aching heart, still rules on the Nindah run,
And no-one knows that he took her heart, who sleeps near the setting
  sun.

THE LAST MUSTER

Muster them up from their countless graves,
    from the plains where the heatwaves dance,
From the sandy dunes, from the river bends,
    from the scrubs where the leaf motes glance.
Stir them awake from their resting place,
    from the towns that they helped to make,
And build them a hall where they'll meet and mix,
    and live for the nation's sake.
Build them a hall 'neath the Queensland sun,
    out where their ghosts go by,
Strong as the dreams that they saw come true,
    'neath clouds or a barren sky.
Build of the stone where their hoofbeats rang,
    build with the rafters red
Of the ironbark trees, like the blood that ran
    in the veins of the waking dead.

Write with a pen that is dipped in gold,
    with words of an opal hue,
Capture the tales of the teamsters' wheels
    that rolled as a nation grew.
Capture the stories of hoofbeats told,
    whispering, galloping, clear,
Muster them all from the winds of time,
    and yard them and hold them here.
Under a roof like the curving sky
    that covered the endless days,
Muster the spirits that sought and found
    what lay in the heat-filled haze.
Cover them all with the blue and green
    and gold of our great wide land,

That they will rest with the things they loved —
and our youth might understand.

Lex McLennan
WHERE TALON FELL

Silent and lone is the mound of stone
    that juts from the Mitchell grass,
And ferns grow rank on the built-up bank
    where few are the feet that pass;
They formed it there with love and with care
    and the rough rail guards it well.
Though years may go it remains to show
    the place where old Talon fell.

The dust was wet where it merged with sweat,
    the saddle was bruised and scarred,
When Talon came like a wind-whipped flame
    to halt at the homestead yard.
The soil was turned and the grass was churned
    like a maelstrom, stirred and spread,
Where hoofs had slipped and had grooved and gripped
    and a horseman bold lay dead.

What were the miles where his pasture smiles
    past flats where the deep creeks flow,
When duty chained to the fates ordained
    that his was the turn to go?
This is the rule of the hard bush school
    that teaches the horsemen's lore:
The Reaper calls when a good horse falls
    who's never been down before.

They were the pride of the countryside –
    tall man and the tall light bay –

Out in the waste where the longtails raced
    and the showring's dusty fray,
And far and wide where the bushmen vied
    for fame in the rodeo,
And they were kings of the lead and wings
    where the brumby-runners go.

The fate they met is a puzzle yet,
    for never a soul could tell,
Save he who's dead and the white-blazed head,
    what happened when Talon fell.
But stockmen say when the dusk is grey
    and the sunset fires grow pale,
That Talon strolls where the wide down rolls
    and stands at the guarding rail.

When homing birds like stampeding herds
    are winging toward the west,
And darkness falls with enshrouding palls
    that cover the brown land's breast,
The old horse dreams as the gold cross gleams
    on the tracks that they knew so well.
He bears the freight of his master's weight
    where the dim star-shadows dwell.

THE SQUATTER'S TALE

When April sunsets redden and set the west aglow –
How clearly I remember an evening long ago,
The dust wrack slowly floating like storm clouds on the sea,
And Bellbird racing homeward while her broken reins hung free.

Somewhere toward the ranges – but where no man could tell –
Somewhere among the foothills the good black filly fell,
And now before the sunset, all pied with clinging foam,
She tore across the bluegrass to bring the bad news home.

Our cooees crossed the ridges, our greenhide woke the stars,
Till the night dew spilt its fragrance on spurs and stirrup bars,
But only echo answered, waning as echoes wane,
Then but the brooding silence that dwells on ridge and plain.

All night the filly whinnied with a weird unearthly wail,
And at dawn she charged the gateway and cleared the high cap-rail.
Oh, the mad leaps to saddle when we saw the vision strange,
For Bellbird, in the dawning, was heading for the range.

The black sweat on her shoulders grew smoky white and creamed,
While rough men chased her hoofbeats and wondered if they
    dreamed.
She was his petted darling, a strange lone man was he,
Who came to learn of cattle from a mansion o'er the sea.

I rode the lead behind her. Though I boast it now with pride,
I would not live it over, the nightmare of that ride,
As sweat-streaked, foam-bespattered and riderless and free,
She swept across the gullies, o'er brush and fallen tree.

Over the broken ridges till I thought each mile my last,
The thorny branches slashed me as the timber whistled past.
Not for the wealth of Midas, not for the world of men,
Would I dash those tangled thickets, would I charge those
    creeks again.

Strange as you find my story, I thought it stranger then;
Nor could I find a reason, such things are past my ken.
My years were spent in wild lands where strange new sights are rife,
But I will not see its equal while I linger in this life.

Hope in my heart was dying for my horse was failing fast,
When I saw her head fling upward and she trilled a piercing blast.
She halted on the hillside where he lay, a battered wreck,
And she nosed his blood-stained forehead with his arms around
    her neck.

Long since, a bold young horseman has crossed the plains of foam
That ebbed and flowed between him and his ancestral home.
Our handclasp spoke our friendship as we parted silently
And I sent the filly with him to cross the leagues of sea.

Long were her years of leisure, and when the old mare died
A grey-haired English squire was kneeling at her side –
He who had long remembered the old undying day
When a filly led us to him in the ranges far away.

And now when April sunsets have set the west aglow
And memories come thronging from the years of long ago,
Plain as a painted picture, the scene comes back to me
Of Bellbird racing homeward with her bridle dangling free.

If I close my eyes a moment I see the sunset wane,
The black speck in the bluegrass, the dust clouds on the plain,
And again I ride behind her down the ridges scarred with stone,
And I hear her hoofbeats echo though fifty years have flown.

Aye, we were mates of the muster, and he writes me now and then,
But the years have put a waver in his bold and flowing pen,
And though our lives are different as lives of men can be,
We two are held together by the black mare's memory.

THE UNKNOWN RIDER

Above Star Valley's stockyards they hung it high and clear:
'None but the best of horseman need ply their calling here.'
They kept a great black outlaw to test the stranger's pride,
A horse that fifty fellows had tried in vain to ride.

Up to the yards at sunrise one still November day
Cantered a sunbrowned stranger astride an iron-grey.
Grey tinged the rider's temples and streaked his tawny hair,
And whip-like scars on his features that bold scrub-dashers bear.

'I've heard of your buckjumper – how far his fame has gone!
But I would ride the west wind if you could leg me on.'
They helped him gear the black horse, who 'struck' the air and pawed.
He scarcely touched the pommel, but vaulted saddleward.

Then from the stockyard railing they watched with hearts aglow
The glory of a horseman no horse on earth could throw.
Oh, splendid was the rider and fiercely fought the black –
He reared with forefeet reaching, and screamed and toppled back.

Death lurks in that swift impact where earth and saddle meet,
But, quickly writhing sideways, the stranger won his feet.
Dusty and now dishevelled, his lean face grey with pain,
He gripped the rising outlaw and mounted him again.

They saw the fight was ending, the first wild surge had passed,
And then, with hot sweat dripping, the black horse stood at last.
The stranger wished the valley a light and swift 'Good-day',
Then calmly doffed his wide hat and swung astride the grey.

Eager, but not yet reefing, the great grey took the road;
Proudly, with neck high-arching, lightly he bore his load.
Far out beside the scrub line, deep in watered glade
Where horses had been hobbled, they found the camp he'd made.

And his ride became legend, a tale the drover tells
When the silent night is broken by the tinkle of the bells.
And still Star Valley's stockmen would sell their souls to know
Who was the master horseman that brought their pride so low.

THE BREAKER'S DAUGHTER

Her skin was the hue of pale floodwater,
Burned and bronzed by the northern noons.
And I was in love with the breaker's daughter
And I wooed her under the mustering moons.
We were midnight mates of the mad moon musters,
When passion flares as the light above,
And the wind that sang in the wilga clusters
Had tuned the hymn of our flaming love.

Then a red moon rose that was wild with battle
When we grasped for more than our hands could hold,
Too big the mob and too wild the cattle,
Too small our band though our hearts were bold.
They were as wild as the winds of winter,
Fierce and resolute, fast and free;
The deadwood under their feet would splinter
And merge with the crack of artillery.

You could turn a lead and that lead would double
And break again on the farthest side.
As moments passed we were all in trouble
But we would not quit for our horseman's pride.
When we pressed them hard they would break and shatter,
The brown earth back from their hoofs would fling;
If they formed a mob it would seethe and scatter.
They would not drift and they would not ring.

Then my horse came down where a break was prising
And I felt the chill of a bluegrass grave.
The leaders split where my horse was rising,
But God knew what of the second wave –

The centre pack that would come pell-melling,
A frenzied horde by the rearguard forced
Behind. Beside them our mates were yelling.
None dreamed a moment I'd been unhorsed.

Trapped in the van of the hoofbeats' thunder,
Loud with the clang of the clashing horn,
The white stars reeled and the cold earth under
Mocked at me with a silent scorn.
A man may think he is smart and clever
When he rides at ease in the tranquil bush,
But his bushcraft goes and his mind will waver
When he comes to grief when the hornies rush.

Through dust and moonlight I saw her coming,
Crouching low on the chestnut's mane.
Through the roar of the hot hoofs drumming,
I sent a cheer down the hoof-torn plain.
She wheeled them off, then my heartbeats halted –
A yearling shot in the chestnut's track.
He hit it hard and he somersaulted
And struck the ground with his burdened back.

While the dust still rose I ran and sought her,
Each moment seeming a year of pain,
But the golden horse and the breaker's daughter
Lay motionless upon the plain.
My hopes were dead and my dreams were ended,
And love of living had taken flight
As the clash of horns and the hoofbeats blended,
Passed and died in the silent night.

I left the North, for the North is only
For nerveless men when the wild leads wheel –
It is no place for a heart that's lonely
Or a man who rides where the grey ghosts steal –
And I returned to the city's pleasures,
Back to the haunts of my boyhood days.
But the joys had fled that vain youth treasures,
And I found no joy in the lights ablaze.

Each night in a hundred breakneck races,
They fight us back to the timber lines,
While low boughs whip at our blood-stained faces
And dead wood crackles and greenhide whines.
And as I cleave the blue surf water
The hoofbeats echo in every wave,
For I left my heart with the breaker's daughter
Who sleeps in a far north western grave.

THE SPIRIT OF THE WEST

'The spirit of the west is dead,' old Cameron said that night,
While yarning on the homestead porch when western stars were bright.
'The life we lived has gone for good,' he said, 'and this I know:
The last remaining link will pass when we old-timers go.'

'The lads are fine when all goes well, but when there comes a pinch
You find them pulling at the rein, to swerve aside or flinch.'
A droving man in youth he'd been but now, by range and creek,
His vast herds roamed the miles untold, so well might Cameron speak.

Next day beyond the Gidgea Yard the restless cattle broke,
And Cameron thundered in the lead before the echoes woke.
At racing pace between the trees, his stout roan stockhorse strode
With hoofs that whistled through the grass and, oh, how Cameron
    rode!

He turned the spreading vanguard in, but as he gathered rein
A wild bull charged him from the side and flung him to the plain.
The old man, stricken, strove to rise, and with a muffled roar
The wild bull, maddened for the kill, lowered his head to gore.

Then riding down the potholed plain, the race that madmen ride,
With blood beads forming on the spurs, young Danny reached his side.
No time to use a stockwhip there – springing as wildcats spring,
He landed on the big bull's head, to nose and horn to cling.

And horsemen speeding to the scene could see him twist and reef,
With not a ghostly chance to throw the raging ton of beef.
They saw the great head dip to toss, the white horns arching wide,
And on the broken gidgea flat the gay young stockman died.

Old Cameron rose on shaken limbs – the old bold breed are game! –
And through his shirt the warm blood seeped, red as the sunset's flame,
While crashing through the undergrowth they heard the wild bull go.
'The spirit of the west lives on,' old Cameron murmured low.

BLUE QUEENSLAND DOGS

The story of their coming, perhaps some greybeard knows,
As through the years forgotten their line of breeding goes,
But where the bushland saga in horseman's gear is dressed,
The brave blue dogs of Queensland are treasured east and west.
Scourge of the mountain scrubber, bane of the mulish steer,
The terror of the wild dog that hunts the homestead near;
The guardian of children, and when the daylight wanes
The comrade of the lone man who camps upon the plains.
Not once or twice it happened that when a good horse fell
And left a battered rider where he alone could tell,
While staunch mates raked the ridges and sought him far and wide
A brave blue Queensland heeler kept vigil at his side.
The good blue dogs of Queensland! The pals of sunbrowned men,
Who brings the range-run bullocks to yard and trucking pen.
And southward to the Murray and westward out to Perth
They bless the great grey northland that gave the blue dogs birth.

THEY MAY NOT RIDE AGAIN

In years that have wafted westward we met on the blacksoil plain,
Where the furlongs rolled like ribbon and the blue grass waved like
    grain.
And we were a country race crowd who played on our picnic day,
When life was as bright as sunlight and war was a world away.

The sunrays shone on the satins and gleamed on the bay and brown,
And the hours were light with laughter as the bush boys rubbed them
    down.
We thrilled to the hoofbeats' music as the reins grew white with foam,
And they swept the bluegrass under and flashed round the turn for
    home.

We met today where the furlongs still ribbon the black soil plain,
And sunrays shone on the satins, but life was as grey as rain.
For the lads with the carefree laughter who rode on the highland runs
Are sighting the cold black rifles and manning the ack-ack guns.

The music had left the hoofbeats and the satins' lustre fled,
And laughter that lived lighthearted is dead as the years are dead.
Our comrades whose sun-browned fingers were fashioned to grip the
    reins
Have bartered their spurs for mortars, their horses for fighter planes.

We'll meet in the years unravelled where the blue grass dips and waves,
When boys from the highland country are sleeping in foreign graves,
And then when the hoofbeats thunder and the dust-wrack leaps like
    flames,
Each inch of the shoe-torn furlongs will ring to their deathless names.

JONAH BELLE

On the pastured wastes of Rawbelle that are rich with memories,
Free to camp through fragrant noondays underneath the shady trees,
Running loose amongst the bluegrass is a gallant little mare
With some roany patches showing through her gold coat here and
    there.
In the homestead, on a mantel where the light and shadows play,
Rests the cup whose incandescence grows not dim nor fades away;
And the story of its winning is a tale the stockmen tell,
And their slow, soft voices linger on the name of Jonah Belle.
Little chance at all they gave her, featherweight or not, they knew
The withering pace of Battle Prince that brought the big bay through
With courage flaunted in his head and thunder in his stride
To triumphs that were gilded tales on the racetracks far and wide.
But the little mare knew better and she reefed into the lead,
Wasting all the store of precious strength her slender limbs would need;
And the furlongs fled behind her, hazed with dust-wrack, one by one,
While they stood and stared in silence at the splendour of her run.
Then the brown horse moved toward her but she seemed to hold him
    clear,
And her stride was still unshortened and the post was getting near.
Oh, the blurring of the colours as they swept around the bend,
And the thudding of the hoofbeats where the turf and steel shoes
    blend.
Gaily down the straight she led them, but a flash of green and white
Through the beaten ruck came sailing, gleaming in the dazzling light,
And the Prince was striding with her and the white posts seemed to fly,
But she bore the station honour – it was either do or die!
Slowly past her heaving throat strap crept the dark and blood-like head,
With its wide eyes flashing fire and its nostrils flaring red –
Only twenty yards to travel, and she snatched the foam-flecked rein,
Racing now alone on spirit still she drew away again.

In the paddocks out at Rawbelle where the sunrays spill their gold,
Idling through a life of leisure on the flats where she was foaled,
Runs the fiery chestnut filly in whose eyes the lightnings dwell
And a horseman's heart goes beating through the years with Jonah Belle.

THE BUSTARD

Low I circle, with pinions flailing,
My wide wings mottled as flood-borne foam;
They bear me on, though my strength is failing,
Back to the plain of my fledging home.
The wheat-wave swirls where the wind has tossed it,
The sorghum burns like a crimson flame;
The land has changed since the day we lost it –
The fateful day when the settlers came.
We were so used to the stockwhips' thunder,
The silver tinkle of gear and spur,
That, floating down with the blue grass under,
We played at our ease where the cattle were.
But new days dawned, and the stockmen's singing
Passed like a dream that was sweet and brief,
And the clank of ploughs and the axes ringing
Sounded a note that was wild with grief.
Little was left in our lives that mattered;
They had cleared the scrub and the land was strange.
With all that were left of our clans shot-shattered,
I headed westward across the range.
I flung behind me the purple passes
And reached the land where the suns go down,
Lost in the drifts of the Mitchell grasses,
Far from the clamour of farm and town.
But still where the clouds from the coastal highlands
Over the wheat-wave dapple the sky,
The lands where the settlers came are my lands
And bustards come to their home to die.

NITA

When dawn was dim on the stockyard she straddled the steel-blue colt,
Who arched his back to the crupper and bucked like a thunderbolt;
But she was set in the saddle, her grip was firm on the rein,
And reefing into the bridle he cantered across the plain;
And, as she swayed to his movement, as only the bush-bred can,
She and the colt were a picture to gladden the heart of a man.
The scowl of her dusky mother merged with the white man's smiles
Had made her a thing of beauty, the pride of the sun-scorched miles.
The black and the white blood mingling had made her as one apart,
But this was the day that Nita rode into the station's heart;
For things went wrong in the wilgas when a heifer broke from the
    herd,
And stockman Jim on the chestnut raced out where the dust-wrack
    stirred.
As, glued to the heifer's shoulder, the chestnut brought her around,
He slipped his foot in a wash-out and fell on the broken ground.
With a twisted stirrup claiming his boot as if it were tied,
Jim clutched at the tail and crupper and hung on the chestnut's side.
Seldom perhaps had a horseman been caught in such ghastly strait,
Chained fast to a plunging stockhorse who answered the hand of fate;
And Nita, holding the leaders, saw Death that was lurking there
And spurs were raking the blue colt whose hot hoofs burned in the air.
The colt was a thin half-broken, and time and time as she tried
To snatch at the chestnut's bridle he twisted away and shied.
She drove him in with the rowels and took the slack of her rein
And fastened a knot securely to a tuft of chestnut mane.
While boughs of the wilgas whipped her and the brown earth flew
    beneath,
She pulled a knife from her belt-pouch and drew the blade with her
    teeth,
And slashed at the holding leather till the stockman tumbled free,

And the horses locked together crashed on to a leaning tree.
The bridle broke with the impact, and she leapt clear of the hoofs
As the blue and the chestnut scrambled, then sped for the station
    roofs.
While dustwirls died in the wilgas as the tasselled grasses waved,
And death in defeat rode outward, the life of a man was saved.
The black and the white blood mingling had made her as one apart,
But that was the way that Nita rode into the station's heart;
And that's why a sunbrowned stockman, far out where the wide floods
    swirl,
Still treasures a raven token – the tress of a half-caste girl.

Richard Magoffin

NO DOGS BARKED

No dogs barked out a welcome as we drove up that day –
No happy cries from yonder where the children used to play –
But everywhere a silence which stole into the mind
And made us feel unwelcome at the home we left behind.

And then a breath of wind began to turn the big old mill
That once poured water down the drain to Cottingley and Rhyll.
A crow on guard flew off the tail and cried as if to say,
'You'll get no friendly cup of tea at Quambetook today.'

And yet we walked in through the gate and knocked upon the
      door;
We knocked but did not enter our home that was before.
For what was once a happy home, except when Mum would rouse,
Stayed silent now – it had become a sad, deserted house.

Where once the lawn grew thick and green, the button grass lay
      brown –
All through the droughts there never was a place so broken down.
Where once the oleanders grew beside the station store,
Our eyes beheld the open downs where trees had been before.

No bougainvillea decked the dray beside the tennis court
Where friends would laugh and cheer at play – what fun those days
      had brought.
But now the dray, in sad repair, leaned peeling in decay –
And oh the silence everywhere the children used to play!

The house all flaking, shabby, grey, with gauze all rusty brown;
The gutter sagging – once so gay – a smile become a frown.
All through the droughts the old home shone, all white by garden
    green;
It doesn't do to contemplate the way things might have been.

Just forty cents an acre then – they'll take four dollars now –
Perhaps they'll paint the place again when profits will allow.
If that's the way the west has gone, it's good we went away;
Old friends are gone, old ways are done, and care just doesn't pay.

No friends to wave us from the gate as we drove off that day;
No calls of 'We'll be seeing you, we'll see you soon, hooray!'
No – just that haunting silence that seemed to mean, 'Move on!
To all of you good riddance – Your days are dead – Begone!'

WHEN THE COOK WAS THE DUNBYDOO DOGGER

Now the Arthur the Fayers is one of those stayers
Who'll work from the dawn to the dark.
He's a business-like man is this galloping Ghan,
Yet he's one who is fond of a lark.

Be it shearing or clearing, or bush engineering,
Or fencing by day or by mile,
Any job he will take if it pays a good stake,
This Arthur is quite versatile.

He will fill every pen with reliable men
When bossing a general shearing,
But if one or two short he will quickly resort
To open and blatant cashiering!

For there's many a man who has worked for the Ghan,
Who has woken up out in the scrub
In the back of a heap after going to sleep
With a hangover back at the pub!

I recall on occasion, on Dongadee Station,
The Ghan made his only mistake –
When he got up and shook and awakened the cook,
He discovered the man was a fake ...

For the cook shook his head, and he hiccupped and said,
'By crikey I'm wounded and sorry.
Now what pub is this? There is something amiss.
How th' heck am I here on this lorry?'

Said the Ghan, 'It's no pub, and we're hungry for grub,
So get out y'recipe book.
Y'brain's missed a cog but it's just from th' grog,
An' I'll have y' know y'th' cook!'

'I'm not y'dashed cook, y'cashiering crook.
Y'shangaied me, Fayers, y'silly rat!
I'm not o'those blokes who doesn't see jokes,
For y'see – I'm the ganger at Gilliat!'

As the ganger of course is the boss of the force
Which attends to the Permanent Way,
The Ghan with a whine took him back to the line
And we loafed for the rest of the day.

But early next morning by picinni' dawning,
Bold Arthur was back with a cook.
When this man out-of-luck rose and fell from the truck,
All the team gathered in for a look.

'Can y'cook?' asked a bloke as he gave him a poke,
'Can y'bash up a reasonable feed?'
'Course I can,' said the man as he sized up the Ghan,
'I can take on whatever I need.'

'I've been a horse-breaker and bush undertaker,
I've wandered from Croydon to Wagga,
But the job that I've got is the best of the lot –
I'm the Dunbydoo Syndicate dogger.'

'By th' scent of y'stink, you are honest I think,
But a dogger no longer y'be.
It's time we were dining so you are resigning –
Y're staying and cooking for me!'

'By hook or by crook, I'll not be your cook,
I've gotta get back to m'traps –
I'll just quench m'thirst and I'll flatten you first,
Then layout the rest o' you chaps!'

He was quite a fair slogger, this Dunbydoo dogger,
But The Ghan is a durable cove,
So we sat in the sun, enjoying the fun,
While they punched and they parried and wove.

Though it wasn't too clean, the fighting was keen –
Piledrivers and uppercuts foul,
They battled all day till the Ghan had his way,
And the Wagga man threw in the towel.

For at set of the sun, the dogger was done
And he gasped as they staggered apart –
'I've had y'dashed hooking, I'll do y'dashed cooking,
What time do y'want me to start?'

And there's no need to say how we all had to pay
For the meals a la Croydon et Wagga,
For there's few live to tell what misfortunes befell
When the cook was the Dunbydoo dogger.

THE MELODY OF RAIN

There's sweet music in the falling of the raindrops when they're calling
With their patter on the gables of an iron roof at night.
I can hear the rhythmic drumming of the downpipes softly humming;
There's sweet music in the raindrops on an outback roof at night.

With a whisper of the breeze as it murmurs through the trees
Comes the chorus of the bullfrogs as they come to life again,
And the melody that's ringing from those thousand voices singing
Is a hymn of praise to Heaven for the steady soaking rain.

There's a musky scent of moisture from the parched and blackened
    pasture
As the cracked and beaten paddocks feel the freshness of the rain;
There's the chorus of the crickets from the oleander thickets
As they play the background music for the bullfrogs' glad refrain.

In the brief but brilliant brightening from the intermittent lightning
There's the white and ghostly glimmer of the water on the ground.
As I stand and look in wonder, there are rolling claps of thunder
And the power of Nature echoes in the vastness of its sound.

Now the drought is broken and these lines are but a token
Of the measure of my pleasure at the coming of the Wet;
It's a joy that's shared by others of my western grazing brothers
And we'll all take up new courage for the squaring of the debt.

When the Mitchell grass is growing and the inland rivers flowing,
When they're swollen with the run-off from the great monsoonal rain,
When the Flinders grass is seeding and the stock are fat and feeding,
We'll forget about the hardships and we'll praise this land again!

Yes, those mystic notes enthralling of the raindrops softly calling
Are the rhapsody of Nature that's the grazier's delight.
As I hear the rhythmic drumming of the downpipes softly humming,
I give thanks to God and Nature for an outback home tonight.

FROM THE LANTERNS

I am sitting, thinking, writing by the bright electric lighting
At a worn and weathered table in the ancient station store,
And as I sit and ponder, my eyes, attracted, wander
Down a row of lonely lanterns from an era gone before.

As I look at them I reckon that they somehow seem to beckon
And my mind in recollection to that bygone era rolls:
As I sit and look upon them, I see history written on them
In the cracks on gloomy glasses and the rust upon their bowls.

Through the cobwebs on their handles and the rust upon their
    mantles,
I can see unknown people and long-forgotten names,
And the folk remembered dearly are reflected smiling clearly
In the glint of chimney glasses in those old and dusty frames.

Though the wicks will never light again and never flicker bright again,
Yet they linger here, survivors, when all the rest is gone;
From a former mellow glory, they remain to tell a story
Of an era and its people that they softly shone upon.

By grime of years encrusted, they are dirty now and rusted,
Their wicks are lost or perished, long gone their evenfall;
Though their substance is neglected, they are good as new, reflected
In their outlines silhoutted in their shadows on the wall.

And as sharp as this reflection is my vivid recollection
Of the people and occasions that these hurricanes recall;
For those years now recollected areas clearly now projected
As the never-ageing shadows of the lanterns on the wall.

Bewitched, my mind meanders to those open green verandahs
Where everyone was welcome those many years ago:
I can see the women darning and the menfolk smoking, yarning
In the mellow, soft and yellow light of lowly lantern glow.

Lo! I hear the lilting laughter as it rolls from wall to rafter
And I see the laughing faces and the love in laughing eyes;
Then, in quiet again prevailing, I hear notes of plaintive wailing
And a mother goes to comfort now the little one who cries.

Now I see again the shining of a table set for dining
By the light of shaded lanterns in those gay more gracious years:
The gravy boats a-winking and the stirling carvers twinkling
And the steaming entrée dishes and the matching muffineers.

And I see the happy greetings at the hack and picnic meetings
When the lanterns lit the dances in the crowded little halls;
And I hear the charleston ringing and those distant voices singing
And I see the lanterns swinging on the corrugated walls.

Though I was just a nipper when these lanterns used to flicker,
They have shone tonight with visions of forgotten yesterday;
As these fancies fade asunder, in silence now I wonder:
I can see the rusty lanterns, but the people – where are they?

My imagination dances on percentage of the answers:
Will Saint Peter write 'All present' when he makes his final call?
Then we can join in laughter when we muster up hereafter
And we'll come and light these lanterns that are waiting on the wall!

CROSSED CHANNELS

Two policemen in a western town
Were resting from the beat:
In squatters' chairs they'd settled down
To try to beat the heat.

The young chap's thoughts were nowhere near,
He gazed out at the sky,
The sergeant quaffed a sip of beer
And brushed away a fly.

The youngster said, 'By cripes it's hot,
These flies'd drive y'mad.
We've had hot days, but of the lot
Today's the worst we've had.

'Eh, Sarge, y'know it's pretty strong,
I think it's pretty weak,
That they can make us stay so long
In spots like Julia Creek.

'I think I'll write to Down Below,
In fact I'll write today.
That Channel Country's where I'll go
If I can have a say.'

The sergeant smacked another fly
And nearly spilt his beer.
'What's that? I thought you'd rather die
Than move to worse than here?

'Who'd ever want to go to towns
Like Birdsville and Windorah?
You wouldn't get me there fo' pounds,
You're off y'block, begorrah!

'The Channel Country's quite the worst –
The blackman's land, I fear.
I fear m'boy y'd die of thirst.
Y'just have no idea …

'The pubs are few and far between,
The beer is always hot,
And have you never ever seen
A man with Barcoo rot?'

'No, Sarge, for sure you've got me wrong,
I pine for city lights,
For go-go girls and shows and song
And other such delights:

'No Sarge, it's not that land you know,
For sure you're off the line –
I mean the land of Channel 0,
Of Channels Two and Nine!'

THE GREATEST MOANER

He was shearing for McCarthy
In the drought of '35,
When I saw him first at Ardbrin
Cursing everything alive.
I was leaning on a catching-pen
Surveying operations,
When I saw him kick an ageing ewe
With sundry lacerations:
'Can't you sit up straight y'worn ol' thing
An give a man a go?
There was never a fossil found
As old as this 'ere yoe.'
A hundred flies enshrouded him,
Sweat trickled from his brow:
'Y'bag o' bones. Y'fangless crone,
Y'fossilised ol' cow.'
At last he'd done and, standing up
(He was a massive brute),
He grabbed the ewe, spat out a butt,
And kicked her down the shute.
'How would you be?' I asked him then
While he was changing tools.
''Ow would I be? 'Ow would I be —
Of all the bloomin' fools —
I'm wringin' wet an' eatin' dust,
M'waterbag is dry,
An' every time I look to see
A fly gets in my eye.
I got a wife an' batch o' kids —
'Ow can I keep an 'ome?
There's not a breath of wind to breathe

An' these 'ere sheep won't comb!
'Ow would I be? Now can't you see?
'Ow do y'spect I'd be?'

In a jungle camp in Java
I was next to hear his cry.
He was sitting on a petrol can
While everything went by.
In the fetid air and steamy
Of an atmosphere offensive,
He was drooping there, dejected,
With a painful look and pensive.
I sauntered up – *'How would you be?'*
I earnestly inquired.
"Ow would I be? 'Ow would I be?'
He sounded somewhat tired.
'Now what the hell; ain't it enough
To fight the runty Japs
Without I 'as to stummick too
You sentimental chaps?
Look at me shorts – they're forty-fours
An' I take thirty-two.
Me boots are both too flamin' small,
What can a feller do?
I haven't slept for near a week
For mozzies thievin' blood,
An' every time I wash me duds,
It rains a blinkin' flood.
Muskita bites on both me arms,
Blood blisters on me toes –
I'd soon be back a' Julia Creek
An' shearin' boney yoes!
'Ow would I be? Now can't you see?
'Ow do y'spect I'd be?'

I heard no more about him
'Till I read that he had died,
And I felt quite sure that Satan
Would consign him to be fried.
Lo and behold, I dreamt last night
I saw him safe in heaven,
Being waited on by cherubs –
There were five or six or seven.
He was lookin' most unhealthy
And his face was rather white.
His halo needed shining
And his gown was far too tight.
I tiptoed up and timidly inquired:
'How would you be?'
''Ow would I be? 'Ow would I be?
'Ow do y'spect I'd be?
St Peter's sainted silverfish
Are chewing up me gown,
Me 'alo keeps on slippin' –
I look a blinkin' clown!
There's a plague of laryngitis
An' nobody 'ere can sing.
There's also dermatitis
An' I'm moultin' from me wing!
Me 'alo's badly dented
But they ain't got no blacksmith 'ere.
I can't afford another
For the price is far too dear.
I keep trippin' on me girdle
An' m'sandles 'urt m'feet,
The climate's far too cold up 'ere,
I'd rather 'ave the 'eat!

Look at me 'arp – th' G string's broke –
Ain't it a lousy crime?
What can I do with band practice
In twenty minutes' time?
'Ow would I be? Now can't you see?
'Ow would I ever be?'

WET WETHER

Now you've heard of the Ghan, that durable man
Of the businesslike, bustling ways,
But the fate of the dogger, the slogger from Wagga,
Is but one of a hundred affrays.

And I feel I must tell of a tale I know well
(Though I'll leave out the terrible end)
Of the poor rouseabout who collected the clout
For fear that the words would offend.

Now the regular man who killed for the Ghan,
A slaughterman, polished and neat,
Had gone down with the flu, so a rousy in lieu
Was detailed for providing the meat.

Now this regular man who killed for the Ghan,
Always hygienically keen,
Took a bucket of water when going to slaughter
To ensure that the carcase was clean.

'Twas the reason no doubt that the poor rouseabout
Made the easy but tragic mistake.
If a sheep he must slaughter, he must have some water –
'Twas a simple conclusion to make.

Now the bucket and steel and the knife made him feel
That this killing was frightfully callous,
But he brushed it aside and, with purposeful stride,
He made for the sheep at the gallows.

Well the time drifted by and the Ghan said, 'That guy
Is the slowest that I've ever had.'
So with the light nearly gone and with night coming on,
He decided to check on the lad.

And the sight that he met, he will never forget,
Nor the rousy the dreadful disgrace.
Where there should have been blood, there was nothing but mud,
There was water all over the place.

For what the Ghan found was a rousy half drowned
And the wether all muddy and wet.
'What th' hell is the matter you blundering hatter,
Why th' hell aren't y'done him yet?'

'He ought to be dead, but he isn't,' he said,
And he looked at the Ghan with a frown.
'To be sure I can't slaughter this sheep in that water.
How the heck do you get him to drown?'

IS THIS THE BUSH?

A tourist, plump and well attired,
One of the city push,
Came in today and he enquired:
'I say, is this the Bush?'

'No, this is not the Bush, my friend;
The bush is nowhere near.
The Black Stump was just round the bend,
But it's no longer here.

'Its borderline was not defined
But it was here no doubt,
Before the modes of men inclined
To move it further out.

'No, this is not the Outback yet,
For we're too up-to-date.
You've come a way, but don't you fret –
Keep on, you'll find it, mate.'

You would have thought, to see him frown,
That I'd been telling lies.
He looked me up and looked me down
With pity in his eyes.

'Good grief! It's not the Bush today?
It's further up the track?
It's Bush enough for me, I say –
From here I'm turning back!'

EH!

Y'reckon, eh? Well, so do I –
It's like their flamin' hide
T'say we all talk different, eh? –
Fair churns me inside!
They reckon, eh, in Queensland, eh,
Y'know eh like they say –
They reckon we talk slower
An' we use a lot of 'eh'.

Eh, bullshit, eh? Y'reckon, eh?
Yair, course it is, eh Joe?
There's no doubt in my mind, y'know –
At least we 'ave a go!
Eh? No mistake! Eh – watch me beer!
Eh – 'oo the 'ell ar you?
Aw – all the way from Melbourne, eh?
Well, sport, how do you do?

We mightin' 'ave an 'Arbour Bridge.
Eh! Watch me bloody beer!
But eh, we got – eh, ridgy-didge –
The min-min light up 'ere.
An' wot about the bloody Reef,
Eh Joe? Y'reckon, eh?
Well like, y'know – beyond belief –
Yair, eh – that's what I say!

Well like, y'know, in Queensland, eh,
There goes me bloody beer!
Eh yair – another Fourex, mate –
'Oo is that bloody queer?

At least we're not the Garden State –
Eh? Not all pansies gay?
Yair, sure y'come from Melbourne, mate –
Eh, lay orf mate – EH! EH!

Bob Magor

COUNT YOUR BLESSINGS

So Australia has failed you, you tell us –
She has squandered your payments of pelf.
That you're cursed with a lack of incentive
And your country's at fault, not yourself.

When fate dealt out the cards for your future
From a pack that was stacked for your ease,
You expected a hand full of aces –
Now despair you were dealt twos and threes.

So you languish inert in self-pity
While your present and future you doubt.
In life's cup, if you put nothing in it,
Logic says you can take nothing out.

Lift the veil on your shallow ambitions –
Smell the freedom that's borne on the breeze.
Get a feel for this land you reside in
And compare it with those overseas.

Stand atop Uluru's ochre grandeur,
Where the sun warms the soul of our land.
Gaze in awe to the western horizon,
At the Olgas reclined on the sand.

Feel the spirit that drives our young nation.
Choke the pride from your chest if you can.
Feel the throb of our land's surging heartbeat
That was pulsing before time began.

Watch the wedgetails who soar on the vista,
Cardboard cutouts hung out on the sky.
They're our symbol of bold self-reliance
With a proud fearless gleam in their eye.

That's the attitude needed to live here
In a homeland where Nature's supreme.
You must bend but not yield to her seasons
If you wish to progress in her scheme.

Stand and gaze from a Nullarbor clifftop
On the lip of the Bight's gaping mouth.
Watch the endless foam leis of the breakers,
Pristine, born from the icebergs down south.

We're a nation surrounded by oceans
And our borders are cleansed by the flow
From the purest of pure ocean currents,
Drawn up deep from vast fathoms below.

Sit a while cloaked in shade 'neath a gum tree
On a sluggish and pale inland stream.
Rig a hook for a sly barramundi
Or elusive and shy silver bream.

Watch the flow, how it glows in the sunlight –
Drink in deep from these arteries of gold.
Sip the lifeblood that nurtures our nation
Pumping still as it did in days of old.

Build a campfire at night in the country,
Well away from a town's neon glare.

Search your soul in the luminous embers
As they warm the night chill on the air.

Then lie back, watch the stars of our country
As they cluster the void of the sky –
Nature's jewellery case standing wide open
With a free fireworks show up on high.

Go and witness the glow of the centre –
Namatjira's stark contrasting hues.
Behold landscapes of bold panorama
Brushed in reds and siennas and blues.

For when nature set up her great easel
And her palate to colour the scene,
Brushstrokes flourished both bold and creative
With her pigments mixed vivid and clean.

Take a swim in the exquisite splendour
Of our garden – the Barrier Reef –
In full bloom with her intricate petals
Of bright flowering blossom and leaf.

See the Daintree kiss white coral beaches
Where a turquoise caress washes o'er.
Was there ever a land more resplendent
With a garland adorning its shores?

Take a journey at dawn from Cooinda
As the Kakadu locals awake.
See the birds, every species created,
On the wetlands and billabong lake.

For there's few places left on this planet
Still untouched for the future to see.
Just feel humble and witness their rising,
For, like you, they're unfettered and free.

When you've sampled the gifts of your homeland,
When you've travelled her length and her girth,
Tell me then what's amiss with Australia –
In this last land of plenty on earth.

For to live and be born in this country
Is your privilege – 'twas never your right.
The best pathways through life travel upwards,
But to climb be prepared for a fight.

Our Australia – she isn't a harlot
Or a mistress to lechers like you.
For her hand, prove your worth as a suitor
With a hard-working heart that is true.

Yes she's hard but she's just, like a mother.
She's a lady, still young but so old.
If you woo her with sweat and exertion
She'll repay your deeds one hundredfold.

Times are tough, always were, always will be.
In life's quest some succeed, others fall.
When the old sit around reminiscing,
It's their battles hard-won they recall.

So don't tell me your land has betrayed you –
Nothing's gained without effort or zeal.

You just shoulder the wheel and remember,
It takes fire to turn iron into steel.

For the price of success is endeavour
And your grit, not your wealth, proves your worth.
Bend your back 'neath the flag of your country,
Our Australia – the greatest on earth.

THE COOPER COMING DOWN

The thunderheads had bunched up
    In the north-west now for days
And the Blackall farmers shook their heads in doubt.
Then the news came in from Longreach
    Of monsoonal soaking rain
And rejoicing at the breaking of the drought.
From the black soil cracks it's spilling,
This is it, if God be willing,
As each watercourse is filling,
Coming down.

And the deluge, unabated,
    Swept the western Queensland plain
With the Thompson and the Barcoo on the rise.
Till they mingled near Windorah
    To become the Cooper Creek,
Slowly spreading like an ocean in its size.
The land's dusty pores are flushing,
Down the Channel Country rushing,
Like an avalanche it's gushing,
Coming down.

Then for weeks the swamps kept filling
    As the Cooper flexed her might,
Ever onward till Lake Yamma flushed with pride.
And at Durham Downs the cattle
    Saw mirages shimmer real
With a spread of thirty kilometres wide.
Oh, the bluebush plains are drinking
As the coolabahs are sinking
And the land is slowly shrinking,
Coming down.

And this floating tide of debris
      Slowly journeyed on its course.
Nappa Merrie, past the ghosts of Burke and Wills.
It funnelled forth its fury
      Down the Cullyamurra Choke,
Progress noted by the haunting ironstone hills.
The bush telegraph is ringing,
And the whistling kites are singing,
Oh what joy the Cooper's bringing,
Coming down.

Then it reached an intersection
      At the Innamincka ford
Where the locals check the levels day by day.
And the wedgetails soar the thermals
      And the pelicans ride high
As the north arm lures the Cooper on its way.
Where the lignum clumps are bending
From this lifeblood nature's sending
With the Cooper never-ending,
Coming down.

Soon Coongie Lakes are brimming
      Like a vibrant inland sea,
And corellas in the red gums screech with pride.
All rejoicing at the cleansing
      Of this jewel in their domain
And the bounty once the countryside has dried.
There'll be grateful cattle lowing
On the native clover growing,
Cooper's verdant passage showing,
Coming down.

Still the Cooper, unrelenting,
        Banks up higher at the ford
Till she shimmers down the dry Strzelecki Creek.
But onward, ever onward,
        On her course toward Lake Eyre,
Proud and rampant slowly rising to her peak.
Down at Moomba, they're berating,
With the gasfields inundating.
There's some problems she's creating
Coming down.

Some three months from Innamincka
        Sees her cut the Birdsville Track
But she's run her race, she ends her proud display.
Lake Eyre may see her next time
        As she spreads to north and south
For a labyrinth of sandhills bar her way.
So her journey now has ended,
Over half a year she wended,
Vast expanses she befriended,
Coming down.

So the Cooper, mighty Cooper,
        Breathes new life upon the land
As the country blooms from passing of her flood.
To this ancient land – this fragile land –
        She's like a living pulse.
She's the country's main life-giver,
To the outback she'll deliver
Not a creek – but mighty river,
Coming down.

SNAKES ALIVE

Now a brown snake's 'bout as deadly
As an Aussie snake can get,
And he'll chase you if it suits him,
So don't keep him as a pet.

And when summer makes him playful
Then he's best left well alone,
Which is easy if you see him
And his presence there is known.

But while cruising on my ag bike
In the fiery midday sun,
I was checking sheep and water
On my dried and southern run.

When I slowed to cross a gully
That turned out a big mistake,
For I crossed the favourite pathway
Of a seven-foot brown snake.

Well, I thought I heard a rustle
But I saw him far too late,
And the snake passed through my back wheel
Like a poker though a grate.

With the wheel still slowly turning
He was picked up like a staff.
Till he met up with the back forks
Which then folded him in half.

Now this bumpy revolution
Didn't do much good.
Through the spokes he saw my pants leg;
He would bite it if he could.

Through the wheel he did a U-turn.
He would strike revenge and pain.
But the forks loomed up to clout him
And he circled around again.

Several times he passed back through the wheel,
His body did disjoint.
A pattern laced amongst the spokes
Like reptile needlepoint.

The snake was now quite angry
As he bit around the seat.
I was lucky that his snappy end
Had shortened by two feet.

For each time he threaded through the wheel
His length contracted some.
By stroke of luck he couldn't reach
The outskirts of my bum.

The snake bit the seat and mudguard
And he bit the rim and tyre.
My legs were on the handlebars;
I couldn't get them higher.

But the snake now had concussion
From each revolution's clout –

A sort of chiropractic nightmare
With his vertebrae all out.

Though just when I thought he'd mellowed
He came back to life again,
When his threshing tail twitched sideways
And caught up there in the chain.

Well that really made him savage,
He'd a tear in his eye,
As six inches of his rear end
On the sprocket passed him by.

Then the front wheel struck a pothole,
From the bike I did propel.
Which ejected me some distance
Off this serpent ride from hell.

As I lay there shocked and bleeding
I reflected on the ride;
Watched the back wheel bravely churning
As the bike lay on its side.

And that snake was madly hissing
Still quite shirty from the fray,
Biting bits of bike at random –
It would need a tourniquet.

Till he bit the plastic fuel line
That protruded from the tank
And spilled out the liquid contents,
Smelling volatile and rank.

It all happened in an instant,
With a spark, a blinding flash,
And a cataclysmic fireball
Turned my paddock into ash.

Yes this Kawasaki comet
Rose volcanic from the ground,
With a half-cooked snake still biting
Every piece of bike he found.

And the bushfire that resulted
Took us several days to quell,
As it burnt out several neighbours
And a national park as well.

And police investigating
To the cause, they called me odd,
And dismissed my brown snake story
With their verdict – 'Act of God'.

Now I grin with some amusement
When a batch of greenies chime
That 'All snakes should be protected
And to kill one is a crime.'

It's quite obvious they're new chums –
Never been outside of town –
And they've never shared an ag bike
With a very snaky brown.

THE DAY I SHOT THE TELLY

I prepared to shoot a rabbit
Which on weekends was my habit
In the sixties, back when I was just a lad.
And I grabbed my gun and bolted –
With the rifle breech unbolted.
I'd been taught the safety practice by my dad.

From the garden Mum was pleading,
Could I help her with some weeding?
Though the rifle now was loaded, it could wait.
For I'd only be a minute,
So I left the bullet in it
And I stood the loaded gun against the gate.

Well the daylight was receding
By the time I finished weeding,
So I grabbed the gun and wandered back indoors.
Where the TV still was going,
It was *Bandstand* that was showing
So I settled back to see what was in store.

Little Pattie looking pretty
And the Delltones sang a ditty
With the legend JO'K all systems go.
All the music highly rated
But the chap I really hated
Was that Brian Henderson who ran the show.

He was talking when I got him
For I drew a bead and shot him.
I said 'Bang bang', but no corpse there could I see.

So I lined up with a snigger,
Cocked the gun and pulled the trigger,
And the world as I then knew it ceased to be.

Cripes, I forgot the gun was loaded
And the TV screen exploded
As I sat in fright cemented to the chair.
Shattered picture tube suspended
And the goldfish bowl upended
As the smell of smoke and gunfire filled the air.

There was valves and things exploding,
My composure was eroding,
As a burst of sparks drew patterns on the wall.
And I got that sinking feeling
Watching shrapnel peel the ceiling
And a smoking cat ran howling through the hall.

I had hit the man dead centre.
Yes, I'd fixed that damn presenter,
Though he haunted me with no time to rejoice.
From a crackling left-hand speaker
Somewhat dry and slightly weaker,
Out this hole that once was picture came his voice.

It was a nasty shock he gave me
Just as Mum rushed in to save me,
But the sight of so much carnage made her stare.
As she viewed the lounge room blasted
I dribbled out, 'I got the bastard,'
And I heard Mum say, 'I'm pleased, but who and where?'

I'd acute smoke inhalation,
Shock and TV screen abrasion,
And I will admit I'd messed myself as well.
Quite relieved it had all ended,
Then a chilling thought descended …
When he came home I'd the old man still to tell.

I was shaking like a jelly
And there wasn't much on telly,
So I went to bed, quite early I recall.
'Cause I didn't feel like eating,
I was bracing for a beating,
And when Dad came home, I heard him through the wall.

From outside Dad yelled and stuttered –
'Someone singed the cat,' he muttered.
He was not a happy pappy, I could tell.
I'd contractions in my belly
When Mum choked, 'Bob shot the telly,'
And the old man had a door to fix as well.

Well I had a nasty time then.
Child abuse was not a crime then.
Father fixed the box and had the lounge re-done.
Though for weeks he weighed the option
Of my name up for adoption …
But he kept me 'cause I was his only son.

THE GHOSTS OF COBB & CO.

The old truckie felt their presence
  As his diesel split the night,
Then he saw the coach reflected
  In a moonbeam's mottled light –
Flying manes and tails a-shimmer.
  Phantom horses' eyes aglow.
For he ran the night shift gauntlet,
  With the ghosts of Cobb & Co.

All the truckies know these spectres –
  They patrol on ev'ry track,
From the black tar super highways
  To deserted roads outback.
They provide a phantom escort
  From those times of long ago,
For the roadtrains and the transports
  All descend from Cobb & Co.

As the truckie stopped for diesel
  He envisaged in the gloom,
The coach passengers out stretching
  Near a mud and split slab room.
They had gold there from the diggings –
  They had mail on top to stow.
It was mailman, vault and taxi
  Was a coach of Cobb & Co.

Then fresh teams were quickly harnessed
  As the spent retired to rest,
With the wheelers backed in sideways
  And the leaders three abreast.

And they trembled with excitement
  As the brake released to go;
They were born to forge a legend
  Were these steeds of Cobb & Co.

As his rig moved out they raced him
  Out across the darkened plain.
They were always there to guide him –
  Be it dust or driving rain –
And they'd lift his sagging spirits
  When the hours were dragging slow.
They protect the highway haulers,
  Do these ghosts of Cobb & Co.

Racing horses' hooves danced firelight
  As they made the gibbers fly.
And he saw the phantom driver
  Silhouetted on the sky.
Outstretched arms with reins entangled,
  Seated proud with hat pulled low.
They were men to be respected
  If they drove for Cobb & Co.

He changed gears down through the cutting
  And the long decline ahead,
But the horses' reins hung limply –
  Down at the breakneck speed they sped
Till the coach wheels sprayed the shadows
  Through the creek bed far below.
So surefooted, bold and fearless
  Was each horse of Cobb & Co.

As the truckie reached the bottom
    He could see them flying still.
And he marvelled at their power
    As they charged the farther hill,
Flashing foam-specked surging muscles
    Never easing for a blow.
Yes, each pony pulled ten horsepower
    In the shafts of Cobb & Co.

The phantom driver slowed and waited
    For the transport in the gloom.
Ghostly guardian of truckies,
    This road rider from the tomb.
And the truckie's hand saluted
    To this friendly spirit's glow –
One of the pioneering heroes
    From the days of Cobb & Co.

Then the apparition faded
    With the dawning shafts of rust,
But he knew the team still paced him
    By the rising film of dust.
For it's with pride he keeps the legend
    That was earned by Cobb & Co.
For it's a route they blazed, he drives on
    From the days of long ago.

THE SHEEMU

Now these days on the farms it's all changing
With diversification the key.
Farming yabbies or deer
Or alpacas to shear –
Growing fish or some fruit-bearing tree.

But one cocky went sev'ral steps further
When he handed convention a shock.
He was Seamus O'Toole,
He was nobody's fool
When it came to the breeding of stock.

For he wanted a beast multipurpose,
With a fleece forty kilos or more.
A lean meat with no waste,
Quite unique to the taste –
Such a blend would be a winner for sure.

So he captured a wily cock emu
And penned him each night with a ewe,
To produce him a sheemu,
Half sheep and half emu –
And I swear that the story is true.

Though reluctant, the sheep were soon mated
By this emu – his breast filled with lust.
But these things with four legs
Never laid any eggs!
And he'd sit in the dust in disgust.

Through the weeks of gestation they waited.
The emu, old Seamus and sheep.
Then they woke with delight
From a cry in the night
That was mixture of baa and a cheep.

And old Seamus beheld his creation –
Woolly legs on each corner they had.
Flapping short stubby wings
With long tail and sheep things
And they wore the long neck of their dad.

Four big drumsticks each beast would provide him,
And he'd neck chops supplied by the yard.
And the meat off the breast
With mint sauce would be best
Though to shear them – well that would be hard.

For their wool hung in locks –rank and curly –
Sprouting out from the end of each quill.
Whether pluck it or shear,
In what pose or what gear,
They were bound to give shearers a thrill.

Although mustering posed quite a problem
When attempting to round up the mob;
They ran round with such speed
Not a fence would they heed –
This was not a conventional job.

But necessity fosters invention,
For the mob later on must be shorn.
His old sheep dog he'd woo

With a buck kangaroo –
So a sheemu round-upper was born.

This result was a grey kelparoo dog
Whose back legs had an accent on power.
Twenty feet was the bound
Of this new-fashioned hound
Which could cruise sixty-five miles an hour.

Things were organised then for the shearing.
Although sceptical – shearers were found.
Wool packs stacked by the score,
Record wool-clip for sure
As the classer swapped wool bins around.

For the necks would go under the table
And the bellies he'd call AAA Breast,
While the pieces and locks
Would be down, quills and hocks,
And the fleece from the wings would be best.

So the muster was on for the shearing,
With the kelparoo bounding ahead.
When the sheemus looked up
At this strange-looking pup,
They baa-cheeped, flapped their wings and then fled.

And they stayed fairly well in formation
As they hurdled each fence in a stride.
And this strange steeplechase
Never slackened in pace
As it vanished to territory wide.

They were sighted the next day out from Birdsville,
Then by drovers on Kimberley's shore.
A Jap tourist in shock
Said they passed by Ayers Rock
And had photos to prove what he saw.

But then never again were they sighted
And old Seamus' fortune was lost.
With the moral, I guess,
If on farms you digress –
Keep your fingers, not animals, crossed.

THE SUBMERSIBLE UTE

The shearing that day had just ended,
I leaned on the sheep yards to wait
As Dad parked the ute on the hillside,
Then walked on to open the gate.
I watched as he spied the young wood duck,
He crept through the rushes to peep,
Then walked past the dam to the gateway
To open a path for the sheep.

I wiped the warm sweat from my forehead
With the palm of my hot grimy hand.
The dirt and the grease blurred my eyeballs
And stung with the bite of hot sand.
My gaze then was drawn to the wethers,
Snow white from the fleece that I'd stole,
They stared at me, yarded like prisoners,
And silently waited parole.

As afternoon shaded the gully,
The sheep and I ended our wait.
I watched the old ute turning homewards
Though Dad was still opening the gate.
Then echoes of swearing engulfed me,
Dad yelled, the problem was plain,
The ute, on its own, it had bolted,
With Providence handling the rein.

I watched it, aghast and astonished;
It sped like a runaway tram
And then, with the spring of an athlete,
A neat swallow dive in the dam.

The bow wave arose quite titanic
And washed all the wood ducks ashore,
While tadpoles and frogs that lay sleeping
Were broken and battered and sore.

Cartoonists could never draw better,
As round the brown water it swam.
The pride of the GMH factory,
An island right there in the dam.
It floated quite upright and stable –
If only a camera I had,
To capture forever the antics
Performed on the bank by my dad.

He addressed it in language unsavoury;
It floated, condemned and accused.
He cursed both its handbrake and gearbox
(Though neither of which he had used).
Our dog, who rushed in, so protective,
And snarled at the monster which swam,
Was seized (as if he were the culprit)
And drop-kicked out into the dam.

I rolled on the ground with laughter;
I couldn't believe it was true.
I watched the ute lurch like a drunkard,
Then soberly melt from my view.
As Dad danced around like a madman
He hurried for home 'cross the flat.
His clenched fists held high to the heavens,
He stopped and he jumped on his hat.

I sprang into action and hurried
With tractor and ropes to the bank,
But by then just a patch of brown bubbles
Showed me the spot where it sank.
But Dad had soon dampened my laughter;
He told me my clothes I'd to peel.
He made me dive into the water
And fasten the rope to a wheel.

The freezing cold depths of that water
I'll remember as long as I live,
As we hauled the old rogue out backwards
And watched her drain like a sieve.
Now Dad had a great sense of humour
But my wit brought a snarl to his mouth,
When I taunted, 'To get the ute going,
Perhaps you should try mouth to mouth.'

I mentioned, 'The ute needed washing.'
He glared unimpressed when I said,
'In future when cleaning the motor
Just try a degreaser instead!'
Years later when talking of faux pas,
One thing that Dad couldn't refute,
Was that afternoon etched in our memory –
The day that he drowned the old ute.

IT'S GONNA HURT

Now a motorbike's essential
On the farming scene these days;
You can cut off speeding yearlings
Or catch up with cunning strays.
No sheep born can hope to beat you
As you race it up the hills;
It's a farmer's greatest pleasure –
Save those death-defying spills.
As you hover close to impact
You sure know, 'It's gonna hurt,'
When the bike and you have parted
And you're headed for the dirt.

When you're rounding up the cattle
And you're racing out to pass,
Then you hit a stump or boulder
Lying hidden in the grass.
You're still sitting in the saddle
But you wear a worried frown
Because now your bike's inverted
And you're riding upside down.
And the revving two-stroke motor
Screams, 'This sure is gonna hurt!'
As the bike begins descending
And you're heading for the dirt.

When your useless bike bolts sideways
With an agonising squeal
And it changes your direction
From beneath the bike's front wheel.
You then feel a strange sensation

Flying forward in the breeze
As the handlebars retard you,
Dislocating both your knees.
As your body's levitating
You sure know it's gonna hurt,
For you're halfway through a cartwheel
And descending to the dirt.

When your front wheel finds the burrow
Of a rabbit now long gone,
And your steel steed concertinas
But your body journeys on,
Now your breeding days are over
And your bike you have to thank
When your manhood's squashed and scrambled
Through the pain of being gelded
You may think, 'No more can hurt,'
Till you contemplate the landing
While descending to the dirt.

As the bike rears up before you
It confirms 'You're going dense.'
You forgot last night you shifted
Your strip-graze electric fence.
And at thirty miles an hour
The fence tightens, snaps and springs,
And the bike and you launch skywards
As if borne on eagles' wings.
Then you land, a twisted tangle,
Your pulsating body hurt,
With a thousand amps now earthing
Through your left ear to the dirt.

As the dust begins to settle
You've survived – though just by chance.
Then you feel the hot exhaust pipe
Cooking slowly through your pants,
For your bike is draped above you
Like a draughty metal tent.
You're alive but badly winded
With a body torn and bent.
And your shoulder isn't working,
There's no limb that doesn't hurt,
And you view the single furrow
That your nose ploughed through the dirt.

Back some years ago I'd revel
In this type of riding stunt.
But the centre of my gravity
Has moved more out the front.
Two-wheeled exploits from my heyday
Through my greying head now floods,
When these days I land ungraceful
Like a sack of wormy spuds.
All my best is now behind me
And my ego sure does hurt
When I fall off just dismounting
And I end up in the dirt.

John James Mangan

WHERE THE BUSH SCHOOL USED TO BE

There's a dozen different places round the district where you'll see
A pepperina growing and a camphor laurel tree,
And a pine tree, not a native, and a fence which leans in need,
Round a garden bed that struggles 'neath a wilderness of weed.
There's a flagpole still upstanding, but no flag to flutter free,
Not a soul to stand saluting where the bush school used to be.

Gone the schools, but not forgotten, written now in history,
And those bush folk who were pupils have a clinging memory –
Yes, the bush folk, they remember, here their future hopes were born,
Here they heard the lilting birdsong on a spring or summer morn.
And those cold and frosty mornings when their feet were numb and
    bare,
And their ponies just like dragons puffing steam clouds in the air.

Oh! the news which passed amongst them 'standing easy' on the line,
How someone's dad was cutting chaff and someone's cutting pine,
And the piebald mare at Jones's, she had piebald twins last night,
The Martin kids have measles and the Smith kids have the blight;
And when the flag was hoisted, to attention at command,
Then the teacher spoke with feeling of a noble Motherland.

Oh! the tang of sandwich dinners underneath the 'dinner tree',
Where I swapped a 'jam' with Mary and she gave a 'meat' to me,
Drab those schools I now remember, though in youth we thought
    them fine,
Each one painted as the other, each one of the same design,
And those teachers, bless the teachers, write their wondrous deeds
    in stone,

Far from home and friends and family, yet they called these schools
    their own.

Now the school bus, warm or chilly, and it's never running late,
Does a pick-up in the morning and delivery at the gate –
Yes the whirring and the buzzing on macadam-coated roads,
Of the flashing cars and motorbikes and trucks with heavy loads,
Drown the jingle of the buckles and the creak of saddle straps,
Spoil the scent of sweating ponies and the sheen of saddle flaps.

When you're driving down the highway and you see a vacant spot,
See a flagpole and a pine tree and neglected garden plot,
Hear the glory of the trilling of the early morning song,
See a pony saddled ready where the grass is growing long;
Pause, and listen for a moment by the pepperina tree,
Hear the phantom songs of children, where the bush school used to be.

Ted Martin

CUTTING CANE

Once again the knives are flashing, cutting sugar cane and thrashing,
I see the stalks go hurtling into bundles by the ton.
Once again the men are flinging rails around, with shoulders swinging,
When they're laying down the portables for sugar trucks to run.

Now they run and grab a bundle and along their arm they trundle,
Half a hundredweight of sugar cane and load it on a truck.
Now they're climbing up the ladders, humping cane and snakes and
    adders.
Loading cane, dear city people, is the hardest work I've struck.

Sure they've got the sugar fever as they fasten chain and lever,
Twitching down the load by inches, like they always did before.
Now they're on the homeward battle and their little Mary's rattle,
When they see the 'cookie' waiting by the open kitchen door.

Seated round the dining table, tired out but fit and able,
Looking forward now to payday when they do their weekly dash,
Dressed like a poisoned finger, placing bets at Longa Linga,
Always ready for a flutter with their hard-earned ready cash.

Suffering from Mondayitis, blisters and imaginitis,
Symptoms of the 'tropic tremins', overhang, and 'dry degree',
Holding a tarpaulin muster, Bluey sheds his knuckleduster,
Representing rocky bottom of his week-end treasury.

But the old time gangs are missing, loving barmaids up and kissing,
They are nearly all cane cockies now or else dispensing brew.
Some have gone along the highways up St Jacob's ladder skyways.
I can hear them tell St Peter all the things they used to do.

And the younger generation understand the situation;
They're a team of willing youngsters that can cut and come again.
If they fly to beer and whisky or the blondies fresh and frisky,
They'll be smashing other records like they are at cutting cane.

Rhana Maxwell

HORSE SENSE

They laughed when they saw him come down the track,
With a stick for his horse and a swag on his back.
His clothes were all tattered and shabby to see,
And the horse that he led was the branch of a tree.

He trotted those sticks as though they were real,
And patted them gently as if they could feel.
He called them fond names and rubbed them both down,
And promised them oats when he got them to town.

They blade him 'G'day,' as he tied up each steed
And invited him in for a yarn and a feed.
They plied him with food, which disappeared fast,
And he talked as he ate of some trips in the past.

For he and his horses spent weeks on the track,
Seeing scarcely a soul in the lonely outback.
He said he was travelling to town for the show,
And his horses he'd sell, as he needed the dough.

They asked him to stay and camp there that night,
But he said he'd be off, and camp on a site
On that flat by the creek, if that was okay,
And his horses could rest and be fresh the next day.

'Sure,' laughed the boss, 'he's a harmless old coot,
And those horses of his wouldn't cause a dispute!'
They laughed as he rode away down the track
With his horses of sticks and his swag on his back.

But the harmless old coot was a wily old scamp
With a hundred good reasons for choosing that camp.
He wanted to rest where the grass was so good,
For not all his horses were fashioned from wood.

One hundred live horses he'd left down the track.
There were chestnuts and bays, and a good-looking black,
A pony or two, a conglomerate lot,
Content to stay put – they were weary and hot.

By the light of the stars he moved his tired mob
And he rolled out his swag on completing the job.
He slept like a lamb while his horses all fed
On that grass by the creek which cushioned his bed.

The men cantered down to the flat at first light,
And the look on the face of the boss was a sight,
For he knew he'd been beaten by the neatest of tricks
By that silly old coot and his pair of old sticks!

Bob Miller

THE WILL

All the tears have long ceased falling from our in-laws and our kin
Since the day my English aunty cashed her chips and chucked it in.
Do not think us heartless scoundrels if we mock this solemn show
But our family's seen recession and we're rather short on dough.
We just viewed her timely passing like some wilting daffodil,
Till a letter from her lawyers said we're mentioned in the will.
Well, Eureka, what a beauty. Just imagine how we felt.
No more we'd live in poverty, no more we'd strain the belt.

This dear old duck was loaded, couldn't count the dough she's got.
We could sell this cockroach castle, build a mansion, buy a yacht.
We'd be livin' soon in luxury. God bless her now-failed health –
And me, her only favourite nephew, surely I would cop this wealth.
So I rang the council foreman, said 'It's me, you ugly slob.
You can keep the pay you owe me and just stick your flamin' job.
No I won't be back tomorrow and I won't be back next year.
See, I'm off to merry England. You'll just have to persevere.'

Then I hurried to the banker, said 'You slimy crawlin' louse,
You can shove that loan I begged for, for that stinkin' little house.
I'll have more than Kerry Packer, and me aunty you can thank.
Not one word, you silly jackass, or I might buy your little bank.'
Hey, this newfound strength I revelled in, I was feeling strong and
    hearty,
But I had to sell the Kingswood for some dough to chuck a party.
As I clambered up the gangplank I then told the watching pack,
'Yeah, the richest thing you'll ever see, is me when I get back.'

261

When they read my dear old aunty's will they started from the ground.
The butler copped the silverware, the maid … a thousand pound.
She left Aunt Doris one Rolls-Royce, old Joe one block of flats,
Then the room was stunned to silence as the lawyer mentioned … cats.
To those mongrel, moggy mousers she'd bequeathed a million quid –
Well, I very nearly fainted and I'm sure Aunt Martha did.
But I knew my turn was coming as the lawyers carried on:
'I now leave my greatest treasure to my sister's darling son.'

'I leave to him my family ring to carry through the years.'
 'A stupid ring!' I said. 'That's all?' I near burst into tears.
I grabbed this lawyer by the throat and I almost run amok.
Saying, 'Give the cat the bloody ring, I'll take the million bucks.'
The hand of fate plays cruel tricks, as I learned on my way home;
For days I leaned across the rail and watched the briny foam.
In a fit of mad depression just for what she'd done to me,
I took old aunty's cursed ring and hurled it, in the sea.

Then I settled back into a chair with a smile upon my face,
But while reading through the papers I collapsed in sheer disgrace.
See, the ring that was still sinking now a thousand fathoms down
Had belonged to Mary, Queen of Scots … worth forty million pound!
I'm back home now, I'm on the dole and living in a tent.
I ponder on my fortune – how it came and sort of went.
I sit each night upon this rock, just toying, with a notion:
Yeah, I wonder just how hard it is to drain that cursed ocean.

THE TRUE AUSTRALIAN

What makes a true Australian? Have they set some stringent test?
Should he ride his trusted stockhorse around some station in the west?
Does he camp at night with ringers when the dust has turned to mud?
Could you smell the eucalyptus that is running through his blood?
Does he drift with sunburnt drovers down the overlanders' track?
Does he gallop through the timber with a stirring stockwhip crack?
Would he rush down mountain gullies wheeling brumbies in the
    scrub?
Would you find him Sat'day evening in some lonely outback pub?

Does he know the isolation of the rolling western plain?
Must he feel the haunting heartache of a season without rain?
If the words of western poets judge the likes of me and you,
Then a person from the city could just never be true blue.
Am I any less Australian on my green suburban block,
Where I've never heard the gunfire as they slaughter starving stock,
Where I can little but imagine tragic tales in times of drought,
As I've never wandered westward to the stations further out?

I have never known the horror when the waterholes go dry.
I can only grasp at glimpses why a drover's wife would cry.
Am I any less Australian 'cause my crops just do not fail,
Or I've never waltzed matilda on a dusty trackless trail?
If I live in easy splendour on a manicured city street,
Is it guilt I should be feeling for the bounty that I eat?
When my taps are never empty and my grass is always green,
Should I feel regret and sorrow for the things that might have been?

Now there's not a single stockman in the circle of my friends.
But they stick like mates together and they'll be there till it ends.
They are plumbers and they're painters and I like 'em just the same,

But they've never ridden brumbies and they've never crossed the plain.
Still they love this sunburnt country and they'd die for her today,
Regardless of poetic words that the western poets say.
Be you black or white or brindle we are equal, we're the same.
Stand up if you're Australian and be proud to bear that name.

THE BREW

When we bought the farm a fair while back
It was real secluded and right off the track.
We gave up a lot and we had to make do –
Too far to the pub so we brewed our own brew

With a couple of cousins from in next door
Who drink a lot ... and always want more.
We soon decided there won't be enough;
We'd need a whopping great heap of this stuff.

So we headed for town in our battered old truck,
We cursed the road and cursed our luck.
We bought sixty tins of Cooper's home brew
And a half ton of sugar just to help it all stew.

Then when it was loaded we roped it all down
And we pointed our truck on the road out of town.
As we drove past the Royal, the old pub looked so nice
We decided to stop ... just to get some advice.

But we downed a cold beer and another one too
While we checked the instructions on making this brew.
We downed a few more, and a few more and then ...
But we lost count at nine so we started again.

Then we bought twenty cartons just to help us get home.
We were long overdue and we hadn't a phone,
All the dogs would be hungry and the women would frown.
We'd been four bloody days since coming to town.

It was high time to make this much needed brew,
So we found a big tank and a boiler or two,
Rigged it all up and we lined it with tin,
Then we chucked the big heap of ingredients in.

We had to stop for a beer so we wouldn't dry out
And we downed a few fourex and a cold case of stout.
When a brainstorm hit Jimmy … at long bloody last:
'If we heated it up it'll brew twice as fast.'

So we fired the boiler with some ironbark stumps
While our outboard motor, she chewed up the lumps.
It bubbled and boiled and we all gave a cheer –
We'd soon be up to our eyeballs in beer.

Then cousin Ed noticed that some pipes were corroded,
But she never let on and the whole thing exploded.
It made such a thunderous, ear-splitting sound
Our bloody great shed was blown to the ground.

The cat went whistling way out through the trees,
Our dog lost his hair and most of his fleas …
Yes, the whole flamin' farm was lookin' real crook.
All the feathers were blown off our poor bantam chook.

Then the sky went dark … yet the air was clear.
It started to rain and it rained pure beer.
All the birds and bees were as drunk as fools
And our yard was covered with beer in pools.

Soon it flowed right into the dam and creek
And it kept raining beer for nigh on a week.

It was better by far then our wildest dreams …
We had beer in buckets and puddles and streams.

So this stuff in our dam is better than gold
There's only one problem … that's keeping it cold.
So Jim goes to town every day, once or twice,
And brings back our truck all loaded with ice.

Yeah, we gave up the brewing. We don't need it now,
And we've fenced off the dam just to keep out the cow.
No, we don't crack a bottle if our friends drop in.
If we feel like a beer … we just go for a swim.

Margaret Millian

THE BALLAD OF BLUEY MORSE

Few shearing shed cooks have patience with books,
I mean of the culinary kind.
They prefer simple fare with plenty to spare
For hearty consumption designed.

For ten men or twenty they have to cook plenty
Of good solid food without stint –
Not for them the rich courses with exotic sauces
Presented in bright glossy print.

Most adhere to the norm and follow the form,
But once in a while you will find
A free-thinking heart who stands quite apart –
Such a character springs to my mind.

One Eustace Morse (nicknamed Bluey of course
On account of his flaming red thatch)
Had a skill and a flair for producing fine fare
That few cordon bleu cooks could match.

Born and bred in the west, his dad thought it best
That he work on the land he knew well,
But the great dream he had, this freckle-faced lad,
Was to cook in a city hotel.

While others lads fished, played football and wished
To be champion riders he'd look
With bright-eyed elation at each rich creation
Displayed in his ma's cookery book.

He'd pore for an age over each coloured page,
Delighting in each fancy dish,
And he made up his mind that one day he'd find
Fulfilment at last of his wish.

Dad fretted and fumed, with anger consumed
That his offspring such softness should own.
No Morse live or dead to his knowledge, he said,
Such unmanly leanings had shown.

But the lad stood his ground and his parent soon found
That his will was the unbending kind:
'Try a year on the land as a shearing cook's hand,
Then we'll see if you're still of a mind.'

Unafraid of hard work, young Bluey would shirk
Not even the lowliest job.
He'd watch and observe, he'd mop up and serve,
And was soon classed as 'one of the mob'.

No effort he spared and new menus prepared
To keep the men properly fed.
And they made him at last, before the year passed,
'Boss Cookie' himself of the shed.

And strange as it seems, the lad's youthful dreams
Faded with time and he grew
So content with his lot that he cared not a jot
His former intent to pursue.

Most people who wish to create a fine dish
Need standard equipment at least.
But dinkum, this cove, on a rough bushman's stove
Could turn out a right royal feast.

His fame grew apace for no-one could lace
An ordinary meal with such class.
His damper so light was a gourmet's delight
But his stews were his real coup de grâce.

Blue was inventive, a man of incentive,
A fellow of wond'rous resource.
He'd whip up a stew of possum or roo
Or his specialty – ragout of horse.

No expensive devices or rare herbs and spices
Did Blue need to foster his art.
With a native-born skill every order he'd fill
As a 'special' or just à la carte.

In the far western pubs his witchetty grubs
Were the subject of talk in the bar,
Nut sweet with flavour and delicate savour
They were fit for a prince or tsar.

From Winton to Weipa, in boxcar and sleeper,
By word of mouth spread Bluey's fame.
Each drover, each swagman, each shearer, each bagman
Sang his praises and toasted his name.

But as years passed at length, Bluey seemed to lose strength,
His eye seemed to lose its bright shine.
His master touch faltered, his whole outlook altered
And he began to go into decline.

Some fellows in bars quaff too many jars,
Earning many a chiack and jibe.
His mates were rum drinkers – strong spirit sinkers –
But Blue was not seen to imbibe.

Yet he grew more unsteady, his hand once so ready
To concoct gastronomic delight
Lost its former great knack, even strength seemed to lack
And he ended a sad, sorry sight.

The shearers all wondered and each of them pondered
The cause of his drooping away.
To the best of their thinking he'd never been drinking
For no-one had seen him that way.

So he sickened and died and everyone tried
To discover what made him succumb.
They were puzzled and swore that the signs that he bore
Were the symptoms connected with rum.

The large funeral over, each shearer and drover
Who'd rallied to pay last respects,
To show that they cared, to his quarters repaired
To gather his simple effects.

A room spartan but clean, a bed with a lean
And a packing case shelf met their eyes.
A coat and hat on a hook and his ma's old cookbook –
But his storeroom contained the surprise.

This storeroom revealed what Blue had concealed
From everyone over the years –
There were empties galore from ceiling to floor
Stacked neatly in gleaming glass tiers.

They all stared amazed, dumbfounded and dazed,
But the irony yet was to come.
A fact was disclosed that none had supposed:
He drank essence of lemon – not rum!

Claude Morris

THE GRAVE SITUATION

When I staggered away from my favourite pub,
The night was dark and still,
And I thought I'd take a short-cut home
That led over Cemetery Hill.
Now I'm not a hero, as everyone knows,
And I have no reckless trends,
But ghosts and the like leave me cold, as it were,
And spirits and I are old friends.

I wobbled along through the cemetery gates,
Begging my legs to behave,
And everything went pretty well, so I thought,
Till I fell down a newly dug grave.
For a moment I thought I had landed in hell,
And ended my earthly career.
I sniffed like a hound for the sulphurous fumes,
Expecting Old Nick to appear.

But reason returned and I staggered erect,
My prison so dark, to survey,
And tested my bones for a fracture or two,
But everything functioned okay.
I made a feeble attempt to get out,
But it needed no more than a glance
To convince me, in my condition,
I hadn't the ghost of a chance.

I reckoned I'd have a lay-off for a while,
And when I woke sober and fit

I'd surely come up with a good idea
That would get me out of the pit.
Just then I could hear fast oncoming steps
That seemed too good to be true,
But ere I could 'Coo-ee' or offer advice,
In the grave there were suddenly two!

By chance he fell in the grave's other end,
With no-one to cushion his fall,
But he rose like a shot with a strangled yelp
And attempted to scale up the wall.
This chap was at pains to be up and away
As the capers he cut plainly told.
He jumped and scrambled and jumped again,
But his fingers and toes wouldn't hold.

I hadn't yet spoken – I'd hardly a chance,
The way he cavorted about,
And I had to admire the way that he fought
To sever all ties and get out.
Of course, he believed there was nobody near;
He thought he was there all alone.
And I got the idea it had entered his head
That the grave was becoming his own.

I felt rather sad for the poor little guy
Now acting a little distraught,
And I thought he'd relax if I gave him the drum
That he wasn't alone, as he thought.
So I walked up behind him and tapped on his back
As he poised for another wild bid:
'You can't make it, mate,' I breathed in his ear –
But by the Lord Harry, he did!

THE RUN-UP

The boss was up before the sun,
Eager to have the muster begun,
But Charlie the backboy never could share
The Old Man's taste for the pre-dawn air,
And had to be wakened day by day
By the Riot Act roared in the Old Man's way.

'When I was young,' he once declared,
'At five o'clock I was up and prepared,
And I'd run two miles, and just for fun,
Jump a five-foot gate at the end of the run.'

Lazy Charlie got up from his seat,
Quite unimpressed by this splendid feat.
'Five foot?' he said with a scornful look,
'An' so you should – look at the run you took!'

TROUBLE BREWING

He came walking through the forest in the summer's glaring sun;
In his left hand was a bottle, in the other was a gun.
His beard was wild and bushy and his hair was shaggy, too,
And his old straw hat was full of holes where tufts of hair came
    through.

I stood and waited for him as he came with steady stride,
And I studied his appearance till he halted by my side.
He wasn't old, nor was he young, but somewhere in between,
And his heavy eyebrows almost hid his eyes of greyish green.

Then he handed me the bottle. 'You must have a drink,' he said,
And I heard him cock the rifle he presented at my head.
'Yes, take a swig of my home brew, and you will be the first
To have the chance of trying out my recipe for thirst.'

The rifle never wavered, and it pointed straight at me,
And that close-up gaping barrel was a nasty thing to see.
I lifted up the bottle with a very shaky hand
And a silent prayer to heaven as I followed his command.

I swallowed twice, and God Above! That brew had come from hell!
I know my head exploded and it drowned my dying yell.
I fell upon the dusty ground and grovelled there in pain,
Vowing he could shoot me but I wouldn't drink again.

When the pain and shock receded and I staggered to my feet,
'It was awful! It was awful!' I could hear my voice repeat.
Then I heard the brewer speaking and he said, 'Yes. I agree!
Now give me back my bottle, and you hold the gun on me!'

A RUM COMPLAINT

The old fellow held out his hands that shook
Like the leaves of a wind-blown tree,
And begged the doctor for relief
From his ghastly malady.

The doctor gave him a thorough check,
With sure and competent touch.
'There's nothing much wrong with you,' he said,
'Except that you drink too much.'

'That's all very well,' the old fellow said,
'You can blame the grog if you will,
But it's not what I drink that's getting' me down –
It's the bloody amount that I spill.'

Jessie Elizabeth Morrow
THE GHAN'S LAST RUN

The great Ghan has moved out; 'twas her last walkabout
Though the depths of primordial lands,
But old ghosts congregate, whilst new eras await –
Salute the past with thin spectral hands.
Tho' they're not of one clan they've farewelled the old Ghan,
Those explorers and settlers and blacks,
For their spirits still dwell in that land dry as hell,
Tho' the desert has covered their tracks.

They still sing their lament thru the wide continent
Where the Ghan once rode down the line,
Where she rocked o'er a bridge or a dark bushy ridge,
Where the last trippers toasted in wine.
As the ghost towns slipped past their bright lights went fast –
Ewaniga, Rodinga, Deepwell
Were soon left in the dark – there were none to embark
And no more will the old clanging bell
Call the trav'lers aboard while the steam puffed and soared
And young lovers embraced farewell.

Now the wind sighs and wails where the Ghan rode the rails
From the Alice to its rail-link in Marree.
And where wheels sang a dirge new paths will emerge
To that far away port by the seas –
And swift transports are with us at last.
So let wine glasses clink to the Ghan and its link
With historical days of our past.

Let's all drink to those days now hid in time's haze,
To those battlers who settled and stayed,
To this land and its heirs and the great world upstairs
When the paths of our airways are laid.
To the lonely outposts where men ride with the ghosts
O'er the desert and dry gibber plains;
Where once caravans passed thru' heat wave and sand blast
With an Afghan still holding the reins.

Now those old times have gone to the Ghans, rumbled on
Like the camel trains lost to 'Lang Syne'
And new wheels will soon come new wheels roll and hum
Down the rails of a new railway line.
But the same moon that shone, the same stars twinkle on,
And the sun's fury waxes and wanes,
And this land calls to men, calls its challenge then
From the paths of the last inland trains.

Colin Newsome

THE GREEN TREE SNAKE

The Green Tree Snake, they called him, his trouser legs were green,
They were cut in stockman fashion out of English gaberdine.
His legs were double jointed at the ankle, hip and knee,
He could wind them round each other just like snakes in ecstasy,
Or wrap them round a brumby while it bucked across the flat
Or bolted for the timber while he flogged it with his hat.

When the Goondiwindi outlaw threw the champions of the west
From Gore to Cunnamulla top riders gave him best.
While he played his concertina on the banks of Reptile Bend,
The Tree Snake read the challenge in a message from a friend.
In puffs of smoke 'twas written on the pages of the sky
By the tribes at Boggabilla to their friends at Mungindi.

The folk of Goondiwindi and Talwood and Toobeah,
When they heard about the Tree Snake, rode in from far and near.
They left the hut and homestead, by river and lagoon,
And billabong and bore drain, for the yards at Callandoon.
And there they boiled their quart-pots and yarned and sat around,
And waited for the Tree Snake while the outlaw pawed the ground.

They mostly backed the outlaw, but the seeds of doubt were sown
When old Red Jack from Texas said 'The Tree Snake can't be thrown.
A man who's double-jointed at the ankle, knee and hip
Must have a big advantage in balance, strength and grip.'
And the young men told the ladies, in the nonsense of the young,
The Tree Snake shed his winter skin and had a forky tongue.

Then, after joke and rumour, gaudy tale and false alarm,
The Tree Snake made his entrance with his saddle on his arm.
He saddled up the outlaw while Red Jack held the reins,
The best man at a horse's head that ever rode the plains.
And the ringers' eyes were bulging, and the ladies held their breath
As the Tree Snake caught a stirrup on the outlaw Sudden Death.

He vaulted to the saddle and he gave a bushman's yell,
And Sudden Death was bucking like a fiend out of hell.
The people cheered and cooee-ed as they saw the Tree Snake ride
Till the outlaw charged the stockyard fence and took it in his stride;
He bolted for the timber, and the girth and crupper broke
As he tried to smash the Tree Snake against a leaning oak.

Then a dust cloud rose behind them and we saw them through
    the blur
With the Tree Snake hanging grimly like a big Noogoora burr.
Perhaps 'twas an illusion of the dust along the trail –
Was the Tree Snake riding back to front and steering by the tail?
We found the broken saddle in the wreckage of their wake,
But we couldn't find the outlaw, and we couldn't find the Snake.

So we reached the grim conclusion that the Tree Snake met his end
When Sudden Death had thrown him in the flooded reptile bend,
And had joined the river brumbies where the channels twist and break,
And the McIntyre River goes winding like a snake.
But they tell another story in the campfire's drifting smoke
And perhaps it is authentic, though it started as a joke.

How the Tree Snake gripped so tightly that he stopped the outlaw's
    breath,

Then he slimed him well all over, and he swallowed Sudden Death.
Then he curled up for the winter in the hollow of a gum
With a side or two of bacon and a gallon jar of rum.
And when the frosts have vanished, then the Tree Snake will appear,
With his scales all bright and shiny and a grin from ear to ear.

FRIENDS AT BALLANDEAN

I, northward on the Roma line,
The golden fleece to shear,
Must leave the land of fruit and vine
So early in the year.
But southward to the Granite Belt,
Where toiled I rows between,
I wave a cheerio, heartfelt,
To friends at Ballandean.

Now I, mid cloying yoke and sweat
Of western shearing shed,
Dream of the folk I'll not forget
Where fruit is ripening red.
Where new year came and old year went,
With joyous times between,
And happy Christmas Day well spent
With friends at Ballandean.

From the stage beside my chute
I see the wool trucks load,
And think of those that cart the fruit
Along the Eukey road.
I wish they would transport me back
To vineyard orchard scene,
And once again I'd take the track
To friendly Ballandean.

I'd sing among the moonlit vines
To strumming of guitars,
And taste home-made Italian wines
Beneath the granite stars.

I'd share my love at twenty-two
With she of seventeen,
The lovely vineyard girl I knew
At good old Ballandean.

Today I feel the loneliness
Of those destined to roam,
And miss the ones who cared to bless
Me with a second home.
I turn to shear the golden fleece,
Where language is obscene,
And thank the times that gave me peace
At friendly Ballandean.

War will change the ways of men
And scatter best of friends,
And all the wiles of word and pen
Will never make amends.
Changes came to them and me
While oceans roared between,
And never more was I to see
My friends at Ballandean.

Note: In desperation, before the Second World War, many swagmen, hobos, itinerant workers and unemployed made Mecca of the Granite Belt for Christmas and New Year, coinciding with the lull in the shearing industry and completion of the wheat harvest.

THE SHAPELESS BLOB

Bill came back from the town with stores
And a man for the timber mill
That sprawled on the banks on Dingo 'Crick'
In the shade of Sugar Loaf Hill.
'The new hand gave no name,' said Bill,
The funniest man on the job.
'In a pinch he'd pass for a chimpanzee,
But he looks like a shapeless blob.'

So we called the new hand 'Shapeless Blob',
We felt contempt for him;
He was scared to ride on the flying fox,
Or chop from a lofty limb.
When payday came with its jostling fun,
We noticed the boss of the job
Gave him his pay in the form of a cheque
Drawn out to the 'Shapeless Blob'.

Shapeless Blob was the butt of our jokes;
Nobody called him 'mate',
And whether he sprang from monkey or man
Was the subject of debate.
We laughed and cheered when the sour old cook
Looked up from the baking dish
To remark he considered the Shapeless Blob
Was more like a blanky fish.

Two brown-limbed boys running wild in camp,
Suspended a dray wheel rim
To sixty feet of lawyer vine,
Which hung from a bluegum limb.

As Shapeless came from the cookhouse door
They called, 'Come and have a swing',
But he turned and tried to sneak away
Like a strange unwanted thing.

We chased him, seized him, bundled him on
And sent him up with a push,
While our shouts and laughter rent the hills
And echoed round the bush.

Up he went with a terrified moan,
A strangled cry and a sob,
While the whole camp stood in a circle to laugh
And jeer at the Shapeless Blob.

He jumped in fear from the crazy swing
And fell with a cry of pain,
Half rose and reeled as the rim returned
And knocked him down again.
Half-crippled, he crept and crawled away
To the shelter of his tent,
While we congratulated ourselves
On a day of rest well spent.

The rains came then with a steady flow
As though they never would stop,
And we turned our ears to their rhythmic beat
For days on the canvas top,
Till a man rode down from the mountain trail
So spent he could hardly tell
Of the flood coming down the left-hand fork
Like a tidal wave from hell.

Then the cry that emptied every tent:
'For Christ's sake men, come quick!
The boys are cut off on a rocky pint
Surrounded by Dingo Crick!'
A group of men unnerved to hear
The sound of a womanised sob
And a pitiful thing at the water's edge
That looked like a shapeless blob.

Shapeless Blob with a coil of rope
Attached to a flying fox
And Dingo Crick that roared and threshed
And snarled amongst the rocks.
Dingo Crick that flung its foam
Like froth from a stallion's bit
Raved and threshed like an angry giant
In an epileptic fit.

The fearless plunge in the current wild,
The struggle, the hero swim
As we stamped around on the slippery ground
And swam each stroke with him.
Tearing of hair and despair,
Suspense, excitement, hope,
Then the boys assisted him up the bank
And relieved him of the rope.

They tied it round an angular rock
While we made our end fast.
Then we sent up a mighty cheer
To know they were safe at last.
The boys came first, hand over hand,
Like a pair of jungle scamps;

They had learned to use a flying fox
Growing up in timber camps.

Shapeless came a short way then stopped.
We realised his plight:
He was scared of nothing else on earth
But terrified of height.
We noticed the sound we must have heard
But heeded not before,
As the wave crashed round the left-hand fork,
Lashing the bank with a roar.

It embraced a wave from the right-hand fork,
And paused as though to confer,
Then tossed a forest giant aloft
As a bull would toss a cur.
The waters embraced, linked arms, and charged
Abreast in a wild advance;
They carried the tree on the foremost wave
Butt first, like a mighty lance.

How the wall of waters drove the tree
To cut the rope like a knife,
And clutch the man to her savage breast
Will haunt our dreams for life.
The corpse we found in the fork of a tree,
Washed up on a rocky knob,
Looked more like the corpse of a noble man
And less like a shapeless blob.

The police came out and took the prints
Of the dead man's fingertips,
But couldn't reveal the secret locked

In the ever-silenced lips.
We wished to bury our heads in shame
And cleave our souls from sin;
None of us knew the dead man's name
Or a clue to his next of kin.

We offered prayerful apologies
As we paid our last respects,
And wept for the child whose photograph
We found in his few effects.
We advertised all over the place,
Describing our mate who died,
Till at last the Police wrote down the words
'Dead unidentified'.

His story spread to the countries' ends
And the earth's extremities,
And a hero known as 'Shapeless Blob'
Made headlines overseas.
Now a guest house stands on the old mill site
To feast on the tourist trade,
Which flows to the town of Shapeless Blob
In the socialites' crusade.

Actors, artists, photographers,
And writers of verse and books
Have gazed on the waters of Dingo Crick
With wistful, dreamy looks;
And a monument stands by a blue-gum tree,
Where the wind comes down with a sob
To blow the dust from the words we carved:
'Here lies the Shapeless Blob!'

FLOWER OF LOVE

All day long I had pruned and picked
Where the fairest flowers grew.
How sweet the aroma and bright the buds,
Only I and the wild bees knew.
I found the loveliest flower of all
With a beauty vivid and deep
When the sun's last rays and the busiest bee
Had gone with the birds to sleep.

I gently sought for the beautiful buds
That bloomed on bosom and lip,
For the fairest rose has the sharpest thorn
For the unskilled fingertip.
The moon above cast a softer glow
On petals of pink and cream
Than ever had been man's pleasure to know
Or dream in his wildest dream.

Some men are destined to crush fair flowers
At the height of their loveliness,
And some are born to stand and admire
And others are quick to caress.
Whenever a man finds the flower of love
He, whom the love gods chose,
Will move both earth and heaven above
To wear his beautiful rose.

Clover F. Nolan

STORM BIRD

Have you heard a storm bird shrieking in the channels,
When the river bed is cracked and powder dry,
And the coolibah trees sadly droop, and wither,
As the sheep and cattle round them quietly die?

Have you heard a storm bird calling from the river,
Its rasping cry, or from the stockyard gate,
And watched the rain clouds roll, and slowly gather,
And prayed they'd burst before it was too late?

Oh, a storm bird's grating song is stirring music
As it screams and hurtles by on rapid wings;
For this bird is the bringer of wet seasons,
An omen, to which every bushman clings.

Martin O'Brien

THE WIND AND THE RAIN

The wind and the rain and the worst of the weather
Bring memories of fear and delight to the child …
The biggest of floods and the driest of summers,
The lightning and thunder in storms that run wild.

A youth now with dreams he can claim his own future,
The seasons now past are like treasures inside;
The wind and the rain and the worst of the weather
The young man with strength and his dreams has defied.

The passing of seasons, one lost in another,
The life of a farmer the years have now slowed;
But still with delight in each raindrop and rainbow
He walks with a limp where he ran with the load.

Some time now to sit and to gaze in the distance,
The worst of the weather he knows is now gone;
Content in the knowledge life reaches fulfilment …
His season has come and he has to move on.

The wind and the rain and the worst of the weather
Will pass o'er the grave where his body now lies;
He sleeps the long sleep of the just and the weary
Till last trumpets sound and the worthy arise.

CATHERINE O'NEILL — THE BULLOCKY'S WIFE

Green walls of the forest stand tall round the clearing ...
A little creek sings where I live with my man;
Some grass for his bullocks ... our house with its garden ...
When I'm not alone, then it's happy I am.

The cow is in milk ... there are chooks by the dozen ...
Our cupboards are full ... *Praise the Lord!* says my man;
Sometimes I do think it's the Garden of Eden,
And yet there are times when it's lonely I am.

Through laughter of children at play in our garden
Come sounds of an axe that is swung by my man;
The forest cries out with its wild birds in chorus ...
For these, all God's blessings, so thankful I am.

I met him and loved him – that wild Irish convict! –
A convict myself when I married that man;
Ah, they were good times when each day I held him ...
But now there are times when it's lonely I am.

Some convicts I saw were like slaves in a chain gang,
But that was not ever the fate of my man;
Assigned as a servant he was when I came for
My fourteen-year term ... but it's free now am I!

We came to the rivers in search of his fortune ...
A dreamer he is ... that's the boy in my man! ...
And times when he's lost in the rum or his dreaming
I wait in the forest ... and lonely I am.

Our kinsfolk back home ... if they only could see us ...
A good women now ... a respectable man! ...
A place of our own, with no landlord to bow to ...
And me? ... it's a bullocky's wife that I am!

We're *Mr and Mrs O'Neill* to the world now ...
Ah sure, that's a change from the past, says my man;
But nights when I think of the faces of childhood ...
Unless he is near, then it's lonely I am.

Our family is only us two and the children,
The others are *oceans away* says my man;
Now seldom he speaks of the troubles of Ireland,
And seldom I dream that it's back there I am.

Though life has its joys, it also has sorrow,
And mine? ... they are wrapped in that very same man;
A life that is changed by each whim of the weather
That takes him away ... then it's anxious I am.

He's here ... but his thoughts are away with the cedar ...
There's little time left now to spend with my man;
Ah, Catherine, he says, *I will love you forever!* ...
He loves ... yet he leaves ... then it's lonely I am.

He sings all the while he is yoking his bullocks ...
Ah, smile now! he says ... Lord, the hide of that man! ...
His bullock whip rings out *goodbye* in the distance ...
But how can I smile in the state that I am?

On some forest track they are traipsing along now ...
Out looking for cedar, both bullock and man ...

A call of the whipbird comes loud from the forest
As if to remind me how lonely I am.

Alone with the children and miles from the neighbours,
A women has fears quite unknown to a man;
Myself, I have buried three babes with his shovel ...
Ah, cheer up! he says ... yet it's worried I am.

A few days, he says ... *that is all I'll be gone, love* ...
He's hopeless with time when he's working, that man! ...
It's nigh on a week since the morning he left us ...
As each day goes by the more lonely I am.

He built this, our home, by the sweat of his labour ...
In truth there are times he's a wonderful man;
Our front door adzed from a slab of fine timber ...
When neighbours come calling, it's proud that I am.

The floor may be dirt, but it's warm in the winter,
And all of our furniture's made by my man;
With flour-bag curtains to dance in the breezes ...
For so much I'm thankful ... yet lonely I am.

Our kettle keeps boiling all day for his coming ...
A lamp by the window to welcome my man;
Too late now ... my hopes must all wait till tomorrow ...
Worn out by the worry of waiting I am.

Our children, so noisy, help fill all my daytimes,
But during those long nights I do miss my man;
A mopoke is calling so clear through the darkness ...
The children, now sleeping ... and lonely I am.

Each morning in hope I look out to the forest
Whose secret alone is the fate of my man;
An answer I seek, not its wild-birds' loud chorus ...
Defiant, it taunts me, and angry I am.

I busy myself with the house and its garden,
A way to forget that I'm missing my man;
A lone dingo howls somewhere near in the forest ...
The children fall silent ... and lonely I am.

Am I just a fool to await his returning?
The cause and relief of my torture, that man!
Ah, sound of his bullock whip rings through the forest ...
No loneliness now ... it's just happy I am!

OLD JIM'S WETTEST YEAR

There may be cockies in the west who talk of dust and drought,
And how long since they saw some rain, or even clouds about;
But here at home amoung the hills and gullies of the coast,
Where there has never been a drought, it's rain we fear the most.

No, not the gentle falling rain that keeps the hillsides green,
But when it rains and just won't stop for months is what I mean.
'Oh, what a year!' Old Jim would say each time we spoke of rain.
'I hope we never see a year as wet as that again.'

'It was the wettest year,' he'd say, 'since Noah built the ark …
It rained nonstop throughout each day, then fell down after dark.
It rained for forty days and nights and then for forty more,
Then rained another forty days – and then began to pour!

'Our dairy cows that used to walk the muddy dairy track
All had to swim to reach the yards – and then they'd all swim back.
The groundsel and the crofton weed grew lank and green and high,
Then caught footrot from all the wet and soon began to die.

'The rising damp had reached such heights that never had been
    seen …
Mildew and mould began to grow where it had never been.
The only time that we could find a place the dry would stay,
Was right inside the old wood stove we kept alight all day.

'It got too wet for all the frogs – they sought a drier place;
The ducks now tried to find some dry, but never found a trace.
Then yabbies left their waterholes through grass now long and rank;
They struggled up the slippery slopes to find a higher bank.

'Ah, yes,' said Jim, 'I've seen some years we'd seldom see the sun,
And times the wet would barely stop before the next begun.
And if you folk were to live as long as I have done,
You may just chance to see a year just like that wettest one.
And I will not forget,' Jim said, 'my memory is still clear,
It rained nonstop with not one break for thirteen months that year!'

Jim O'Connor

THE RESCUE

Floodwaters flowed down on a little bush town
And the local lads looked to their boats;
Then word got about, there wasn't a doubt
That the flood has entrapped the town goats.
Two lads jumped aboard and a small engine roared,
The skip took the tiller with pride,
So, as his one-man crew would have plenty to do,
I thought I'd go along for a ride.

She purred like a dream as we headed upstream
And the skip, in the stern, wore a smile,
Then as we angled east the current increased,
And that wiped the grin off his dial.
The skip's visage looked bleak as we hit Emu Creek,
Our progress upstream was quite slow,
And when we caught sight of the goats packed up tight
We still had some distance to go.

They stood belly deep on a fence, in a heap,
With the nearest dry land half a mile.
Things looked kind of grim for those swine wouldn't swim,
And that kind of dampened our style.
Now the captain chipped in with an unconcerned grin
As he caught one old girl by the snout.
He said, 'They won't swim, but things aren't so grim.
We'll just have to ferry them out.'

Now that was a chore I'd not tackled before
And I wondered just how it would go,

But with sixty or more to be ferried ashore
I knew progress would be rather slow.
We had nothing to tie 'em but skip said, 'We'll try them,
We'll sit them all up and in rows,
If they can't move about they shouldn't fall out
And it's not far across, heaven knows.'

We packed them in tight and they looked quite alright,
One pull and that small motor roared.
With a smile and a cough the skipper took off,
With a wave he called out, 'All aboard!'
With a knowledge uncanny, one big-titted nanny
Stood up and looked over the side,
The skip swore and fought her as the boat took in water
And quickly went into a glide.

As the boat settled lower her speed became slower
And quickly she got out the hand,
Then each mongrel goat deserted the boat
And struck out on its own for the land.
Now the skipper and boat were no longer afloat
And I heard the lone crewman then quip,
'It seems quite uncanny, we saved every nanny,
But the captain's gone down with the ship.'

This story's retold as they sit drinking 'gold'
In the bar of the local at night,
But this version is true, as I've told it to you,
I was there so I know that it's right.
It's hard to refloat a sunken steel boat
In floodwaters up to your lip,
But we did it that day when the goats swam away
And the captain went down with his ship.

THE WET

From the Bay of Bengal, by the way of Sumatra,
Borne on the monsoons, so active again,
Then crossing the coastline and bearing on Darwin,
Comes the first teeming downpour of monsoonal rain.
Then down from the Top End to flood the dry inland,
And turn a dry dust bowl to bottomless mud,
Each gutter and gully, each creek and each river,
Contributes its quota to the inland in flood.

Then crossing the border, it pours into Queensland,
A great rain depression, the width of the state,
Then filling and flooding, it pours forth its fury,
'Ere it loses its force and begins to abate.
The Georgina is full, she's running a banker,
The Barcoo in flood is a great sight to see.
In Blackall they're using rowboats in the main street;
On the edge of the town there's a cow up a tree.

At Longreach the Thomson is out on the flood plain,
There's brown water lapping at three sides of town.
Drowned sheep, bobbing slowly, drift by on the current;
They'll tally their losses when the water goes down.
At Stonehenge and Jundah she's high and still rising,
A few miles beyond, she'll meet the Barcoo,
From there on they call her the mighty old Cooper,
At Windorah they'll toast her in a long neck or two.

Then thirty miles wide, she'll continue her journey,
A great inland sea, what a sight to behold.
Brown water, red sandhills and miles of green lignum –
To those down the bottom she's plain liquid gold.
Onwards she creeps, still spreading and filling
The great waterholes and lakes everywhere,
The drinkers will see her creep past tiny Birdsville,
Six months from the Top End she'll enter Lake Eyre.

'Old-Timer'

BABBLER'S SONG

Mixin' flamin' brownie, settin' of me dough,
Cookin' stoo an' roastin' lamb an' jumpin' to an' fro,
Up at flamin' sparrer' chirp, stokin' up me fire;
The bloke who reckons life is sweet's a rotten ruddy liar.

Gotta keep me mouth shut while the greasies skite,
Gotta keep the tucker up t' stay their appetite.
Some don't like me pumpkin, some won't eat me rice –
Flamin' ringer had the cheek t' order cheese an' spice!

Gotter toil on wet days, though the others spell;
Y'orter see 'em hangin' round, waitin' for me bell.
Sundee flamin' mornin', think they'd go away –
Strike me fat, they're hungrier than any other day.

Listen to 'em skitin' how they shear so neat,
Struth, what I could tell y' of the sheep they eat!
Hungry lot of blankers, 'nough t' make y' weep –
Bet their flamin' grinders are chewin' in their sleep.

Penners-up an' pressers – got the flamin' blight,
Gallopin' consumption, day an' flamin' night.
I'm weary an' I'm anguished, I wanter stop an' rest –
Some greasy wants a pint o' tea t' pour beneath his vest.

Heaps o' things I could ha' bin – could ha' went t' sea,
Might ha' bin an actor or a hotel licensee,
If only I'd ha' knew before, what measures I'd ha' took
T' make dead sure I never was a flamin' shearers' cook!

GOING HOME

My port is packed and labelled, I've bought my brief to go
To Walgett on the rattler, then the coach to Widgeego,
Which is out beyond Culgoa, on the road to Tilboroo,
And there I'll pick up Maynard and his dusty droving crew.
I feel a sort of tightness, like a pleasant kind of pain,
And my feet are sort of aching for the stirrup bars again.
My eyes are tired of glaring lights, they're yearning for the sun,
And I've got a job with drovers on a western Queensland run.

I can hear the engine panting like a prisoner in pain;
By morning she'll be racing out across the blacksoil plain.
I've been in town since Christmas, doing odd jobs here and there,
Spending much, and much too freely, which don't get you anywhere.
The picture-shows have tired me, I'm sick of crowds at fights,
And though the streets are full of life they're lonely in the nights.
There'll be fires on the stock route when the day-long stretch is done,
And I'll do my trick of night work on a western Queensland run.

I wonder how the stock are where the muster will begin;
I always like an easy mob to break my muscles in.
I must, of course, be pretty soft from living in this place,
But I bet I'll foot it with 'em when the heelers set the pace.
I can hear the yearlings bawling as we start 'em on the road,
And the stockwhip cracks are ringing, though they'll scarcely need a
    goad.
I'll bet my horses know me, both the chestnut and the dun,
And be glad to take me droving on a western Queensland run.

It's grand on sunny mornings, when the young stock take the lead,
When a lithe young sunburned stockman rides in front to hold the
    speed.

On the wing you'll find me singing, sitting easy in my seat,
While we keep them moving lively in the rising morning heat,
We'll spell 'em in the noonday and the cook will have the tea,
Piping hot and thick with sugar, in a camp beneath a tree.
I'll bet – good Lord, the whistle, and my journey has begun …
I'm off to join the drovers on a western Queensland run.

Glenny Palmer
THE BRIDE OF ST CLAIRE

Will you ride with me to the rails tonight
To the yards at old St Claire;
Will you stride with me in the pale moonlight
And stroke my auburn hair;
Lay aside the whips for my ruby lips
(I'll give you a blossom fair),
One ride, my love, for a lifetime's thought,
Before you leave St Claire?

Will you lie with me by the wattle tree
In the clover at St Claire;
Will you tie for me with its humble blooms
A garland for my hair;
Will you keep the tryst if I ever whisper
Naught of the sweet affair,
Transgression's kiss upon Virtue's lips
Before you leave St Claire?

Do you long for me, now the wanderlust
Sings far from old St Claire;
Do your songs for me linger mournfully
On the wandr'ing western air;
Does a lover's pain tempt the horse's rein
To the call of the weeping prayer,
That I, with child, whispered every day
In the chapel at St Claire?

For the youthful spell I remember well
Was woven at St Claire,
On a moonswept night, in the clovered site
The virgin love laid bare;
And a heart was lost, while a heart was gained,
Our son, with a faint despair,
Asks why he has not a father here
To love, at old St Claire.

So I taught him trust, and I taught him true
How to watch from old St Claire;
And he listens too, as I do for you
On the distant evening air;
Though I'm weary now, for I'm wan with age,
Confined to the rocking chair,
In my harrowed heart, I will ever be
Your fair bride of St Claire.

GOOD LOOKER

I have a place for everything
And all is in its place,
But when my hubby's searching
Things just vanish without trace.

He opens up the cupboard door
And says, 'It's not in here.'
I think he's waiting for the thing
To wave to him and cheer.

'It must be in there somewhere,
You just used it yesterday.'
'Nope,' he says with arms still folded …
'Not in here, no way.'

By now I'm getting crabby
'Cause I've got my job to do,
But for the sake of peace
I take up searching for it too.

I reach inside the cupboard
And I shift a tin or two.
Do you believe in miracles?
The thing comes into view.

And does he hug and kiss me
'Cause the flamin' thing is found?
Not on your life, that's when
He turns the situation round.

He accuses me of hiding it:
'You shouldn't shove it here.'
'I haven't shoved it anywhere –
At least not yet, my dear.'

So now I'm an inventor
And I'm working on a plan
To make a see-through cupboard
That will liberate my man.

The shelves are all transparent,
Things are set to wave and cheer
Automatically, when
Someone says, 'It's not in here.'

R. C. Pearce

THE FLIGHT OF THE SKY QUEEN

The great gale raged o'er hill and street,
Palms bowed to the wild wind's wrath;
On the echoing beach the great waves beat
And all day long on a blinding sheet
Fell the rains of the tropic North.

Brolga Station called for a doctor there,
For a sick child wracked with pain:
'The rivers are flooded everywhere,
Our only hope is from the air,
You can land on the Brolga Plain.'

The pilot is ready and willing to try,
Ready and willing the doctor too.
One glance they give to the rain-filled sky,
No words they waste in the curt reply:
'The Sky Queen's going through.'

With head to the racing clouds and fogs,
She revs with joyous roar,
Then on the makeshift runway nearly bogs,
And narrowly missing two stray dogs
She slowly begins to soar.

And now aloft she fights for height
In the teeth of the raging gale.
The great clouds race by left and right,
The rain clouds strike with terrific might
And they rock her head to tail.

The altimeter moves by slow degrees
Till it shows 'two thousand, dead',
Then all of a sudden the pilot sees
Through the clouds the ghostly loom of trees,
It's the high Coast Range ahead.

With rising spurs to left and right,
Sharp banked is the little plane;
A few miles she must retrace her flight,
But foot by foot she is winning height
As she comes at the range again.

She is over with a few score feet to spare,
Below great jungles lie,
Then granite mountains, gaunt and bare,
Like crouching lions with surly stare
That watch the plane go by.

And now beneath grey waters show
A slender winding thread.
The pilot speaks: 'Every mile I know,
It's the Wentworth River that runs below
And Mount Margaret's just ahead.'

But the blinding clouds close in again
To shorten the pilot's view,
While the propeller bites in the driving rain,
Still the engine hums the same refrain:
'The Sky Queen's going through.'

At the homestead now she circles round,
Yet circles twice again,
Till certain the safest spot is found,

Head to the wind she comes to ground
And lands safe on Brolga Plain.

With a patient aboard she is soon away,
Once more on the skyward track,
And coast towns hear near close of day,
Amid the driving clouds of grey,
The Sky Queen's coming back.

OF OTHER YEARS

Do they still, the old hands yarning, talk of tin on 'Black Cow' yet?
Do they still make plans for working at the 'Perry' through the wet?
Are there still the same old 'nitwits' in some poor creek, slaving hard,
Who can tell of wondrous gullies, going two 'bags' to the yard?

Do you ever ride down Stony, where the sprightly whipbirds call?
Ever stay and gaze in wonder at that mighty waterfall?
Are you ever East of Clean Skin mid the flood gums, tall and white?
Near the lorne and lonely jungle where the Scrub Hens call by night?

Do cassowaries down 'Raspberry' in the scrubs play hide and seek?
Is the view now just as lovely from the pocket of Mack's Creek?
With the sweeping ranges northward rising wild and bold and free,
Do the dawns break just as golden out to eastward, cross the sea?

Do fireflies on 'Bluewater' still at night flash living gold?
Is the platypus just as shy there, and the 'Brandy' just as bold?
Does the stinging tree still catch you, is the curse still cunjevoi
Do they still find sleepy adders around the Fox and Yalleroi?

Are the black bream still down Michael where the current swirls and
        swills?
Do the whiptails still go hopping over the slate and granite hills?
And the plump slate-coloured pigeons, do they still fly south in flocks?
Are there camps on Silent Gully, shooters still on Pigeon Box?

Yet these perhaps are idle questions for there's likely little change
In the lives of all the wild things or the beauties of the range,
And it seems the years fly backward as again in dreams I see
The storm-girt crest of Grahame and the fog clouds round Mount Lee.

In those distant days we battled, times seemed mostly lean and tough,
But we learned to face things gamely, taking smooth things with the
    rough.
There were days of joy and sorrow, nights of laughter tinged with tears,
And the old bush music playing, always playing down the years.

LONELINESS

She comes to us with pallid face,
With hollow haunting eyes,
From the depth of skylined space
To blacken all the skys.
She comes from sorrow's rivers far,
To every lone address –
We know her by each falling star,
The Queen of Loneliness.

She is the Queen and her grey steed
Will never need a rest;
From bit and harness never freed
It goes from breast to breast.
With swinging stride it carries her
Across the city's rush,
She speeds it on with ship and spur,
Where the mountain torrents gush.

The miner in the ranges camped,
The bushman in the west,
They both must find their feelings damped
When Loneliness is guest.
On the single bride her hand is dealt,
On the deceived one her caress,
They both have shivered and have felt
The breath of Loneliness.

She rides where roads of life are brown,
She rides in flooding rains;
Every man is going down
Has touched her bridle reins.

The swagman gathering to his load,
The dead leaves of the past,
Has seen the print upon the road,
Her luckless shoe has cast.

At home alike on sea or shore,
Although a friend to none,
A thought will bring her to the door
In dark or rain or sun.
When hands we love have ceased to shake,
Whenever friends grow less,
The rich and poor alike may take
The hand of Loneliness.

Neil Peters

THE BUSH RACES

Today is the day for the races
And excitement is rife in the air –
They'll be backing for winners and places.
There are horsefloats and trucks everywhere,
And the women are looking fantastic
With their dresses and hats and their smiles,
And their waists all pulled in with elastic
Will excite all the 'ringers' for miles.

The 'bookies' are all looking solemn
As they write up their price on the boards,
And they carefully work out each column
So the punters won't think they are frauds.
The owners and trainers conferring
Will know who will win and who'll lose.
(But the jockeys with judgment unerring,
Will be doing their best to confuse.)

The track really isn't a fast one,
And to stay up in front is a must,
For the jockey who's riding the last one
Can't see where he's going for dust.
And the 'weigh-in' is never a problem,
For the system they use doesn't fail –
If the winner is 'light', the head steward
Just stands with his foot on the scale.

The judge is hand-picked for his eyesight,
So the placings are seldom in doubt.

(Though sometimes if his lenses don't feel right,
When the race starts he just takes them out.)
And because of the 'caller's' delusion
(He can't tell a horse from a tree),
To avoid any further confusion
They restrict nominations to three.

When the time comes for giving the prizes,
It may not seem right, I suppose,
But in my very honest opinion
The publican wins by a nose.
For the speed of his hand was unequalled
As the problem of thirst he resolved.
And though often he's called by the stewards,
There's never a protest involved.

When the sun puts an end to the races
(As it settles away in the west),
The girls all start looking for places
To 'get changed (as they say) into their best.'
And liberal proportion of powder
Is applied to the body and cheek,
While the menfolk's ablutions are louder
As they wash off *their* dust in the creek.

Then with hair done and nice shiny faces,
They all head along to the hall.
If the girls have to suffer the races,
Then the men have to suffer the ball.
And the girls mostly dance with each other,
While their 'idols' pour beer down their throat,
And the pianist (the publican's mother)
Gets a cheer when she strikes the right note.

The male conversation's enlightening
As they change from the weather to flies;
And a newcomer finds it quite frightening
For he can't tell what's true and what's lies.
And the womenfolk wonder what good is
Their pleading looks sent from afar,
As they all sit around where the food is,
While the men congregate at the bar.

But at last comes the time for departing
(For the band has collapsed on the stage);
All the cars and the horsefloats are starting
To move off like a funeral cortege.
Though it isn't apparent on their faces,
I'm sure if you asked one and all:
The men had a ball at the races,
But they'd rather not race to the ball.

Morva Power

SONG OF THE SEASONS

There's a hint of spring in each early morn
   when the dawn winds gently sing,
When the world wakes up to wonder
   what the coming day will bring.
There's spring in the step of a lively colt
   when the saddle leathers creak
And you're mustering wild cattle
   along some scrubby creek.
It's the spring of life when we take the road
   on our journey just begun;
Let us dance to the tune the fiddler plays
   and dream of what's yet to come.

You can feel the touch of a summer's day
   every time the sun rides high,
So our working life will run its course
   as years fly swiftly by.
A mighty good horse is our Summertime,
   fully trained for every job,
Be it stop a beast that's breaking
   or simply drive the mob.
As we wend our way through the summer of life
   making plans for the years to come,
Let us swing in the march with head held high,
   in step with the beating drum.

The cool autumn comes in late afternoon
   as the sun dips to the west,

When the shadows slowly lengthen
and the world considers rest.
Our autumn's a smart little dapple grey
striding carefree through the trees,
While the falling leaves float past us
on the chilly evening breeze.
In our autumn years, as we're steadying down,
let's reflect on days just gone;
We can dance to a slower tempo now
and sing as we waltz along.

With the darkness comes faint winter's breath
when the night birds hoot and scream;
Now's the time for reminiscing
in the campfire's cosy gleam.
Poor winter's a weary and spent old horse
with a slow and steady gait,
Spending his last days in clover.
Our time's near done, old mate.
In our winter days, may we reap the rewards
for those years we gave our all;
Let us amble along with peace of mind
to go when the pipers call.

Carmel Randle

THE DARKEST HOUR

Another sultry summer's day has shuffled to the west
As I slip into a squatter's chair to snatch a moment's rest
On the open cast verandah, where the moon, just past its prime,
Silhouettes the gidyea by the creek and boundary line.

Just two of us, each lost in thought. A moon has come and gone.
No rain this time … a dry moon! Lord, what ARE we doing wrong?
How can two lonely women carve a little hereabouts
When all we get are dust storms, searing heat, and flamin' drought?

Myself – I shared a dream with John. This was his family's soil.
For many generations it had seen their loving toil.
We'd dream about the future as our boys grew into men,
And feel the circle of our lives turn over once again.

John taught them basic outback skills as soon as they could walk –
They knew of stock and native plants as first they learned to talk –
And in between their schooling, well, they learned to shoot and drive,
And mend a fence, and fix a pump. They'd need THAT to survive!

Then college years … how Jack just couldn't wait to come back home,
But Jim there found a new life very different from his own …
A 'guru' all-important … How I wish he'd keep in touch!
We hope he's happy, safe and well … but miss him, oh, so much!

Then Jack came home with Lorna as his lovely blushing bride –
Just the sort of friendly girl to take things in her stride.
Consoled me when the hand of death smote keenly at John's heart;
Here to give a focus lest our dreams should fall apart.

And she gave us Jan, and little John – they're such a bonny pair!
Now snuggled safely in their cots, they sleep without a care.
They prob'ly won't remember much about their daddy, Jack,
'Cause no amount of wish or prayer can bring my eldest back!

No cure for his cancer – there was nothing we could do –
And now his lovely Lorna is a lonely widow too.
So we sit in friendly silence as the moon climbs up the sky
And grapple with the reasons why our menfolk had to die.

We wonder where our Jim is … will he ever change his mind
And come again to share his life with those he left behind?
Why should we bother staying here in drought and dust and sand?
Deep in our hearts we know we feel this is our Tribal Land!

Sure, I miss the quickened heartbeat when my John returned each day,
His smile across the table, and the teasing things he'd say,
And the heartache weighs so heavy in the middle of the night
When I long to throw my arms around my love and hold him tight!

So I sit here, bathed in moonlight, and I ponder on the worth
Of striving for a lifetime to retain this piece of earth …
Would my forebears rise and haunt me if I ever should give in?
Would 'to quit and run away' be termed 'a grievous mortal sin'?

And I think of Jan and little John – perhaps they wouldn't care …
They'd find 'Home's Where the Heart Is!' true if those they loved were
    there.
And the years until they're old enough stretch grimly out ahead
As they lie there wrapped in silence in their comfy baby bed.

Don't treat my cogitations now with scorn or faint derision –
When the agent rings me back I must have made the right decision

'Cause he's pressing for an answer, and it's me who must decide …
Will the city or the country be the future for our tribe?

The moon has gone. Is that the dawn … that rosy eastern glow?
A sleepless night with worry fraught, but now at least I know.
I'll dial the agent's number – Help me, please, Lord guide my hand!
The answer's 'No! I cannot … will not … sell my children's land!'

Terry Regan
WINTER SUNSET

Winter sunset, close of day,
What a royal cloud display.
Purple, mauve, blood-red and blue,
Tinged with pink and orange hue.

Flashes of pure opal fire,
Silhouette of yonder spire.
Warm rays wage a losing fight
Against cold fingers of the night.

Valerie Reid

THE BANKS ARE MOVING IN

A neighbour telephoned today, distressed and overwrought:
'I thought I'd ring to let you know my farming land's been bought.'
'I didn't see a "For Sale" sign. Why are you leaving, Jim?'
'I've got no other option, mate – the banks have done me in.'

I heard a sob in ev'ry word; my heart near broke in two.
Jim's family had owned that land since eighteen ninety-two.
They'd battled flood and fire and drought and never given in;
That same proud pioneering will was born and bred in Jim.

I felt the fear crawl in my guts. I had a mortgage, too.
The payments o'er the past five years were far between and few.
Like Jim we, too, have never known another way of life;
We'd all been born to farm the land, and bred to cope with strife.

When flooding washed our crops away and drowned our breeding
    stock,
Jim had come, without demand, to help us save our flock.
And when the bushfires threatened Jim, we'd worked day and night,
And cried with him o'er blackened plains – a truly dreadful sight.

You can fight a fire, fight a flood, but drought's a different thing;
If it goes on year in, year out, disaster it will bring.
Your feed dies off, the water goes, your stock gets thin and weak;
You shoot the bawling cattle first and then the starving sheep.

I couldn't say a word to Jim; his news had struck me dumb.
I knew that if I tried to speak a flood of tears would come.

We'd known each other all our lives – like brothers we were now –
And he had telephoned to say that he was moving out.

I looked across the seared plains where hot mirages played;
I looked into the clear blue skies and, once again, I prayed,
'Oh, God, please send us some relief; we've been to hell and back.
We've paid our penance, Lord, it's true, and we're about to crack.'

We've had hard times and seen them through, my old mate, Jim, and I;
We've watched our paddocks turn to sand and seen our dams go dry.
But now the banks are closing in and selling farmers out,
I reckon that, compared to them, our kinder foe's the drought.

Ray Rose

WE'LL NEVER GO DROVING AGAIN

Maybe just an old packhorse but he's more than that,
  there's memories surround his old frame,
He still lifts his head and walks out of the mob,
  in the yard, when I call out his name,
He rubs his old head down the front of my shirt
  and I pull the burrs out of his mane,
And I know we're both sharing, the same line of thought,
  no we'll never go droving again,

And there, in the timber, he'd dodge every tree,
  and he'd never walk under low limbs,
No, he'd never roll in the bed of a creek,
  though the sand looked inviting to him.
The thousands of miles this old horse has been,
  the weeks and the months on the road,
The long and the short trips, they all were the same,
  he seemed to make light of the load.

I'd broke him to pack in the long ago now,
  when our lifestyles were easy and free,
And nothing would change but the seasons, it seems,
  now it's all just a fond memory,
And the smell of old leather, and cattle, and dust,
  and the big gidgea scrubs after rain,
Yes, this old horse is part of a life that is lost,
  for we'll never go droving again.

Now he feeds with his mates on the flats by the creek,
  their days on the road now are done,

No more the sweat lathers, the breastplate and girth,
 as they plodded on 'neath the hot sun,
And the packs that they've carried hang there in the shed,
 with hobbles and gear packed away,
Horse bells and halters, with old greenhide ropes,
 all remnants of old droving days.

Yes, he's just an old packhorse, the last of his breed,
 and his stories are fading with time,
Each year sees the number of horses like him
 grow smaller, in steady decline,
And the pads that we followed are now overgrown,
 as they wandered o'er mountain and plain,
And the fate of my old mates, guess I'll never know,
 for we'll never go droving again.

And the fate of my old mates, guess I'll never know,
 for we'll never go droving again.

GIDYEA AFTER RAIN

Let my stirrups graze the Mitchell with its late in summer seed,
Let the brown leaves of the Flinders brush the big mobs while they feed,
Let the smell of dust and woodsmoke, and the damper in the coals,
Let the sweat of horse and leather stay with me as I grow old.

Let the whirr of quail and plover fly before me as I pass
Through the lignum and the clover, nardoo, the Channel grass,
Hear the dawning chime of horse bells and the clink of hobble chain,
And let me smell and ne'er forget the gidyea after rain.

Let me ride across the country where the wedge-tail eagles fly,
See the rush of flooding channels, and the creek beds in the dry,
Let me always remember things I'll never see again,
The flower of gum and wattle, and the gidyea after rain.

Let me feel the easy rhythm of a stockhorse in his stride,
Feel him prop, and wheel, and shoulder, and toss his head with pride,
Let me feel the bond of mateship, let it linger and remain,
Like the moonlight glint on horns and hide, and the gidyea after rain.

Let my mind always remember, in my youth's wildest years,
And at times let me be saddened by a loss with grief and tears
When I face my final sundown, guide my hand on redhide rein
To my journey's end, on the river bend, and the gidyea after rain.

Let my stirrups graze the Mitchell with its late in summer seed,
Let the brown leaves of the Flinders brush the big mobs while they feed,
Let me always remember things I'll never see again,
And let me smell, and ne'er forget, the gidyea after rain.

THE LEGEND (OF ARANDA)

He sat there in the dust on the edge of the camp,
In the shade of a desert oak tree,
Though his clothes they were ragged and covered with dust,
He still bore a quiet dignity
His people walked past him, and young children played,
Their world was so far from his own,
For his old eyes weren't seein' these material things,
They were not from the land he had known.

His skin was the colour of the fire's charcoal,
You could guess at the suns it had seen,
And the wisdom embedded, behind yellowed eyes,
Was more than most mortals could glean
His face was the kind of which legends were made,
That no pen nor no words could describe,
And no-one could guess at the life he had led,
Nor the customs and ways of his tribe.

His old suitcoat worn over the torn khaki shirt,
Bore the brunt of the winter nights' chill,
Though the worn corduroys had seen better days,
Like his old hat, they serviced him well.
But he longed to discard all these civilised things.
And roam his old grounds, proud and free,
But he knew he could never, it was only a dream,
A long way from the reality.

And what of the tourist who scarce gave a glance,
And who read from their little guide book
Of the wonders that lay before them to see,
The souvenirs and the photos they took

In too big a hurry, their schedule to keep,
On a bus-guided itinerary,
So they lost their one chance to talk to this man,
A legend of lost history?

Oh, but how could he tell them, or hope to explain,
Of a world that they never had seen,
Of the legends surrounding his people and race
In a land where the dreamtime had been,
And the spirits that spoke from his old tribal grounds,
Now shrouded in lost mystery?
No, these things must remain locked far back in time,
They were not for a stranger to see;
No, these things must remain locked far back in time,
In the mists of dreamtime reveries.

Philip R. Rush

OLD JIM'S MOTORBIKE

On a farm away out yonder
Where few folk ever wander,
Old Jim had lived for sixty years or more,
He was lean and tough and wiry,
And was obstinate and fiery,
But a dinkum Aussie battler to the core!

He had beef and sheep a-plenty
And his son, a lad of twenty,
Said, 'A motorbike would help us with our stock.'
'No, son, you can't beat horses
On hills and watercourses,
Where there's precious little else but sand and rock.'

But in the weeks that followed,
Old Jim's opinion mellowed,
And maybe that was due to more than fate.
For his horse, one morning, propping,
Found Jim no way of stopping
And he landed on the barbed-wire paddock gate.

On being so upended,
Jim's body slowly mended,
But, still angry with the horse that threw him down,
He took his car and trailer
From the outback of Australia
And drove for several hours to reach the town.

The bike that took his liking,
To say the least, was striking –
A monster of a bike with lots of chrome –
And so Old Jim acquired
The bike he most admired
And got into his car and headed home.

And when, at home arriving,
Despite his hours of driving,
He sat upon the bike and switched it on.
His son, who stood beside it,
Said, 'Father, can you ride it?'
But before he got an answer Jim was gone!

With a roar that split the silence,
The bike, with sudden violence,
Careered across the yard and through the gate.
As it raced towards the mulga,
Old Jim, with language vulgar,
Clung grimly as he waited for his fate.

His son, though none too clever,
Did decide, however,
That maybe something should really be done.
He drove the car and chased him,
But the motorbike outpaced him
As it headed west towards the setting sun.

Through the mulga branches whipping,
Jim's skin and clothes were ripping,
As he struggled to remain upon the seat.

With blood he was bespattered
And a mob of roos he scattered
From where they rested in the evening heat.

Jim struggled with the steering
As he wildly went careering
Across riverbed, and saltpan and ravine.
Emus jostled one another
As they hastily sought cover
From Jim upon his murderous machine.

Every bump and corrugation
Caused further aggravation
To the bruised and bloodied body on the seat.
As sense and hope were going,
Jim felt the engine slowing,
Then it stopped – and his journey was complete.

Jim's immediate survival
Depended on his son's arrival,
Who was still negotiating scrub and roots.
When he came, a little later,
He was stunned to find his pater
Bruised and battered and unclothed, except for boots.

Still seated, stiff and gory,
On the bike, in all its glory,
Jim was senseless and his son thought he was dead.
But, on listening intently
He heard father moaning gently,
So he took him home and put him straight to bed.

Jim stayed in that condition
Of the seated, stiff position
For a week upon the bed where he was laid.
And recovery extended
For months before he mended
From that fearsome motorcycle escapade.

And no more is there debating
When stock need relocating
As to whether horse or motorbike is best.
Jim continues using horses
Through the scrub and watercourses,
And the motorbike has long been laid to rest!

OLD JIM'S COW

Driving home from who knows where a little while back,
I saw a rathered battered cow beside the gravel track.
She looked somewhat the worse for wear, with cuts upon her knees,
As there she stood, a mite bemused, amongst a group of trees.

'You know, I'm sure,' I said aloud, 'that's Old Jim's Jersey cow.
He keeps a mob in Paddy's place, and she's escaped somehow.'
'You'd better go and tell him then,' says Yvonne, she's my wife,
'Cattle wandering on the road can cause a bit of strife.'

Well naturally I agreed with her, and so we motored on.
Jim lived ten mile up the track, just past my brother, Ron.
We hadn't gone a half a mile when, stone the bloomin' crows!
We found another damaged cow with blood upon her nose!

She looked a little dazed as well, like she had hit her head,
'Looks like she's got concussion, but that can't be,' I said.
'She does look quite bewildered,' my anxious wife replied,
'And look, she's got a nasty gash right along her side.'

We went another mile or two and reached McDonald's Hill,
And there we found another cow, lying very still
Right across the gravel road – I leant upon the horn,
And as she slowly looked around I saw her ear was torn.

'There's something fishy here,' I said, and since I couldn't pass
I helped the cow get to her feet and walked her to the grass
That grew quite thickly by the road, then motored on some more,
And there, a little up the hill, we found cow number four!

She, too, was sagging at the knees, and looking rather crook,
Her eyes were opened very wide and had a starry look.
'This poor old thing is seeing stars, and lucky she's alive.
And look – another stumbling cow – that makes it number five!'

We hurried on to tell our friend, and on the way we saw
Not one or two of Old Jim's cows, but half a dozen more!
A final right-hand turn we made, and reached the old bloke's gate,
But we could see quite plainly that we'd come a little late.

Old Jim, a glazed look in his eye, was sitting in his truck.
His wife was there beside him, we thought they might be stuck.
But no – they were not stuck at all – just simply staring back
At a cow that stood beside them on their rather muddy track.

We stopped our car and walked across in time to hear him say,
'Isn't that a cow of ours we loaded up today?'
He gave a start when I replied, 'Too right it is, my friend,
You've left a cow along this road on almost every bend!

'We noticed one along the track with blood upon her face,
Just up from where you keep the cows in Paddy Murphy's place.
We thought we'd come and tell you, and we've seen a dozen more –
Next time you load up cattle don't forget to shut the door!'

OLD JIM'S CHRISTMAS

The year had been long, and the year had been dry,
With no decent rain since late in July.
And now, close to Christmas, the harvest was down,
And the grass in the paddocks was withered and brown.
Jim looked at his stock; they weren't sleek any more,
The condition of most a bit forward of store.
Old Jim wiped his brow with the back of his hand,
Then, adjusting his hat, the horizon he scanned.
On the distant blue hills, through the shimmering haze,
Was a large plume of smoke where the bush was ablaze.
'No threat to us here,' he muttered aloud,
As he gazed at the far-away, billowing cloud.
'Unless a strong northerly blows up, of course,'
He said as he patted his faithful old horse.
'But then, me old girl, it'd take half a week
To get our boundary down there by the creek.'

He flicked with the reins and returned to the house,
And there he was greeted by Gladys, his spouse.
'Judy and Alan have arrived with the boys,
But the baby's asleep, so don't make any noise.
You promised to get them a tree when they came,
To put up at Christmas, I guess one the same
As we've had every year, can you get me one in?'
'I know what you want,' Jim replied with a grin,
'A branch of a cherry, the native one here,
I'll see that you'll have one this arvo', my dear.
But first for some lunch – have a bite to eat,
And take a break from this dreadful heat!'

It was later that night and the boys were in bed,
When Alan, Jim's son, to his father said,
'There's a smell of smoke in the air tonight,
And the moon is tinged with a reddish light.
That fire on the hills that I saw today,
There's every chance of it getting away,

'For the wind is up, and it's northerly, too,
Is there anything more I can help you to do?'
'No! The trailer's right, and the firebreak's done,
I've completed the fire preparation, son.
I'm feeling weary, I've been busy today,
I think it is time that we all hit the hay.'

By the following day Jim was ill at ease,
For the fire had spread on the northerly breeze,
And was racing across the desolate plains,
And never a chance of a sudden rain.
On the day before it was Christmas Eve
Old Jim and his son decided to leave and join in the fight to
    control the blaze
That had burnt unchecked for so many days.
As they started the ute and prepared to go,
Old Jim heard the voice of his grandson, Joe,
Who said to his Pa, with a hint of alarm,
'Will the fire keep Santa from reaching the farm?'
'I think he'll be here, and he won't forget
There are kids on the farm – he hasn't missed yet!
We hope to be back before Christmas Day,
And meanwhile, lad, we can hope and pray
For the wind to change and the rain to fall,
Or it could be a difficult time for all.'

Old Jim and his son went away to fight,
And they didn't come home at all that night.
And on Christmas Eve they were still away,
And so, at the end of a worrying day,
Young Joe went inside, and on bended knees,
Prayed for some rain, and a southerly breeze.
But the weatherman gave a prediction bleak,
And, later that night, fire jumped the creek,
And, to Jim's dismay, it went racing again
Through the withered grass on the windswept plain.
And the captain announced to his wary troop,
'It's back to the house, where we'll all regroup.
It'll give us an hour, or a little more,
Before it approaches the homestead door.'

As the men drove back through Old Jim's farm
The northerly died, and an eerie calm
Proclaimed the arrival of a smoke-filled day.
And to everyone's amazement, the skies were grey!
As the south wind blew, and the raindrops fell.
The exhausted men gave a thankful yell,
And a soot-stained Jim, with his reddened eyes,
Was greeted by the noise of his grandson's cries.
'I prayed for the rain, and the south wind, too,
And Santa Claus came, and so did you!'
He leapt in the arms of his Grandpa Jim,
And his Pa shed a tear as he cuddled him.
He turned to the men, and his family there,
This weather-beaten bloke with the snowy hair,
'Strange things have happened in my life before,
But nothing like this has surprised me more.

'I'm all overcome, don't know what to say,
'Bout the miracle that's happened this Christmas Day.
But I thank you all, and the captain, too,
And the very best of Christmases to each of you!'

DEATH OF A GIANT

I found a fallen giant today,
What caused its death I cannot say.
Old age? The wind? White ants, or rot?
Whate'er the cause, it matters not.
For centuries, maybe, it had grown
And not a sign of weakness shown.
It had withstood the heat and frost
And, when the winter tempest tossed

Its fiercest storm, the tree had stood
Unbowed, as mighty giants should.
But now it's dead. Its broken back
Forlornly lies across our track.
Last afternoon it filled the sky,
And now upon the track will lie
Subject to gradual decay.
Farewell, O giant of yesterday!

John Russell

OUTBACK WOMEN

(Charters Towers)
She crawled out through the stockyard rails, with blood upon her shirt,
Her hat and boots and tattered jeans all caked with sweat and dirt.
And through her wet dishevelled hair a half-smile crossed her face,
And I thought if fate were justice she deserved a better place.
But she'd not trade her dusty hat for any jewelled crown,
Nor swap her dirty old blue jeans for any ballroom gown.

(Quilpie)
She poured me out my whisky with a friendly 'There you are';
It was 112 on the hotel porch and 101 in the bar.
She shared a joke with the shearing team who'd just cut out the mob
And jollied up the busted ringer, waiting for a job.
And while I drank the bottle dry I heard her history;
She dreamed that one day she would own a cottage by the sea.

(Cairns)
She swung the battered diesel round and took the Cape York road,
The Christmas gifts crammed in amongst the big wet season load.
Her weathered face seemed softened by the salon's new hairstyle;
There'd be six months' isolation with the next 300 mile.
'Old man's a real no-hoper, ay – she runs the bloody show;
I reckon she might make it, but you wouldn't bloody know.'

You will find them though you travel down the harshest inland track,
And they are the very backbone and the heart of our outback;
They are our western women, who have helped to mould this land,
And through every trail and obstacle, courageously they stand.

And the vision of the outer-back would not seem half so grand
But for our western women; they're the pride of our great land.

For they love the very land that seeks to ravage and enchain,
And they're always there to share the joy, the hardship and the pain
Of the droughts that seem unceasing and misfortune to endure,
With their will and fighting spirit and support so strong and sure.
And the gum trees and the wattle blossoms never bloom so fair
As do the women of the outback, with the hope they inspire there.

THE YEAR'S FIRST BRANDING ROUND

The station stirs 'fore the break of dawn
    For the year's first branding round,
And the camp cook's gong midst the clanking plates
    Is an appetising sound.
The ringers walk with a jingling step
    And a mincing hasty tread
Past the yards and dip near the old airstrip
    To the door of the saddle shed.

The horses yard with a nostril flared
    And an eager pounding stride,
And the stockmen cut the brood mares out
    And check those fit to ride;
And the plant stock ring in a frantic bid
    To keep with their kin and kind
As they draft the doubtful youngsters out
    And the bay with a lame off-hind.

The ringers mount 'midst the yells and cheers
    From their mates perched round the rails,
For the horses yet are spelled and fresh
    With a kink in their necks and tails.
But the humps are smoothed by a lap or two
    And a turn round the main yard fence,
And they cross the lane on an easy rein
    Though highly strung and tense.

The mob drones in 'neath a cloak of dust
    As they march the last mile home
Through the laneway down to the stockyard gate
    At the edge of the aerodrome.

And the cattle tramp through the force and draft
   To the yards where they low and stand,
And the stockyards sing to the slap and sting
   Of the greenhide rope and brand.

I sit and dream on the latticed porch
   And again I can live it all.
I can taste the dust, hear the rattling hooves,
   I can hear the cattle bawl,
I can smell the yards, hear the stockwhip crack,
   I can feel the old greenhide;
But it's time for tea, and my son helps me
   And my old wheelchair inside.

Dan Sheahan

THE SERGEANT'S COW

Old Billy was one of the hard-headed push –
All wily and wise in the ways of the bush.
Full many a creek and dry gully he's crossed
By day and by night and he never got lost.
He kept in his shop on the side of the street
Where he sold saveloys with the best of good meat –
He was not too keen about killing his own
If he had to do so he'd sigh and he'd moan.

But bullocks you know don't fall from the skies –
If happened he ever went short of supplies –
He'd go in the night-time to places he knew
And there with a rifle he'd get one or two.
When many a fat one had taken the knock
The station woke up he was killing their stock.
The police were told as a matter of course
When Rafferty became a big man of the force.

They took him to court but old Bill had them tricked –
A wise poddy dodger is hard to convict.
Big Raff had a set on committers of crime;
He patiently waited and bided his time.
He worked the old head and thought out a plan –
One that would finally fix up his man.
He'd go to the yard at the foot of the hill,
The place where the butcher would usually kill –

And there up a mango he hid 'mong the leaves,
All ready to drop on top of the thieves.
The stars were all paling as Bill and his mate,
Both driving a 'killer', came up to the gate.

He got off his cuddy – went quizzing around –
And spotted the print of a foot in the ground.
'Twas surely the work of a giant in his stride,
About half a yard long and half a foot wide.

And only one man in the whole river flat
Left marks that could come within inches of that.
He surmised at once 'twas the big-footed Celt
And he wasn't there for the good of his health.
He had an intuition that trouble was brewing
So he thought it was better be up and be doing.
Says he, 'This old codger has dogged me for months.
He cannot be now in two places at once.

'He's been after my scalp since the first time we met;
I'll teach him a lesson he'll never forget.'
He winked at his cobber, saying 'Sharpen your knife,
Then gallop and go for the lick of your life.
A red Illawarra hangs out by the creek
Her udder is big – she's fat and she's sleek.
Cut open her gullet and do the job neat.
The boys of the village are waiting for meat.'

He never looked up at the leaves hanging dense –
Gammoned a while to be fixing the fence.
He gave work away – 'twas getting too hot –
And took himself off to the pub for a pot.
Meanwhile the big sergeant perched up in the tree
Had torn his tunic and hurted his knee,
But still he hung on by the skin of his teeth
And fought with the flies that came up from beneath.

When chances of capture had faded away,
He skidded to earth and he called it a day.

Down in the mouth, all embittered with life,
It was a sad man that went home to his wife.
And sullen and surly she stood at the gate
Saying 'Sergeant my boyo what kept you so late?
I wonder however I met such a man;
The meat I have cooked has gone cold in the pan.

'I'll dish up a feed but there's one thing I lack.
The cow never came – you must drink the tea black.'
The sergeant was silent – he ate and he ate –
He swallowed the tea and polished the plate,
And when he had finished he picked up his hat
And went on a walkabout down to the flat.
He came to a clump of lantana and scrub –
The place wouldn't be half a mile from the pub.

There, plain as the daylight in front of the rail,
Were hooves and horns and part of a tail –
And battered and blooded beneath a green bough,
Right there was the head of the little red cow.
He stamped, went berserk, and ground his false teeth,
He cursed the whole world above and beneath.
He pulled at the hairs that were left in his head
And wished all the butchers then living were dead.

There was a business he couldn't live down –
Tomorrow he'd be all the joke of the town.
And how could he face up to people he'd meet?
The ringers would laugh when they looked at his feet.
Now, both those old-timers have both passed away –
They're both in the boneyard this many a day –
But people laughed then and they laugh at it now,
When told how the butcher killed Rafferty's cow.

THE RED RUM OF BUNDY

It's strange how the sons of all nations will toast
Their own native land in the booze they love most.
For thirsty Sinn Feiners of Erin the Green
Are partial to porter and pots of poteen.
The sons of the Saxon their tummies regale
On 'liquor of Lunnon' – John Bass's brown ale.
The dew of the Hielands in Scotia is known
For strength and a flavour that's all of its own.
But sons of Australia, where gum trees grow tall,
Vow Red Rum of Bundy the best drink of all.

Let Dutchies foregather and squander their tin
On insipid toddies of sugar and gin.
'Vin Blanche' and 'Vin Rouge' please the Poilus of France
And vodka in Russia makes Bolsheviks dance.
The German can yodel and toast his fraulein
On lager and pilsen – good brews of the Rhine.
But by our own tonic we'll stand or we'll fall –
The Red Rum of Bundy, the best drink of all.

This fair land of freedom, should war ever come,
We'll put all our trust in our own native rum.
'Twill steady our nerves and 'twill stick to our ribs,
Make strong men of wasters and brave men of squibs.
With a tummy full each we'll not care a cuss
For all Hitler's hordes or the millions of Muss.
Though rifles be few and our numbers be small,
With Red Rum of Bundy we'll conquer them all.

Let Fritz have his lager and Frenchie his wine,
Good luck to them both – they can have it for mine.
I'll stick to the booze of my own native sod,
The life-giving juice that's fit for a God.
And when I line up for the final parade
To meet with St Peter I'll not be afraid
If some of my cobbers will put a small flask
Into the box where I'm sleeping my last.
I'll take off the cork and give Peter a sniff.
He'll scratch his bald head and stroke his long ziff,
Then say, 'Come inside with me, Danny Asthore,
'Tis devil's own pity you never brought more.
For even the saints up in heaven will fall
For Red Rum of Bundy – the best drink of all.

VENABLES' CAT

By campfires at night-time strange stories are told –
Of horses and cattle, wine, women and gold.
You're certain to hear of the Gundagai dog,
The drunk that the Peeler main chained to a log …
But tales often told become stale and go flat
Now wait till I tell about Venables' cat.

A hybrid he was, half Kilkenny and Manx,
So short in the tail and so lean in the flanks.
In fight or in foray he stuck to his guns;
He'd dozens of daughters and numerous sons.
Was never his equal at yarding a rat –
A wonderful mouser was Venables' cat.

And Tom might have lived till the end of his days,
But fate butted in with its ficklesome ways.
While lolling at ease in the afternoon sun,
A New Aussie came with a long-barrelled gun.
The shooting stick spoke and the leaden hail spat,
And there in his gore lay poor Venables' cat.

The assassin, then doubting his victim was dead,
Drew out a long dirk and then cut off his head.
He saved all the blood, not a drop did he waste,
Then pulled off the pelt of the unlucky baste.
And soon in a cooker with onions and fat,
All ready for supper lay Venables' cat.

Then guests came in great haste to join in the feast –
I'm thinking there would be a dozen at least.
To head, tail and torso with curry and rice

They all helped themselves once and some came back twice.
They all kept their minds on the job they were at,
The night that they gobbled up Venables' cat.

Now food must have something to do with blood –
Give Scotty his porridge and Paddy his spud
Beef-eaters, of course, will be hard to convince
The tail of the cat is a feed for a prince.
But gourmets who've dined on the frog and the bat
Had vowed they had not eaten better than Venables' cat.

Now Tom he has gone to where good felines go,
Wherever that is – well, I'm sure I don't know –
But at midnight's lone hour when a waning moon spills
Its sickly light over Nalwogarre's hills,
A spectre is seen around Atkinson's Flat.
They say it's the ghost of poor Venables' cat.

THE DEATH SONG OF THE CANE BEETLE

I'm a beetle, a bug, an object of hate
To people that live in this part of the state.
It was twelve months ago that I first saw the light
In Elphinstone Pocket one hot summer night.
I was puny and small and my living was plain,
Hidden away 'neath a tall stool of cane.

But slowly I grew as I fed on the shoots
And sugary sap of its wide spreading roots,
Until I developed into a fine grub
As oily and fat as the boss of the pub.
I was happy as Larry I'm telling you true,
With plenty to eat and nothing to do.

The wet season ended, the weather got fine –
Cane growing above me soon started to pine.
From Emerald of Erin it changed into brown
And one windy morning it all tumbled down.
The cocky came round and he gave a roar;
He jumped on his hat and he cursed and he swore.

He called up a meeting where I was abused –
You'd blush if I told you the language they used.
They ended by putting a price on my head;
They outlawed the greybacks, both living and dead.
I got a bit windy and altered my berth –
A hollow way down under two feet of earth.

'Twas dismal and dark but it suited alright
Till my wings grew in length and were ready for flight.
Then I had a notion I'd like to see life –

To meet my kindred and look for a wife.
So touring the pocket I acted the sheik
With young lady beetles at Elphinstone Creek.

There from a green sapling, as evening was nigh,
A dainty young flapper gave me the glad eye.
No intro was needed, we started to spoon,
And then flew away on a grand honeymoon.
Splitting the ether – Amy Mollison's bus –
For grace or for grandeur had nothing on us.

We viewed the Dalrymple and other grand scenes,
And lobbed on a fig tree near Seddy McQueen's.
Ah me! When I think of those hours of bliss
I never had notion I'd finish like this.
But fate in the shape of a man called a 'boong'
Strolled into the shade of the tree where we hung.

I slipped and I fell when he'd shaken the tree.
His wife underneath it, she pounced on me.
To regain my freedom I tried every plan,
But she bore me away in a black billycan.
My pleading for mercy she paid no regard,
But raced to the cocky to claim the reward.

My story is ended, I'm scanty of breath –
I feel it within me the coming of death.
At dawn of tomorrow I won't be alive
But in Elphinstone Pocket my breed will survive.
The cow of a cocky who caused my downfall –
Next season his Trojan will pay for it all!

JOHN OTTAVI'S MULE

You've heard of Snips and Dargan's grey,
Phar Lap and Gallinule.
Now you listen and you'll hear the lay
Of John Ottavi's mule.

His father sprung from Baalam's ass
That lived by Jordan side.
His mother's forbears nibbled grass
Along the banks of Clyde.

Though somewhat peevish in his ways,
Still tough and strong as wire,
He worked through long hot summer days
And never seemed to tire.

One night while munching in his stall –
All in a sullen mood –
He thought upon life's bitter thrall,
As mules will sometimes brood.

He felt that all it held for him
Was years of sweat and toil,
From dawn till dusk a battle grim
To cultivate the soil.

His frame was stiff – his skin was sore –
He hated human rule.
'I'll clear out bush and work no more,'
Says John Ottavi's mule.

'Here goes,' he said, ''twill be a change
And flew across the fence –
And beat it for the Cardwell Range
Where scrubs are deep and dense.

When John awoke and found him gone
He offered a reward
To black or white – to anyone
Who'd bring him to the yard.

Young cocky boys with shining spurs
And wide sombrero hats,
Pursued behind by yelping curs
Came from the Ingham flats.

They lost the truant on broken ground –
They lost themselves as well –
And whether they have since been found
Is more than I can tell.

Stone River Joe and Sambo came –
Australia's dusky sons –
Bold riders who long knew the game
On rugged basalt runs.

They chased him over gullies rough –
By flat and mountain peak –
Till tired and sore they cried, 'Enough!'
Down by Dalrymple Creek.

George Croton tore up from the blocks –
He swore he'd run him in –

He raced him over scrub and rocks,
He raced him back again.

They thundered up the Seaview Range
And when they reached its crest
The hybrid headed for The Grange
And George then gave him best.

A score of others came and tried –
They galloped long and cruel –
But never one could touch the hide
On John Ottavi's mule.

You'll find him at Dalrymple Gap –
He lives a life of ease –
And calmly takes his midday nap
'Neath spreading Leichhardt trees.

He snorts at all the passers-by –
He's ready for a duel –
But no-one cares to have a try
To yard John Ottavi's mule.

Ian Simmonds

THE MATRIX OPAL

We bottomed on concrete in number ten shaft
And recklessly blasted it out as we laughed,
For the wonderful prospects lie under this band
Of waterworn boulders cemented with sand.
Then under the rubble I picked out a blob;
A specimen matrix to sell for ten bob.
Silicified sandstone with colours that fade,
They're oval like eggs that a dinosaur laid;
Regarded good traces by luckless in hope.
I coeed to Joe as he wound up the rope.

Joe fondled the scintered grey surface and said,
'It's possible inside the outside is dead.
But also it's possible, under the skin,
A kernel of opal is waiting therein.
A buyer like Gerhardt might gamble a "brick"
And treble his profit or lose it all quick.'
We looked at the matrix, each other, and grinned;
Discussion unneeded with luck in the wind.
For gougers afraid that a flutter will fall
Can hardly be counted as gougers at all.

I gave him the snips as he scanned it alone,
For carelessness also could shatter the stone.
Then suddenly striking a dynamite blow
He sheared off a sliver and, oh, what a show!
The mother-of-opal's placenta was tight
With the colour exploding out into the light.
Bedazzling beauty awoke to the sun;

Imprisoned for aeons since earth was begun,
When sunrays had sabred the rainbow to shreds
And buried them deep in the Permian beds.

We gaped for a moment, so stunned by the sight,
And awed by the knowledge we gave it the light.
Then out came a whoopee not caring who saw
(The keeper of secrets is always a bore).
We studied its pattern of harlequin hues,
The crimson of ruby and amethyst blues,
The shades of the sapphire to chrysoprase green,
The yellow of beryl to soft olivene.

While marvelling how all these colours could leap
In multiple layers from out of the deep,
I realised why only the dozen gems pretty
Adorned the foundations of God's Holy City.
No mention of opal in John's Revelation,
For all gems combined made this perfect creation.

We named it the 'New Jerusalem Stone'
Then sold it for ninety before we got home.

Bruce Simpson

GOODBYE OLD CHAP

You may rub your head on my coat, old chap,
As you stand by the gate in pain,
While I loose the knot in the greenhide strap
That you never shall wear again.
You may nudge my hand as you've done so oft
In the days that have gone for aye,
For you'll carry me never again on watch
Round the mob at the break of day.

You will draft no more as the grey dust swings
From the camp on the blacksoil plains;
You will prop no more by the stockyard wings
When we yard for the cattle trains.
No more you'll wait for the mob to splash
By the light of a storm lit sky,
Mid the thunder's roar and the timber's crash
Round the camp in the Muranji.

Ne'er again by the night horse break you'll doze,
In the chill of a winter night,
When the south wind moans and the back log glows
And the stars wink cold and white.
We may find another with swinging gait
To hack through the trucking town,
And there'll be others to quietly wait
By the break as the sun goes down.

We may find another to match your pace
Through the scrub when the fireworks start,
But never another to take the place
That you hold in a horseman's heart.
Your mates have stood on the camp since dawn,
You are watching, alert and keen,
The packs are on and the girths are drawn
But the fence stands there between.

The plant is off on the road again
And here by the paddock gate,
In the days to follow, and all in vain,
You'll whinny and watch and wait.
And often out on the Wave Hill track,
When the evening shadows fall,
Our thoughts will turn to the gamest hack
And the best night horse of all.

Actor farewell! Till your last long sleep,
May never the creek run dry,
May the grass be whispering fetlock deep,
Forever, old chap, goodbye.

AND YET SOMETIMES

Now the droving is done and no more from the scrub
Come the drovers to camp by the Newcastle pub;
They are gone from the routes with their horses and packs
And the tall grasses blow o'er their deep trodden tracks.
Now there's never a campfire the stock route along,
For the transports have silenced the night-watcher's song.
And yet sometimes on nights filled with thunder and rain,
In my dreams I am back on the stock routes again
With a wild restless mob, ever ready to rush
On a camp mid the antbeds and dry underbush.

'Twas a grim hundred miles down the Muranji track
Where the night camps were bad and the scrublands were black –
A vast wasteland unwanted that seemed without end,
From the scrub-covered jump-up to Bucket Creek bend –
Then we prayed for fine weather, a clear autumn sky,
When we entered the scrubs of the grim Muranji.
And we doubled the watches and cursed long and plain
When the Muranji met us with thunder and rain,
For when the mobs rushed, there was little recourse
Save to trust to your luck and to trust to your horse,
And there many a drover, when things went amiss,
In the Muranji scrublands faced grim nemesis.

And the big bullocks knew, for they gave us no rest
As they grudgingly walked from their runs in the west,
For they sulked and they pined for their far distant hills
And they scorned the long troughs at the Muranji mills.
They would moan soft and low for their pandanas springs
And they watched us like hawks from the lead and the wings,
But they'd ring in rebellion and baulk in dismay

When the Mitchell grass plains stretched ahead and away.
Now there's never a campfire the stock route along,
For the transports have silenced the night-watcher's song.

There is bitumen now where the big diesels roll
And the dead men grow lonely by Muranji hole.
Now the shy curlews wail and their sad chorus swells,
As though missing the music of Condamine bells.
For the droving is done and the drovers no more
String their mobs to the lake by the Newcastle store.
They have hung up their whips and like me settled down
In a job that's secure mid the comforts of town,
And yet sometimes on nights filled with thunder and rain,
In my dreams I am back on the stock routes again,
With a good horse beneath – with the timber acrack –
Round a mob of wild stores on the Muranji track.

WHERE LEICHHARDT LIES

Is this the land where Leichhardt lies,
Unfound though the years have fled?
Stark red desert 'neath blazing skies,
Where the ghostly pools of mirages rise
From the claypan's barren bed.
Where is the spot that he lies at rest –
By channel or gibber plain?
Did he grimly hold to the journey west
Or, disillusioned and sorely pressed,
Did he turn to the north again?
Did he turn to the north as the Israelites
Once turned to the promised land?
Through days of torture and nightmare nights
To a fate unknown went the ill-starred whites –
To death where no crosses stand.

This is the land where the whirlwind goes
In the path of the men who fell;
Where the stars are pale and the min-min glows,
And the sandhills shift when the storm wind blows
From the south like a blast from hell.
Sweeping north go the dull red waves,
Storm-crests of a long-stilled sea –
Deep down under in smothered caves
Do they shield forever the long-lost graves
And the key to the mystery?
Did he die a hero or die accursed
By the comrades he had led?
Did he fall to fever or blinding thirst?
Was he trapped by flood when the channels burst
And the north-spawned waters spread?

This is the land where the desert blacks
Still wander, a scattered band.
Do they mutter low of the 'debil tracks'
In the long-ago, and of fierce attacks
In the heart of their sacred land?
Where the fine red dust of the Centre cloaks
In a close embrace and strong,
The spinifex hills by the rock-bound soaks
Where the twisted limbs of the desert oaks
Are crooning a deathless song.
Is this the land where Leichhardt lies –
Land of the 'great unknown'?
Grim red desert and blazing skies,
Guard well your secret from questing eyes
For this is his land alone.

ONE MAN'S POLICY IS ANOTHER MAN'S POISON

A life rep drove the western roads amid the dust and flies,
His hopes of selling policies as barren as the skies.
He braked beside a rutted track that led off to the right
To wind behind a gidgea hill, then disappear from sight.
Will I, he thought, or will I not go touring down that track
To vanish as poor Leichhardt did or bring some business back?

Be positive, he told himself, and fortify your will.
He psyched himself, brainwashed himself, then drove in for the kill;
He pulled up by the station yards and there, back-bent in toil,
He found a callow country youth, a real son of the soil.
The life rep tried out every trick he knew upon the lad;
He even dug out selling aids he never knew he had.

The long youth grinned a vacant grin. 'Me dad's the one to see,
You'll find him up there at the house, he has a policy.'
Ah! the life rep thought, at last I've struck the crock of gold,
A fellow who has purchased once can always be resold.
He drove down to the station house and there, beside the door,
A weather-beaten giant stood with grimly jutting jaw.

The life rep introduced himself, he said: 'Here is my card,
I'd like to talk to you about your son down by the yard.
Protection on that young man's life a wondrous boon would be;
I'm sure that it will interest you – you have a policy?'
'I have at that,' the squatter said, 'a simple one, it's true,
It's sooling flamin' cattle dogs on salesmen such as you.'

Just then from out behind the house and not too far away
There came the guttural growls of dogs preparing for the fray,
Our hero stayed to hear no more, he wished no further goad,
And with the dust clouds blowing back he vanished down the road.
The moral of this story is: Though reps may try to please,
At times they meet a snag who holds quite different policies.

VALE, RUSTY REAGAN

Old Rusty Reagan's cashed his chips,
No more he'll go on droving trips,
And no more grog will pass the lips
Of drunken Rusty Reagan.
He died of drink, or so they say,
Or pure neglect, but anyway
The sands of time have slipped away
For luckless Rusty Reagan.

Although he camped upon the flat
The bar was his true habitat,
And home was underneath the hat
Of drifter Rusty Reagan.
There's none to say from whence he came,
Not sure in fact if that's his name;
To Rusty though it's all the same –
Dead finish Rusty Reagan.

No relatives with reddened eyes
Will weep at Rusty's sad demise;
No lowered flag at half-mast flies
To honour Rusty Reagan.
We'll miss perhaps his ugly dial,
His raucous voice and toothy smile,
We'll miss him for a little while,
Then forget Rusty Reagan.

Perhaps somewhere someone will wait –
A mother, sister, brother, mate –
Who'll wonder as they vainly wait
For absent Rusty Reagan.

I'd like to think some tears might fall
For Rusty's ilk, no-hopers all,
Who answer that last trumpet call
Unmourned like Rusty Reagan.

TRAVELLING STOCK – 1969

Southward the road trains thunder,
On through the hours of light,
Never a halt this morning,
Never a rest tonight.
Hollow, and gaunt and hopeless,
Dusty, and dim of eye,
By night and day on their weary way,
The travelling stock go by.

On through the noonday silence,
On through the dust dry air,
Away with the drought-time harvest,
The loadings of dumb despair.
Weary, and weak, and wasted,
Famished and sinking fast,
Two tiers high 'neath a brassy sky,
The travelling stock go past.

A TALE OF TERMITES

Stranger please pause by this old bungalow,
For it hides a grim battle that ebbs to and fro –
A primitive struggle, devoid of romance,
Twixt the Camooweal drunks and the giant white ants.
No quarter is given, no mercy displayed,
In this fight to the death with the termite brigade,
But if their rampaging is not soon reduced
You can all say goodbye to the old ringer's roost.

There are termites to left and termites to right,
And their molars are grinding by day and by night;
They raid and they ravage and plunder unchecked,
And they're larger, much larger than one would expect.
By wall plate and rafter they stealthily creep,
And God help our hides if they catch us asleep,
And if we can't turn their attack mighty soon
We'll be under the stars by the change of the moon.

There are white ants below and white ants above,
In the floorboards and battens and rafters they love;
They deploy to the left and attack from the right,
And their molars are grinding by day and by night.
They break up our parties and ruin our rest,
And they are, in a nutshell, a damnable pest,
And if we can't deal them a kick in the slats
I fear it's the end of these batchelor flats.

We've tried every method to stop their advance,
We've fought them with poison and baton and lance,
But it does little good for in thousands they breed
And they sharpen their fangs as they look for a feed.

An expert once called in to give us a quote,
But as soon as he entered they sprang at his throat.
He fought himself free with the leg from a bed
And, 'One flick and I'm going,' he screamed as he fled.

They've ravaged our larder, our furniture too,
And one night they punctured a carton of brew,
Then the word got around to the whole of their tribe
And they bunged on an orgy I couldn't describe.
They've cleaned up our woodheap, our outhouse as well,
The 'Man who comes round' said he'd see us in hell;
They've eaten our moleskins and eaten our Bex –
Two novels by Thwaites and a pamphlet on sex –
And if very soon we don't stop their advance
Then I'll transfer the deeds to the flamin' white ants.

RETURN

She held in the colt as he raced from the stockyard,
And gaily she laughed as they sped by the mill;
With a rattle of hoofbeats they passed from the valley,
Along the rough track round the brow of the hill.
The evening star dipped by the gap in the ranges
Where the fires of sunset had long ceased to burn,
As they waited in vain on the homestead verandah
For the hoofbeat and song that would sound her return.

The horses were run to the yard in the morning,
With never a glow where the daylight first starts;
And there as they saddled their mounts in the starlight
As cold as the dawn was the fear in their hearts.
On the short cut that ran from the ford to the township
Across the rough hills, through the pine thickets there,
They found where she lay by the broken top railing,
The reins in her fingers – the dew in her hair.

She sometimes returns when the grey twilight deepens,
When soft drapes on darkness descend over all;
Down the rough track she rides that re-echoed her laughter,
By the little bush home with the creeper-clad wall.
She rides when the Cross marks the south like a beacon,
When the crest of the ranges are swaddled by night,
And she rides a grey colt shod as light as a moonbeam
And as swift and as sure as a kestrel in flight.

There's never a dog breaks the stillness that settles,
There's never an owl breaks the hush by the creek.
The possums grow quiet in their play by the stockyard
And a silence dwells there that seems almost to speak.

Then wraith-like she comes and as fleet as a shadow
As the night wind caresses the gums on the hill,
But the song that she sang and the lilt of her laughter,
And the rattle of hoofbeats forever are still.

SAM FULLER'S THOROUGHBRACE

Sam Fuller's was a well known face on stock routes yesteryear,
And Fuller bought a thoroughbrace to shift his droving gear.
A spanking coach it once had been in days of Cobb & Co.,
That carried mail on roads between the Reach and Jericho.
Converted to a wagonette, Sam Fuller thought it grand
Despite the fact he'd still to get a team of five-in-hand.

We loaded on the gear and swags, we roped them into place,
Then culled the plant for likely nags to pull the thoroughbrace.
We draughted five from Fuller's mob, the progeny of sin,
Then readied tackle for the job of breaking outlaws in.
'We're wasting time,' Sam Fuller cried, 'we're shifting camp, you know.
We'll have some fun with them untried, we'll break 'em as we go.'

The boss's word was law of course, somehow the job was done,
We caught each wild unbroken horse and harnessed every one.
We battled hard to keep control, then placed as Sam decreed
Two snorting brumbies in the pole, three others in the lead.
As ringers held each horse's head – five time bombs all alive –
Sam Fuller turned to me and said, 'They tell me you can drive?'

In shaking hands I took the reins with, 'Steady, whoa there, whoa!'
Then five mad horses hit the chains as Fuller shouted 'Go!'
At reckless pace away we sped, the horses running blind –
Escape they knew was up ahead while hell was close behind.
They bolted out towards the track, the bits between their teeth,
The dust and grasses billowed back, the stones flew underneath.

They held to scorn the heavy load, the smoking brakes they spurned.
And when we reached the Jundah road we all but overturned.
The Jundah track was fast and dry and faster grew our speed

For not a hope in hell had I of pulling up the lead.
I held the reins in hands that grew white-knuckled with the strain
As hooves beat out a mad tattoo and gravel flew like grain.

The leaders bowed the spreader bars, with harness all a-fail
They cleared the road of motor cars and scattered them like quail.
The thoroughbraces pitched and rolled, the camp gear rattled free
Like cargo in a clipper's hold that braves the stormy sea.
I rode the wildly swaying seat, one foot upon the brake,
As ringers yelled, 'You've got 'em beat', and galloped in our wake.

We thundered through a flock of sheep, the poler shied in fright,
But Lady Luck chipped in to keep the wagonette upright.
I waited for the pace to ease, I knew it couldn't last,
But still the dusty gidgea trees like phantoms flitted past.
I saw at last the chains go slack beside the heaving flanks,
And as I reined the leaders back I said a prayer of thanks.

The weary horses ceased to fear the vehicle at their backs
And with the brake shoes riding clear they trotted on like hacks.
They swept past distant station roofs and by a stony hill,
With arching necks and drumming hoofs now bending to my will.
What seemed at first a hell-bent trip was now a Sunday drive
As, septre-like, I raised the whip above the team of five.

The big wheels sang the same refrain they'd sung in days of yore,
With dust clouds following in train and flying heels before.
The braces gently rocked the load and oh! but life was grand
When spinning down the Jundah road with Fuller's five-in-hand.
In fancy's flight I rode with men who drove for Cobb & Co.
Oh! I was young and foolish then but that was long ago.

The bush is not the same today, for time has turned the page,
And out Stonehenge and Jundah way trucks roll on every stage.
Long gone is Fuller's wagonette – long gone the plunging team –
But memories that linger yet enshroud me like a dream.
Once more I feel the braces sway as, at a cracking pace,
Down distant roads I'm borne away on Fuller's thoroughbrace.

ASSIMILATION

A fighting son of a warlike race,
Woodinga strode with a hunter's grace
To the very brink of the cliff's rough face,
Blue shadowed by afternoon.
He snarled at the white men camped below
Where a precious spring seeped sweet and slow,
Then his challenge rang like a hammer blow,
For he was a Kalkadoon.

Jimmy Quartpot sweats on the smoko bell
As he cleans the yard at the bush hotel,
Though no-one expects him to do it well
As he's only a flamin' coon.
He'll spend his pay on the cheapest booze,
And the lockup floor is the bed he'll use,
For his wits are all he has left to lose,
And he is a Kalkadoon.

PAST INVERWAY

Oh! the west seemed full of promise
And the bush asked little from us,
When we rode the track that led us
Out to where our future lay.
And we left but few hearts grieving
At the prospect of our leaving,
Like the wild geese heading westward,
Further out past Inverway.

With the plant shod up, we started
On our pilgrimage, light hearted,
With the hobble chains a-jingle
And the loaded packs a-sway.
But we'd little more to guide us
Than the faith that rode beside us,
When at first we travelled westward,
Further out past Inverway.

Then the wattle scent was spreading
And the boughs, their blossoms shedding,
Made a golden fairy carpet
Where the dappled shadows lay.
Then the wet had not long ended
And the grass like wheat extended
From the old road heading westward,
Further out past Inverway.

When we camped the evening found us
With the virgin bush around us,
While the horses grazed in hobbles
Lest they wander off and stray.

Down the flat their bells were ringing
As the Southern Cross was swinging
Up above the darkened timber,
Further out past Inverway.

As the night wind, softly blowing
Set the back-log embers glowing,
We yarned of future triumphs
Where the last frontier lay.
We awoke each dew-drenched dawning
To the music of the morning,
As the bush birds gave us welcome
Further out past Inverway.

Then we had no qualms, not knowing
What awaited us, when going
Out to where the wild geese gathered
And the brolgas danced at play,
For the sap of youth was flowing,
And our spirits soared when going
Out to Kimberley, our Mecca,
Further out past Inverway.

GOLD STAR

The sun went down and the storm clouds rose,
Dark browed with the threat of rain,
As they put the mob through the netting fence
To the camp on the blacksoiled plain.
'Twas a short half mile cross the plain just there,
From the hills on the western side
To the gloomy depths of the myall scrub,
Where scarcely a man could ride;
Near a mile across and as bad a scrub
As ever a stockman saw,
Then a bluegrass flat and a twelve-foot drop
To the river that ran before.

As quiet as milkers the bullocks seemed
As they moved on, feeding slow,
With heads all turned to the cattle camp
In the sunset's ruddy glow.
But a spark remains in the quietest mob
That can leap to a roaring flame
In a maddened rush, as the ringers know
Who have followed the droving game.
They had splashed a bit when we took them first,
As the Gulf mobs often do,
But they settled down to the dull routine
Of the road in a week or two.

For they learnt the lesson the drovers teach
To the tune of the whip's barrage,
And seldom it was that a mob played up
When Mac was the man in charge.
For he'd served his time when the game was tough,

In the days when the west was young;
When a man was judged by his bridle hand
And his skill when the scrubbers rung.

A sunburnt son of the far north-west,
Where the fenceless stock routes are,
And the pride and joy of the drover's life
Was his chestnut mare, Gold Star.
I had heard tales told in a hundred camps
Of Mac and his chestnut mare,
From the Gulf Coast down to the New South side,
Ere ever I met the pair.
A thing of beauty she was to see,
And a tower of strength to ride,
With a lean game head and a lion's heart
And a free and swinging stride.

There was never a night horse foaled, Mac swore,
That could stay with the chestnut mare
Through scrub or holes in the mad pell-mell
Of a rush 'neath the lightning's flare.
For a dozen years she had served him well,
And always the mobs were held,
But he rode her only at odd times, then,
When the fresh store mobs rebelled.
A favoured pet with the plant she ran,
From the bridle and hobbles freed,
But she watched the mob with her soft ears pricked
As it spread on the plain to feed.

Mac came to me as I hobbled up
By the camp in the failing light,
And I heard him say as I caught the bays,

'Better tie up the mare tonight.'
'Better tie up the mare' was all he said,
But he spoke with a troubled frown
And I saw him glance at the thunder heads
That had grown since the sun went down.
I went on first round the sleeping mob,
While the quarter moon on high
Was blotted out by the leaden clouds
As the watch dragged slowly by.

It was Jim's watch next and, stepping down
By the fire I called his name,
Then the heavens split in a blinding flash
And the whole camp seemed aflame.
I stood transfixed by the startled bay,
Then cursing I swung around,
For merging low with the thunder crash
Was an other and grimmer sound.
I offered a silent prayer of thanks,
For a night horse that knew the job,
As the bay horse reefed at the bit and raced
Round the wing of the rushing mob.

But the lead was off to a flying start –
A start that was far too great –
And even then as I urged the bay,
I knew we would be too late.
They hit the scrub with a splintering crash
And, strong on the storm wind borne,
Came the pungent breath of the fear-crazed mob –
The tang of the hoof and horn.
I had eased the bay to a saner pace
And pulled out a little wide,

When I heard Mac's shout, then his chestnut mare
Was galloping by my side.

'Ride as you never have ridden, lad,
No matter what risk or cost.
We must beat them out on the further side
Or half of the mob is lost.'
Mac was never a man to flinch at night,
In scrub or to ease the pace,
And I'd never relive for a thousand mobs
The span of that nightmare race.
A gully loomed in a lightning flash,
It was strewn with stumps and wide,
But the old mare rose in the lead of me
With never a change of stride.

As game as ever, she took the jump,
We were but a length between,
But the power and strength of her quarters then
Were not what they once had been.
She landed badly and blundered on,
Striving to rise in vain.
She turned clean over while time stood still,
Then the darkness closed again.
The bay horse lit and his shod forefeet
Struck fire from the jutting stone,
With a backward glance and a bitter oath
I rode on through the scrub alone.

Rode on alone through the wind-swept scrub,
Though that dark-clad rider, death,
Rode stirrup to stirrup with every stride

And I cursed him with every breath.
The roar of the storm and the timbers crash
Were hell's own mad refrain,
And I threw the reins at the bay horse then,
And rode like a man insane.
The bay was bred where they know a horse
And value the old game breed,
But we burst at last from the myall scrub
Too far from the flying lead.

Then high and shrill rose a horse's wail
That died in a kind of sob,
And Gold Star passed like a bird in flight
Down the lead of the rushing mob.
The poley saddle was empty then,
And the loose irons swung beside,
No brown hand gathered the flying reins
To steady and urge and guide;
Her mane and tail were as burnished brass
In the lightning's vivid flood,
And the foam that she flung from the bit-rings back
I saw then was red with blood.

With a wicked light in her kindly eyes,
Ears back and her teeth laid bare,
She wheeled them back from the river's edge
With nothing but yards to spare.
She wheeled them back from the yawning brink
Till they rung on the narrow plain,
And I rode and sang till they settled down
With their backs to the slanting rain.
I was looking for the chestnut mare

But never a shadow stirred;
When I heard Jim's voice and the song he sang,
Was the finest I'd ever heard.

We watched them there through the lonely hours
Till the dawn broke chill and grey,
And showed the spot by the timber's edge
Where the chestnut night mare lay.
Jim called to me and I rode across
As he knelt by the dead mare's side;
She had wheeled the lead as her life blood flowed
The faster with every stride.

They buried Mac as he would have wished,
For he does not sleep alone,
By the posts and railings that guard his bed
Stands a rough built mound of stone.
They rest together, the man and mare,
Where the shy scrub cattle feed
On the narrow flat by the river's bank
Where Gold Star wheeled the lead.

Jeffrey Simpson
THIRTY FEET BELOW

The valley's shadows lengthen as I pause to take a rest
And I read again the letter Darcy wrote me from the West,
For Darcy say he's mining where the sandstone ridges run,
And I find myself daydreaming as I laze here in the sun.
Soon I watch a fiery sunset as it sets the sky aglow
In the West where Darcy's gouging some thirty feet below.

Although the orchard stretches with it ordered rows of trees,
With the branches, heavy laden, swaying gently in the breeze,
It seems above the rustle comes an old familiar sound
Of miners' picks on sandstone as they labour underground
Where Darcy's working mullock in the bright electric glow,
While the bucket rattles upward from thirty feet below.

Yes Darcy's opal mining for he's fallen 'neath the spell,
Old-timers could have warned him if only they would tell,
But when the opal fever strikes no victim wants to hear
Of fortunes lost, of fizzer claims, of wrecked and broken gear.
For only those who mine this gem can ever hope to know
The thrill of striking opal when you're thirty feet below.

The darkness slowly deepens and the campfires flare and gleam,
But Darcy goes on working for he's on a colour seam.
Perhaps it is that Lady Luck has guided Darcy's hand;
Perhaps kind fate has shown him a hidden colour band
That indicates a parcel near that waits the final blow –
A fortune may be feet away when thirty feet below.

And as I sit here at my ease my back against a tree,
I think I envy Darcy, for I know that he is free.
For him the union never comes to seek another rise;
No women's lib annoys him with their cries to equalise.
The muggings and the murders and the violence seems to grow.
It seems a whole lot safer working thirty feet below.

The bankers here are telling us that mortgage rates must rise;
The treasurer has sternly said we must economise.
I know the day must surely come when, cursed by mounting bills,
I'll roll the swag and call the dog and head out thru the hills,
Away across the black-soil plains where western rivers flow,
And try my luck like Darcy, working thirty feet below.

Jack Sorensen

GOING SOUTH

A warm wind in the Leichhardt pines is whispering of rain;
The sergeant working on his own uplifts a song of cheer:
'Old mates, we saw the wet go out and now it comes again,
But we're heading south tomorrow, for the northbound troops
    are here.'
It's no drum – we're going south;
At long last we're heading south,
Where there's warm love and cold beer at our home towns in the
    south.

The rich green moss is on the road that winds through giant teaks,
The hothouse air is heavy with a dank smell of decay,
The vapours from the valley shroud the ranges' ragged peaks
As the battle-weary regiment moves down towards the bay.
They're embanking for the south,
For relief has come from south,
And their dream things will be real things when they're resting
    in the south.

The man who dwarfs his slant-eyed guard is looking at the sky,
Regardless of the battleplanes out there manoeuvring;
His stern brown face has softened and a light is in his eye
As he watches in the distance homing wild fowl on the wing;
And he says, 'They're flying south,
Lucky blighters going south –
God in heaven speed the hour when we, too, will travel south.'

THE CALL OF THE NORTH

Oh! the western wind is blowing
So there's rain and storm in store,
And the teams have long been going
Down the road to Glindawor:
To where tropic sun is gleaming
And the fragrant winds blow free;
I've awakened from my dreaming
And the North is calling me.

Oh! the steam is in the boiler,
In the expert's room below,
While upon the board each toiler
Waits to hear the whistle blow:
For the shearing is beginning
And my heart is fancy free,
And the friction wheels are spinning,
So the North is calling me.

From the southward to the nor'ward,
Where the long brown tracks wind down,
All my mates have hastened forward
To the wilderness from town:
Gone! by stony hill and hollow
To where I now fain would be,
Where they lead I needs must follow,
For the North is calling me.

What's this news I have been hearing?
Tidings strange to me indeed.
Bidgemia now is shearing,
With Sawallish in the lead;

Straining camel teams are swaying
From the Junction to the sea;
Why so long am I delaying
When the North is calling me?

And so northward I am going,
For I cannot linger here,
Now the starting whistle's blowing,
And the guns are into gear;
So to be there I am yearning,
I will hail the sheds with glee,
For the friction wheels are turning,
And the North is calling me.

Note: Robert Sawallish was one of the fastest shearers in the world.

BOOMERANG DAY IN THE NORTH

As the new jackaroo set out on a ride
To look o'er the station first day,
The man from the outcamp rode up to his side
And cried in a horrified way:
'Go back to the homestead, keep out of the way,
'Tis peril today to ride forth,
It's the ninth of October and Boomerang Day,
Yes, Boomerang Day in the North.

'In England you choose your fair Queen of the May,
And the Yanks have the fourth of July,
But we celebrate in our own little way
By making the boomerang fly.
We rush round in circles in primitive glee
And terrible, too, is our wrath,
When we first sight a stranger from over the sea
When it's Boomerang Day in the North.'

The jackaroo glared, in his saddle he swayed,
And his voice rang defiant and clear:
'I'm Captain McCall of the Nineteenth Brigade,
And McCalls are all strangers to fear.
Forever you'll find them where fiercest the fray,
Defying the enemy's wrath,
So why should I tremble and hasten away
When it's Boomerang Day in the North?

'It will never be said that McCall bowed to fear,
So lead, and I'll go where you go,
And should there be danger confronting me here

I'll ride with my face to the foe.
So hand me a boomerang, stranger, I pray,
And I'll whirl it around and ride forth,
To help them to celebrate Boomerang Day,
Since it's Boomerang Day in the North.'

Ron Stevens

OF MEN AND BOYS

I was almost down to Elders when I saw him at their door,
So I turned and sought a refuge in the nearby hardware store.
It's unlikely Ernie noticed how I dodged him yesterday
But he surely must be asking why I haven't called his way.
Over forty years we've managed to be open and enjoy –
In a word that's out of fashion – being *cobbers*, man and boy.

When I've needed help, trust Ernie to appear upon the scene,
Whether flood or bushfire threatened or my bank was turning mean.
His assistance started early (in a twist of golden rule)
When he thrashed the playground bully at our single-teacher school.
Until then schooldays were dismal, but at seven life began
To be brighter, thanks to Ernie, who was nine – almost a man.

Being manly suited Ernie, who developed strong and straight.
In his work or weekend football he would always pull his weight.
With a smile and soft 'goodonyer' he'd encourage weaker types
And was never known to harbour any grudge or pretty gripes.
Yet this champion sagged at Elders, like a scarecrow, fate's rag toy,
And I slunk, a furtive dingo, from my cobber, man and boy.

Was he there to sell the homestead? Will he toss it all away?
He'd have given me the answers when I saw him yesterday
If I'd walked right up to Ernie, gripped him firmly by the hand,
And enquired about his future, told him, 'Mate, I understand
The enormous blow you've suffered … Is there anything I can …
I mean *anything* … Remember we've been cobbers, boy and man.'

It sounds simple but I'm certain I'd have weakened into tears
And embarrassed my old cobber, as I've done throughout the years:
Like collapsing at the graveside of his lovely wife Kathleen,
To be helped along by Ernie who retained a stoic mien;
Or awash with tearful pleasure when my lad and Ernie's Roy
Shared a swag of high-school prizes. They were mates, our shining
    boys.

Now today I try to muster all my strength but fear I'll cry
As my son and I stand tortured by a grave's unfathomed *Why?*
I'm confused but humbly grateful that my boy's alive and well
Though poor Ernie's Roy went stumbling into unimagined hell,
Then, by adolescent impulse or closely guarded plan,
Tied a noose beneath a rafter to destroy a youth … and man.

For his father's not the Ernie that I knew two weeks ago.
He has shrunk, his eyes are rheumy and his tread is shuffling, slow.
I can feel my son's frame shaking and I whisper, 'It's okay'
Through my tears, across the gravesite, as the parson starts to pray.
I see Ernie nod agreement and his smile, devoid of joy,
Seems to argue, 'Grief's a refuge, as is laughter, man and boy.'

Douglas Stewart
SOMBRERO

In a cowboy hat and a dark-green shirt,
Lithe on a piebald pony,
The blackfellow rode through the coolabah trees
Where the creek was dry and stony.

Here's fifty horses from Pandie Pandie
To drove to far Marree,
But before I start on the track again
I'll boil up a billy of tea.

Oh he was dark as the gibber stones
And took things just as easy,
And a white smile danced on his purple lips
Like an everlasting daisy.

The horses strayed on the saltbush plain
And he went galloping after,
The green shirt flew through the coolabah trees
Like budgerigars to water.

And then what need had he to sigh
For old men under the gibbers
When he was free as the winds that blow
Along the old dry rivers?

He had the lubras' hot wild eyes,
His green shirt and sombrero,
He rode the plains on a piebald horse
And he was his own hero.

Milton Taylor

QUEENIE LUCINDA O'TOOLE

Sweet Queenie Lucinda O'Toole,
I muse by your graveside today
How fate should, so callous and cruel,
Banish young bones to the clay.
What grevious and heinous a mischief
Committed, dear Queenie, by you,
Ensures that your beauty eternal
Lies hidden forever from view?

Were you wilful and headstrong or wicked,
Precocious, or sinful and wild?
Did you lie, did you cheat, did you slander
To earn your grim bed, precious child?
While there's many the villian still living
Who has yet to be paid his full due
For sins that have long gone unpunished
And deserves this drear grave more than you.

Two years and five months was your lifespan,
Your tenure here sadly too brief,
And the loss of unquarried potential
Adds more to the bleakness of grief.
What talents lay latent within you,
To bloom as in stature you grew?
An artist, a dancer, a teacher?
The answers, my love, sleep with you.

Frustration's keen blade twists inside me,
Unanswered these questions I've hurled;

Why the blossom must wilt in the desert,
Fade away with the petals still furled?
Why a babe, with a name like an angel
Was finished before she could start?
Why a story untold, merely guessed at
By a stranger, can claw at his heart?

And I wonder which stroke of misfortune
Was the cause of your sorry demise –
An accident, sickness, a fever?
Who knows? One can only surmise.
Perhaps you were felled by our climate,
The fierce breath of north Queensland heat,
Too ruthless in pitiless onslaught
For a fragile wee lass to defeat.

Did your passing stretch faith to its limit,
Put stoic belief to the test?
Were the faithful in agony shaken
As your tiny form lowered to rest?
Did your parents cry, desperate in anguish
As they knelt by your deathbed to pray?
Unheeded, their pleas for His mercy:
'We love her, Lord, please let her stay.'

Beside you sleeps dear Mary Allen,
From Sligo's fair country she came.
Like you, she was graced with the beauty
Of bearing a blest Irish name.
Do you fancy, in far-away Sligo,
Where winds kiss soft valleys of green,
That they sigh as the whisper in sorrow
For the loss of their bonny colleen?

How different from Sligo and Antrim,
Stark contrast to Connaught or Cork,
Is this harsh weathered earth of Cloncurry
Where the shy leprechauns never walk,
Though I feel sure the gods of the Dreamtime,
Surveying the realm of their rule,
Gaze fond on their flower of adoption,
On their Queenie Lucinda O'Toole.

Sweet Queenie Lucinda O'Toole,
I muse by your graveside today
How fate should, so callous and cruel,
Banish young bones to the clay.
But futile and fruitless my musings,
Too few now my tears, far too late,
Not mine is to challenge life's history
Nor to question the dictates of Fate.
For Fate plays no favourites, my darlin',
She's unkind, she'd unjust, she's cruel,
And I weep for my angel departed,
For my Queenie Lucinda O'Toole.

GREY LAUGHING EYES

A lifetime of slaving he'd left far behind
And now lay bedridden, worn out and near blind.
He'd shorn his last wether and ground his last comb,
Now waited to die in an old people's home.

The young nursing sister stood close by the bed
Of the frail, tired, old shearer. She stroked the grey head.
As his weary eyes focused, he briefly saw clear
The girl, and he whispered, 'I'm so glad you're here.

'For in days of my youth I held an ideal,
A dream I pursued with missionary zeal,
A dream of a girl as fair as spring skies,
A slim, lovely girl with grey laughing eyes.

'As onward I ventured e'er seeking my dream,
A vision before me ever present, did seem,
To beckon and call in perfection's pure guise
A slim, lovely girl with grey laughing eyes.

'A standard she'd set to judge others by,
Oh, that mere mortals should be held as nigh
To an angel, unfairly, comparison lies,
To my slim, lovely girl with grey laughing eyes.

'Met girls I did, and lovely ones too,
And grey eyes had they, and brown ones and blue,
But none had the aura that could mesmerise,
Like my slim, lovely girl with her grey laughing eyes.

'Loved them, I did, but always we'd part,
For I never could give them all of my heart,
For always, she'd be there, sweet compromise
My slim, lovely girl with her grey laughing eyes.

'As I grew older, good sense did prevail,
I knew that my search for perfection must fail,
An intangible goal, like Galahad's prize
Was my slim, lovely girl with grey laughing eyes.

'And so I forgot her until, into view
There came a slim lady, that lady was you.
I looked, disbelieving, with joyful surprise,
My slim, lovely girl with grey laughing eyes.

'My treasure of years! My soul then I bared
At the vision of beauty before me I stared
With frank admiration I scarce could disguise,
At my slim, lovely girl with grey laughing eyes.

'After all of these years our paths now do meet
Oh, grey eyes you have, love, and as ever so sweet
But, too late for me now, to capitalise
On their beauty, slim lady, those grey laughing eyes.

'When I leave I'll go happy just knowing we've met,
My happiness tinged with a hint of regret
That the years have escaped us, but please, realise
I have loved you forever and your grey laughing eyes.'

MY UTE

I'm a kelpie, a collie, a cattle dog blue,
Labrador, Doberman, Dalmation too,
Poodle, retriever or foxie-pom cross,
In the back of my ute, mate – I am the boss!
My ute is a Holden, a Datsun, a Ford,
Toyota or Mazda, when I spring aboard
I bask in the glory, the power one feels
When guiding my wonderful kingdom on wheels.
Be it brand new and shiny or battered and old,
Black, white or purple or three shades of gold,
The colour's no problem, the brand name no sweat,
As long as it gets me where I wish to get.
My ute is the best, crème de la crème –
Ute and dog, dog and ute, oh boy what a team!
Surveying my realm I'm bursting with pride,
Enjoying my wondrous triumphal ride.
You'll all hear my challenge, my bark of defiance
Commanding attention, demanding compliance
As my ute makes its progress, hear the sound ring
From the king of the ute, in the ute of the king.
Other dogs howl as they strain to compete
With my regal position, Lord of the Street.
Their utes are quite nice, I bear them no malice,
But compared to my marvellous travelling palace
They're damned insufficient for one of my stature,
They can't cause euphoria or bring about rapture
Like my splendid ute can, it's one of a kind,
Most noble of utes – that ute is mine!
On the footpath or street I'll do you no harm,
But dare touch my ute and I'll chew off your arm.
The eye of the tiger and, lurking beneath,

The heart of a lion with crocodile's teeth!
Docile no longer, ablaze with aggression,
Guarding my treasured, most valued possession.
What causes this change, this strange transformation
From friend to all men to scourge of the nation?
If man's home is his castle, then a dog has one too.
Nought else can approach what a ute does for you,
And the pride, the contentment, I tell you it's beaut
Just being a dog in your own bloody ute!

Lennie Wallace

HOBBLE CHAINS AND HORSE BELLS

Hobble chains and horse bells, the plant is coming home;
Jim's in the lead on Dancer, young Ernie's riding Foam.
Six weeks ago they left the yards, their horses fat and dancing,
The Dancer's still up on his toes, but Foam's no longer prancing.
There's Baldy with a pack on, and Dot and Cyclone too,
While underneath that topload it looks like good old Blue.
There's Nellie looking pretty tired, and Gay Girl's not so gay,
Then there's Red Cloud and Hornet, the chestnut and the Bay.

There's movement at the station now the men are almost here.
Old Biddy's woke up from her sleep, she's working with good cheer;
The piccaninny's stirred herself, she's sweeping up the yard;
Inside there's sounds of washing up, they're working good and hard.
Six weeks the plant's been on the run, branding up and speying;
Six weeks they've all been going flat – they've had no time for playing.
It's great they'll soon be home again, it's good to see their faces
When they're sitting down to dinner in their old familiar places.

Jim said he left the cattle at the old Big Paddock gate,
They should yard up quite early – let's hope they won't be late!
Hot tea, hot scones and chocolate cake should make a welcome change
From the damper and the brownie in their home out on the range.
All hands will turn out at the yards when they bring the cattle in;
Mate greets mate, man yells to dog above the dust and din.
The six weeks that they've been away seems more like two or three
When, the cattle being drafted, we all squat down to tea.

And then the talk soon gets around to pikers that were thrown.
Each man tells of his mate's good work – keeps silent of his own –

And someone asks the question they've been betting on all day.
'Has Sweetheart got a foal yet?' 'Is it piebald?' 'Is it bay?'
The questions and the answers are interspersed with tea,
While the other fellow's mishaps are related full of glee.
'We struck six head that galloped, just above the Dingo Yard,
Old Rocky hit a melon-hole and did that ground feel hard!'

'You should've seen old Whiskers with that bull just close behind,
With one tree on a great big plain – I'll bet his thoughts weren't kind!
But anyhow he made it, and old Rocky wasn't hurt,
Though I'll bet he felt uncomfortable with that bull pawing up the dirt!'
And now the man who runs the camp has risen to his feet:
'We'll put 'em through and get 'em out and try and dodge the heat.
The branders in the round yard, the speyers in the pound;
Weaners in the shady yard with that old bull we found.

'Better keep the killer back – leave him in the pen.
Shove the others through the dip and we'll turn 'em bush again.'
It's great to have them home again, hear them yarning after teas,
While Jim tries out a new song with his guitar on his knee
And Ernie's in a corner trying to write his girl a letter –
If he thinks nobody's noticing he'll have to hide it better.
Yes, it's good to have them home again, though they'd rather be by far
Sitting round the fire at night out where the cleanskins are.

A RINGER'S FAREWELL TO HIS QUART POT

Goodbye old bungie, old mate of mine,
Looks like you and me must part.
Though you're old and finished and lost your shine
It cuts me to the heart.
There's two big dents in your front and back
And a hole where there shouldn't be one,
But you've been a good friend all along the track
And I hate to part with you, son.

The first bash you got was when Rover fell
When we struck that galloping mob.
You lost your pannikin cup as well
But I still got me tea on the job.
Those old stags hiked it fast that day,
I though we'd never catch up.
Once Rover was right we made them pay,
But I'm sorry you lost your cup.

You were underneath when Sailor reared back
And flattened me on the ground.
He hit the ground with a helluva whack –
Thank goodness me bones are sound.
And bungie, old mate, I can still say yet
There's none can beat you to boil.
You'd be bubbling enough to double me bet
While the others looked stiller than oil.

It's hard to part with you, old friend,
But I guess it must be so.
I'll hang you here down the Boundary end
Where the drovers come and go.

And you can look down from your perch up here
On the quart pots lined in a row,
But there's never a rival among them to fear –
You're up where the good quart pots go.

Veronica Weal

GOLD AGAINST THE GREY

The wattle trees are flowering bright along the river track,
And my head is bowed in sorrow as the years go rolling back,
The sky is dark and cloudy with the threat of coming rain
And my mind is filled with memories that only bring me pain.
Twenty years ago it happened, on a day just like today,
When the wattle trees were blooming, gleaming gold against the grey.

She was all I had to live for since the day her mother died,
And she grew just like her mother, she was all my joy and pride.
She was beautiful and headstrong, with a spirit free and wild,
At an age to make her wilful – half a woman, half a child –
And her chief delight was riding through the bushland far and near
On the handsome dappled pony that she held so very dear.

They were meant to be together, wayward girl and flighty grey
Who would fight the hands of others, but his mistress would obey.
He had stamina and spirit, with the boldness of the brave;
He was king of all her kingdom, she his owner and his slave,
And the bond was strong between them, for he'd answer to her call
With a whinny shrill of greeting from his paddock or his stall.

She rode the dappled pony, rain or shine, throughout the year,
But best of all she liked to see the wattle flowers appear,
For when she went out riding on those mornings crisp and cold,
She'd adorn the dappled pony with a spray of green and gold.
'It makes him look so pretty,' she would smile at me and say,
'With the wattle in his bridle, gleaming gold against the grey.'

I never felt concerned for her, she rode him very well,
And the dappled grey was nimble for he never tripped or fell.
They knew every ridge and gully in the country where they'd roam,
And I knew that I could trust the grey to bring her safely home.
So many times I waved and watched them canter down the track
Until, one grey and cloudy day, they didn't canter back.

I searched with rising panic while the endless minutes passed,
And the light was slowly fading when I found them both at last
Where the ground beside the river bank rose gently to a hump,
Surmounted by the big grey log I'd told her not to jump.
The pony's neck was broken, and beneath him as he lay
I could see her shining tresses gleaming gold against the grey.

Twenty years ago it happened, twenty long and dreary years,
Yet still the sight of wattle makes me blink away the tears,
While skies so grey and gloomy, when the misty clouds hang low,
Make me feel afresh the sadness that will never let me go.
And the memories flood o'er me as I quietly kneel and pray,
With the wattle on her gravestone gleaming gold against the grey.

MURPHY'S JERSEY BULL

Murphy was a battler, forever trying to grub
A living from a holding which was mainly stone and scrub.
He had seven hungry children, so he greeted with dismay
The announcement from his missus that the eighth was on the way.

He was flat-out feeding seven, but he had to manage now,
So he begged and borrowed money and he bought a jersey cow.
She was very near to calving, and he watched her udder swell;
There'd be plenty for his children, the remainder he could sell.

The cow was quite a beauty, it was Murphy's frequent claim
That her breeding put the scrubby local cattle quite to shame.
When she dropped a sturdy bull calf, with delight he proudly said
That he'd start a herd of jerseys (only slightly inter-bred).

The neighbours envied Murphy, for the calf was fine indeed;
He grew to be a really prime example of the breed.
His mother's milk was plentiful, the richest to be found,
And her calf became the finest bull you'd find for miles around.

Murphy watched him often, and he rubbed his hands with glee;
He would use him as a stud bull at a hefty service fee,
And the beast was so impressive that the neighbours, sure enough,
Brought their cows and heifers over for the bull to do his stuff.

But although the bull looked macho, all the heifers he ignored,
His admiring bovine harem left him, frankly, rather bored,
He had no desire for dalliance, and Murphy bore the brunt
Of the taunts from friends and neighbours, all unmercifully blunt.

Then Murphy, nothing daunted, to the ribbing called a halt
By announcing to his critics that the bull was not at fault.
'It's your scrawny low-bred cattle that's the problem, goodness knows.
He'd have to be quite desperate to fancy one of those!

'He's a bull of class and breeding, with discriminating mind,
And he's obviously waiting to meet others of his kind,
So we'll put him with the jersey and he'll show what he can do,
And then those scraggy cows of yours will see a thing or two.'

When the jersey cow was ready, Murphy's bull was shown his mate,
And he galloped off to meet her at a very rapid rate.
He was so enthusiastic Murphy shouted, 'Told you so!'
But the sudden yells of laughter very quickly laid him low.

Instead of going over her – poor Murphy's face turned red –
The bull approached the jersey and went under her instead.
He gave a joyful bellow as he fell upon his knees.
And he sucked the jersey's udder, just as happy as you please.

He drank until the cow was dry and all her teats were sore,
He wouldn't leave her side at all, and still he wanted more.
Murphy got no milk that day, and all he got instead
Were some very ribald comments which are better left unsaid.

But Murphy had his vengeance, for before the week was through
He invited all the neighbours to a monster barbecue.
The steaks were rich and tender, and when everyone was full
They all agreed that fine indeed was Murphy's jersey bull.

MORNING RIDE

It's grand to ride when the fading stars
Throw shadows dark and deep
In the cold grey dawn of an early morn
When others are fast asleep.
As I pass through the dark and silent bush
To the track where I often ride,
I'm alone, the world's my own,
And my cares are cast aside.

I can tell by the feel of my restless mare
She's as free of care as I,
For it seems she moves on spring-shod hooves
And a gleam lights up her eye.
She snorts in sudden, startled fear
At a sinister object black,
Then rolls her eyes as she leaps and shies
At a shadow across the track.

Then the sun comes up and the land so fair
Is flooded with golden light,
And the shadows grey seem to melt away
In the wake of departing night.
The sunlight gleams on the bay mare's coat
And her shoulders flecked with foam,
But time won't wait, and it's getting late,
So I turn her head for home.

She tosses her head in an eager plea,
And I let her quicken her pace.
I can feel the pride in her lengthened stride;
She knows she was born to race!

And I wonder if ever the whispering wind
Tells of horses galloping free,
Of the desert sands of an ancient land
And Arabian ancestry?

And what of this other sunburnt land,
Do the wandering breezes know
Of the fate untold, of explorers bold
In the days that were long ago?
Could they tell of a land to break the hearts
Of all but the hardiest few?
Could they tell of the tears of the pioneers,
And their joys and triumphs too?

But phantoms and fantasy fade away
As the present replaces the past,
And I check our flight for our home is in sight –
The pleasures of life don't last.
But no matter what fortune may bring my way,
Whether sorrow or tears to hide,
These I'll endure, for I've found the cure
In an early morning ride.

THE BREAKER'S TALE

Breaking horses had been my trade
For more than twenty years –
Skill and knowledge bought and paid
With my blood and sweat and tears.
Roan and piebald, grey and black,
Chestnut and brown and bay,
Draught and thoroughbred, pony, hack,
They all had come my way.

Some were stupid and some had brains,
But in time's allotted span
They bowed themselves to the leather chains
Of their servitude to man.
With patience, kindness, and a little force
Their load they were taught to bear,
And I never failed to break a horse
Till I met with the chestnut mare.

She was foaled way out on the western plains
Where the earth and the sky collide,
And the fire of freedom filled her veins
With a fierce and stubborn pride.
Born of a renegade station mare
And a rebel brumby sire,
With a savage temper to match the flare
Of a coat that burned like fire.

The brumbies fled as the stockwhips cracked
One day in the early dawn.
They galloped blindly, bunched and packed,

And we yarded them all mid-morn.
We drafted, sorted and culled the mob
In a welter of hide and hair,
And when we finished I tackled the job
Of breaking the chestnut mare.

I started slowly, as I recall,
For I wanted to win her trust.
I knew some tricks and I tried them all
But she dashed my hopes to dust.
I was the enemy – hated, feared –
And she fought me with all she knew,
With slashing hooves as she kicked and reared
While the dust and the curses flew.

Attack was all the defence she had,
And her heart was filled with hate
She fought like a demon – blinded, mad
With fury that wouldn't abate.
I was a breaker of some renown
But my courage began to fail
When, five days running, she threw me down
And smashed me against the rail.

At the sight of men she went wild with rage
But she saved the worst for me,
And she fretted and pined, in her wooden cage,
For the plains where she longed to be.
She would never submit, and I tossed and turned
As I lay in my bed at night,
While deep inside me the conflict burned
As I battled my moral fight.

I knew in my heart she deserved to live,
With her spirit no man could tame,
But the baser side of me couldn't forgive
That she'd sullied my nerve and name.
In the grey of the morning my injured pride
Refused to admit she'd won,
I went to the mare that I couldn't ride
And I carried a loaded gun.

Ahead in the yard was a flash of white
And I stopped, with a sudden start.
Then a wave of terror held me tight
And fastened around my heart.
The boss's daughter, three years old,
Was calmly standing there,
With her laughing face and her curls of gold
In the yard with the chestnut mare.

I raised the gun, but the rails were high
And partly obscured my aim.
I stood like stone, for a word, a cry,
Would have set the mare aflame.
In less than the time that it takes to tell
Of my anguish and dump despair,
'Pretty horsie,' said little Nell
And she patted the chestnut mare.

The mare was shaking, but stood her ground
And I watched, with my mind awhirl,
As her lovely head came slowly round
To nuzzle the little girl.
Did she scent the innocence, sense the love
That came from the tiny mite?

Nell fondled the velvet nose above
And gurgled with sheer delight.

'Bye-bye horsie,' she softly said,
Then climbed through the stockyard gate.
I ran to meet her, arms outspread,
With a joy I can scarce relate.
I held her close, then I turned about
And the gate pulled open wide.
With a buck and a whinny, the mare shot out
In a blur of chestnut hide.

The station fences that stood nearby
She cleared like a bird in flight,
And we watched her galloping, Nell and I,
Till she disappeared from sight.
And today the mare is running wild
On the plans where the brumbies dwell,
For she spared the life of a tiny child
And she saved herself as well.

Robert Whyte

VANISHED HOMESTEADS

Resting place of lost romances,
Those old homesteads by the river!
There is one, with cattle camping
'Neath the hardy pepper tree.
Planted in the good old days
Our father thought would last forever,
When the shepherds lined the frontage
With their big flocks running free.

There's a single chimney standing
Where the trace of smoke still lingers,
But the old slab walls have fallen
And are overgrown with grass.
Where the broken palings seem to point
Like gnarled and twisted fingers
And the garden is a-litter
With old tins and broken glass.

You may faintly trace the bush course
Where we held the shearers' races,
And the horses and their riders
In your fancy visualise,
Now the thunder of the finish,
Glimpse of gleaming, bearded faces
Where the bets were plug tobacco
And a bridle was the prize.

There were dances at the cut-out
And the neighbours all came over,
Lads and lasses blithely riding
From the homesteads, small and great.
Fifty miles was little matter
For a horse that grazed on clover,
And the reins were rarely tightened
As they loped from gate to gate.

There are rabbits in the stockyard
Where the wildest colts were ridden,
But the posts and rails are leaning,
Charred and blackened from the drought.
Bush fires, here, their toll have taken,
But their work is partly hidden.
By a kurrajong that's growing
Tall and stately at the gate.

Gone are rouseabout and shearer;
Tough old-timers of the stations
Rolled their swags and faced the sunset
As the flocks spread further west.
Most by now are soundly sleeping
At their final destination,
Gathered in the last great muster
Gone to their eternal rest.

Col Wilson

THE TRAILER

In my very early childhood, I learned to crawl and walk,
To use the potty on command, to gurgle, goo, and talk,
And in good time I went to school and learned to read and write,
To co-exist in playgrounds – to run and jump, and fight.

When I grew up I got a job, a wife and family too.
In short, I did the kind of things that most men get to do.
And whilst my life may not have gained the ultimate success,
I can say with modesty it's not a total mess.

That's why I find it difficult to contemplate my failure;
Despite my years of trying to, I still can't back a trailer.
All my friends who have one seem to do it well,
So why do my attempts end up a journey into hell?

When I bought my trailer, six by four and painted green,
I thought it was the nicest one that I had ever seen.
I hooked it up, and drove it home, determined to arrive
In a blaze of glory, by backing up the drive.

I knew the theory: left hand down to back it to the right;
Right hand down to guide it left. As I said before, I'm bright.
But theory into practice, though it may sound commonsense,
For me seemed quite impossible, and so I hit the fence.

Quite a crowd soon gathered round. Advice was far from lacking,
With every new arrival saying: 'Having trouble backing?'
I finally unhooked it, and wheeled it through the gate,
Up the drive, and round the back, so I could concentrate

On learning how to back it, this trailer so perverse,
Instead of getting better, though, I kept on getting worse.
You can see where I've been learning, my area of practice –
The woodpile fence is broken, and all the shrubs are cactus.

The corner of the garage is gone, no trees are left alive,
And I've completely flattened both the downpipes in the drive.
The clothes hoist has a nasty bend, the sprinklers are no more,
And the imprint of the number plate is on the toilet door.

My backing reputation now is legend in this town.
I'm down the street. Some smart-arse says: 'Hey Blue it's left-
    hand down.'
But since I've bought my trailer I have to persevere.
Accidents don't worry me. It's ridicule I fear.

So when I take it to the dump I pray no-one's around,
But the news just spreads like wildfire. Spectators abound.
They hope I'm going to duplicate that trailer-backing sin,
And go too near the edge again and drop the damn thing in.

But finally, I've solved it. The problem's not so hard.
I only drive it forward now when I'm not in the yard.
In the matter of reversing, there's really nothing to it.
When I need to back it I just get the wife to do it.

GRANDKIDS

The grandkids are coming. They are? They are?
Quick, hide the computer and lock up the car.
Lift everything breakable onto the shelves.
Teach grandfolk the art of defending themselves.
Take plenty of vitamins, A, B, and C,
For strong and resilient you'll need to be.

Say goodbye to harmony. Goodbye to quiet.
Your home will resemble an out-of-hand riot.
Make sure that you check out your washing machine
(Those washing nappies will know what I mean),
And don't let the two-year-old near the TV –
There might be a program you're wanting to see.

Hang on to your patience with both of your hands,
The dear little darling will not understand
If you shout 'Will you stop it. You must not touch that.'
Or 'Don't kick the dog' and 'Put down that cat.'
'Don't wake the baby by yelling and screaming.'
And 'Isn't it time you were in bed and dreaming?'

There's Erin – two months and queen of the castle –
Food in one end, and waste out the other.
How can one baby, so tiny and frail,
Be so possessed of such ear-splitting wail?
And how does she know, when she's starting to squeal,
That the rest of the family are having their meal?

But how can you pretend to be cross,
With the queen of the castle. The princess. The boss.
When she looks up and smiles, gurgling and gooing,

You don't have a choice. You just stop what you're doing
And pay her the homage of which she's deserving.
She makes the demands, and you do the serving.

Now Matthew, he's one of the terrible twos.
No wonder some grandfathers get on the booze.
They christened him Matthew, but I have a notion
He should have been christened Perpetual Motion.
They say that it's cruel to keep them in cages
And that they grow out of it, slowly, in stages.

But the question that hovers on everyone's tongue,
Is 'How long does it take to stop being that young?
And tell me, wise counsellor, what guarantee
Can you give to grandparents they're better at three?'
If it wasn't for *Play School* on the TV
We'd be in a rest home, Grandmother and me.

He is ever so charming, ever so sweet,
His capture of Grandmother's heart is complete.
But I am his grandfather, I am much sterner,
Or is it perhaps that I'm just a slow learner?
When he looks up at me and says 'Gamfarver. Cuddle?'
All thoughts of discipline melt into muddle.

I have to survive, or turn into a rover,
If the grandchildren's holiday isn't soon over.
And it's true, they are going, I'm sad to relate,
But we'll sleep for three days when they go out the gate.
And following that, we must build our physique,
For the other three grandkids are coming next week.

MY MOWER

I have a motor mower, an abortion of a thing,
And my hate for it increases with the coming of each spring.
When first I bought my mower, the written guarantee
Said that it would start the first time with just one sharp pull
    from me.

I fill it up with petrol. Make sure I've turned the switch.
Move the throttle. Check the choke, and try to start the bitch.
I pull it once. I pull it twice. I pull my sacred guts out.
Surprise, surprise. It gives a cough, a wheeze, and then cuts out.

And if, by some strange accident, the mower starts to run,
I race to cut the lawn and then – the catcher comes undone.
I put the catcher on again. The motor stops. Guess what?
No way is there to start this bloody mower when it's hot.

You wonder that I don't complain. What would be the use?
They'd send an expert to my house. He'd pick me for a goose.
He'd give one pull and start it. I'd lose again, you see,
In the never-ending battle between machines and me.

The bloke who sold it to me, he says the mower's okay.
(I bought the chainsaw off him, too, and lived to rue the day.)
He says that I'm the problem, that motors hate me. Then
He's got the hide to tell me I should shop at Mitre 10.

My wife can start it. Kids can too. The woman down the street.
Everyone can start it, but that bugger's got me beat.
I'm sure it sees me coming and decides to have some fun,
And though I pull, and pull, and pull, I can't get it to run.

My family quite enjoys the show. I know the neighbours do.
They like to see my face turn red and watch the air turn blue.
I can't reveal the brand name of this cursed pain-inflicter,
But here's a clue: you'll never guess – it rhymes with boa constrictor.

Alf Wood

BOOLEM

Have you been told of Boolem in the Never-Never Land?
The farmers harvest gibbers and they dam the drifting sand;
The sun dries the mirages as they float across the plain,
But no-one talks of drought because they've never heard of rain.

The stock they raise are hardy goats with fleece as fine as silk,
And from the herd they get supplies of dehydrated milk.
They haven't any trees there, not even fallen logs,
For years ago the trees pulled out and went to look for dogs.

A stranger came to Boolem with his throat all parched and raw;
They offered him a drink and said, 'It's water from the bore.'
'Good grief!' exclaimed the startled man. His eyes grew round and big.
'I hope you can assure me that it is a healthy pig!'

The fishermen of Boolem are the best in all the land;
The fish they catch are gropers and they grope for them in sand.
A youngster caught a tiddler once and kept it in a dish;
His mother poured some water in and drowned the muddy fish!

If tourists visit Boolem Town, they always want to stay,
Pretending it's the climate spilling sunlight every day.
But when they come to Boolem and they want to stay a year,
The reason is the water's off and all they drink is beer.

ROCK PAINTING

Only the hawk hanging silent and still
Noticed Wondahba move over the hill;
Slide through the bush like a shadow half-seen
On to the valley where stricken rocks lean.

Wondahba thought of his dreams and his hopes,
Panted and clambered up rock-tumbled slopes,
Climbed over chasm and narrow ravine
On to a cave with the scrub as a screen.

There in the niche hid from impious eyes,
Safe from the tempest and heat from the skies,
Wondahba moistened the ochre and clay
And sand as he painted to make the dream stay.

Softly he sang of the totem he drew,
Chanting the myth of the grey kangaroo,
Flesh of his flesh that he never must harm,
Held in his dreaming and sung like a psalm.

Down the steep mountain he clambered again,
Back to the laughter and life on the plain,
Leaving his painting in secret to share
Silence and peace with the early dreams there.

Wondahba's people no longer remain
There in the mountains nor down on the plain.
Legends and paintings on rock-walls, it seems,
Are all that remain of their doings and dreams.

THE WALHALLA BULLOCKY

There's bullockies and bullockies
With stories that are strange,
Moving timber near Walhalla
As they worked along the range.

There's Olsen that was boasted,
'He's the champion' they would tell;
He would use the strongest language
And he cursed his team to hell.

He would crack the leather flailing
And spare them not the least;
As they strained in yoke together
He would single out each beast.

The air was dark with cursing
As those bullocks pulled with fear.
There was language in those mountains
Not fit for man to hear.

He swore with raucous anger
As those bullocks tried to climb,
And wild of eye they struggled
As he roared along the line.

He was giving of his strongest,
With words of fiery heat,
When a parson travelling through the bush
Heard the words I can't repeat.

He said, 'My good man, why expletives,
To make the bullocks heed?
I'm sure that they would work as well
With kinder words, indeed.'

Olsen dropped his curling whip,
Turned round movin' slow,
And eyed the parson as he said,
'Why don't you have a go?'

Now the parson being Methodist,
A missionary and all,
Said, 'I'll show you heathen bullocky,
I'll answer to the call!'

So the parson gave a little prayer,
Then spake into the air
With words of love and tenderness
Those bullocks found quite rare.

Those honeyed words beseeching,
The team all settled calm,
And listened to the preaching
And the message of the psalm.

That parson gave a sermon
With a warning oh so grim,
You could almost hear an organ
And the singing of a hymn.

Well, Olsen blinked with teardrops
That came tumbling down his cheek.

'Such words,' he said, 'are wonderful,
And make me feel quite weak.

'It's made of me a new man,
I have to give myself a pinch …
But have you noticed please, your reverence,
Those bullocks haven't moved a *bloody* inch!'

Bibliography

ANTHOLOGIES

Australian Bush Verse, selected by the Winton Tourist Promotion
Association, Ure Smith, Sydney, 1976.
North of Capricorn, Elizabeth Perkins and Robert Handicott (eds),
James Cook University, Townsville, no date.
Off The Shelf, A.K. Thomson (ed.), Jacaranda, Brisbane, 1960
The Bronze Swagman Books of Verse 1972–1998, published by Winton
Tourist Promotion Association, Winton. Later by Vision Winton
Incorporated, Winton.

WORKS OF AUSTRALIAN POETS

Allen, Geoff, *Ballads of the Kimberley,* published by the author,
Balgowah, NSW, 1991.
Campbell, Ellis, *Eye of the Tiger,* published by the author, Dubbo,
NSW, 1997.
Clark, Louis H., *Second Step,* The Clyde Press, Thornbury, Vic., 1949.
Dixon, Kelly, *From a Drifter's Pen,* published by the author,
Camooweal, Qld, 1997.
Garvey, Keith, *Songs of a Shearer,* Hutchison, Hawthorn, Vic., 1984.
Garvey, Keith, *Cattle-Camp Collection,* published by the author, Glen
Innes, NSW, 1987.
Garvey, Keith, *Verses of a Vagrant,* published by the author, Glen Innes,
NSW, 1990.
Green, Jean and Fitzgerald, James, *McLennan's Way,* Hesperian Press,
Victoria Park, WA, 1994.
Haig, Janine, *I Hope Yer Sheep Get Fly Blown,* Red's Books, Eulo, Qld,
1997.
Kelly, Jim, *The Voice of the North,* Shire of Derby/West Kimberley,
Hesperian Press, Victoria Park, WA, 1993.

Magoffin, Richard, *We Bushies,* published by the author, Kyuna, Qld, 1968.

Magoffin, Richard, *Down Another Track,* Mimosa Press, Charters Towers, Qld, 1982.

Magoffin, Richard, *Laugh Your Way Through Queensland,* Matilda Expo Publications, Kyuna, Qld, 1998.

Magor, Bob, *Blasted Crows,* published by the author, Myponga, SA, 1990.

Magor, Bob, *Snakes Alive and Other Verses,* published by the author, Myponga, SA, 1995.

Magor, Bob, *Donkey Derby and Other Verses,* published by the author, Myponga, SA, 1998.

Maskell, Irene, *Dan Sheahan: Bush Balladist,* published as a Hinchinbrook Bicentennial Community Committee Project, 1998.

Newsome, Colin, *The Green Tree Snake,* International Colour Productions, Stanthorpe, Qld, 1981.

O'Connor, Jim, *Look Before You Leap,* published by the author, Longreach, Qld, 1997.

Pearce, R.C., *The Scrub Bull and Other Verses,* published by the author, no date.

Simpson, Bruce, *The Territory Rouseabout and Other Humorous Verses,* published by the author, Caboolture, Qld, 1994.

Simpson, Bruce, *Packhorse Drover,* ABC Books, Sydney, NSW, 1996.

Wilson, Col, *Blue the Shearer,* published by the author, Wellington, NSW, 1995.

PERIODICALS

The North Queensland Register
The Bulletin